THE LIFE OF
JOSEPH HODGES CHOATE

Joseph Hodges Choate
From a photograph made in 1898
by Mrs. J. Montgomery Sears

THE LIFE OF
JOSEPH HODGES CHOATE

AS GATHERED CHIEFLY FROM HIS LETTERS

BY
EDWARD SANDFORD MARTIN

INCLUDING
HIS OWN STORY OF HIS BOYHOOD
AND YOUTH

VOLUME II

LONDON
CONSTABLE & CO., LTD.
1920

CONTENTS

CONTENTS

XI

ILLUSTRATIONS

THE LIFE OF
JOSEPH HODGES CHOATE

JOSEPH HODGES CHOATE

CHAPTER VII

THE NINETIES (*Concluded*)

INCOME-TAX CASE—HIS ARGUMENT—MR. SOUTHMAYD'S BRIEF—CONSTANT ACTIVITIES—THE VENEZUELA SENSATION—DUNRAVEN—AS SEEN IN ACTION—IRRIGATION CASE STANFORD CASE—McKINLEY ELECTED—THE BACCHANTE—HE RUNS FOR SENATOR—TOBACCO CASE—HIS SON'S CLASS POEM—NAUMKEAG—TAMMANY TRIUMPHS—THE ADDRESS ON RUFUS CHOATE—ROOSEVELT FOR GOVERNOR—JUDGE DALY—RUMORS ABOUT AN AMBASSADORSHIP—IN WASHINGTON—APPOINTED AMBASSADOR TO ENGLAND—HIS LAW PRACTICE REVIEWED

In March, 1895, Mr. Choate made an argument before the Supreme Court against the income tax and reargued it in May of the same year. It has been considered his greatest argument on a matter purely of law. His record is full of celebrated cases. He once said his most famous exploit at law was the Fitz-John Porter case because two court-martials had decided it adversely and the true facts were very hard to gather and put before a court. But then he did that comparatively early in his practice, which perhaps made him look the more kindly on it. Mr. Strong says that the Sage-Laidlaw case provided jury trials as famous as any in the New York records, but neither the Porter nor the Laidlaw case had much to do with the law. The lay pubic inclined to suppose that Mr. Choate was not much of a lawyer, but was a considerable humorist, but in the income-tax case he had no compunction about furnishing the evidence to destroy that theory.

He thought the case was of great importance to civilization—a case that would build a proper rampart around the rights of property, which he seemed always to feel were the real underpinning of civilization. As to that, "Holland," a very well known New York newspaper correspondent, said in the Philadelphia *Press*, May 7, 1895:

"If Mr. Choate meets the expectations of his brethren of the bar in this city with the argument which he proposes to make to the Supreme Court upon the rehearing of the income-tax case, his speech will probably rank with those greater efforts like Webster's in the Dartmouth College case, which have served the country so well in influencing a constitutional interpretation of incalculable value in securing the protection to property and the liberty of individuals. When Mr. Choate went to Washington in April to make his first argument in opposition to the constitutionality of the law he was inspired far more by the impulse of the patriot than the professional zeal of the lawyer. He felt very deeply upon this question. To him it seemed as though a decision affirming the constitutionality of the law would be the most dangerous influence in its results which this country has met with since the pro-slavery men of the South determined upon secession. It seemed to him if the Supreme Court should find itself impelled to declare this law constitutional, that then we should have the most startling illustration of the influence of Populism, and he felt as though such a decision would in the impulses which would follow it simply accelerate the purposes of the Populists so that the next legislative attempt of theirs would be greatly to increase the amount of taxes taken from the wealthy and also greatly to increase the discrimination in favor of those who have not great possessions.

"After Mr. Choate returned from Washington he had astounding evidence of public sentiment. His mails contained many letters, not all of them from men of wealth, speaking in the highest terms of the statesmanlike view which he took in his argument. He found that there were thousands of citizens who felt exactly as he did, that this discrimination against the rich was to be, if maintained, only the beginning of greater and greater discriminations of that sort. He found that the Bar Association of this city with but few exceptions approved his argument and its purely legal elucidations. When it was determined to ask for a rehearing, it being believed by the lawyers that the Supreme Court would grant it, and had in fact intimated so much in the earlier decision, Mr. Choate gave every moment that he could spare from his other duties to further study of this question. He became more and more impressed with the great danger involved. He spoke with very great seriousness of the crisis, and he was persuaded that upon another argument it was reasonable to hope that a majority of the court would become convinced that the law, tainted in part, was tainted in whole.

"I have heard a number of lawyers speak of the argument which Mr. Choate had in mind to deliver to the Bench, and they spoke as though they expected one of those masterly addresses which are fully equal to the great occasion which inspires them. Whether Mr. Choate gave his friends some idea of what he would say or not, I did not learn, but it was evident that the bar of this city expects perhaps the finest of Mr. Choate's powers in this address."

Mr. Choate lived to see the income tax that he abolished restored and paid, but at least he must have approved of what the money thus raised was spent for.   His old friend and antagonist, James C. Carter, was the big gun among the distinguished lawyers opposed to him.   *The Tribune*, March 13, 1895, says:

"Mr. Carter spoke two and one-half hours, and was immediately followed by Mr. Choate, who, in the remaining forty minutes of the session, made the preface of his argument and outlined its scope.   In the beginning he said: 'If the Court please, after Jupiter had thundered all around the sky, and had levelled everything and everybody by his prodigious bolts, Mercury came out from his hiding place and looked around to see how much damage had been done.   He was quite familiar with the weapons of his Olympian friend.   He had often felt their force, but he knew that it was largely stage thunder, manufactured for the particular occasion, and he went his round among the inhabitants of Olympus, restoring the consciousness and dispelling the fears of both gods and men that had been prostrated by the crash. It is in that spirit that I follow my distinguished friend; and shall not undertake to cope with him by means of the same weapons, because I am not master of them.

" 'It never would have occurred to me to present either as an opening or closing argument, to this great and learned court, that if, in their wisdom, they found it necessary to protect a suitor who sought here to cling to the Ark of the Covenant and invoke the protection of the Constitution which was created for us all, against your furnishing that relief and protection, that possibly the popular wrath might sweep the Court away.   It is the first time I ever heard the argument presented to this or any other court, and I trust it will be the last.' "

The World, *The Tribune* and other papers had summaries of Mr. Choate's argument. That in *The World*, March 30, 1895, is signed by David Graham Phillips and runs as follows:

"When future American historians fix the due proportion and value of events they will give more space in their histories to the great debate upon the income tax before the Supreme Court of the United States than to the whole four years' administration of many Presidents. 'I do not believe,' said Joseph H. Choate, closing this debate, 'that any member of this court ever sat or ever will sit to hear a case the consequence of which will be so far reaching as this.' And he spoke from a profound and just conviction.

"The Supreme Court, the court of final resort for 70,000,000 people, the custodian and final judge of our rights and liberties under the Constitution, has considered and decided many great questions and has heard the splendid eloquence of many a great lawyer. But never was a question more vital presented to it in the arguments and rhetoric of lawyers more eminent or more famous. Of these lawyers three were pre-eminent— Joseph H. Choate, the most famous throughout the nation; George F. Edmunds, most admired of constitutional lawyers, and James C. Carter, whom lawyers call the leader of the bar in the United States.

"The matter about which the battle raged under these distinguished leaders was the power of Congress to tax the people. As we all know, taxation has been the great question in all histories. It is the goad of taxation that has driven oppressed people to free themselves. From taxation have come the longest and bloodiest wars. It was taxation that made our own Revolution.

"In this particular issue the two sides divided upon two irreconcilable views of the Constitution. Those under the banners of the Attorney-General and James C. Carter held that the income tax was legally laid by Congress; that the Supreme Court had practically no power to halt or limit Congress in the exercise of the taxing power. They held that this tax was a just and necessary correction of the unequal burdens of our present system of taxation, by which the rich escape and the poor and those of moderate means bear all the expenses of Government.

"On the other side, under the banners of Choate and Edmunds, the contention was that the income tax was the beginning of socialism and communism, the carrying of the outer intrenchments of property rights. They held that the tax had no warrant in the Constitution, and that a decision for the tax meant the restriction of the rights and liberties guaranteed by the Constitution —indeed, the destruction of the Constitution itself.

"As *The World* has believed that the income tax is just and necessary, it is fair that a full hearing be given to the other side. And no better presentment could be made than the speech of Mr. Choate. That eminent gentleman, profound, acute and witty, of the highest type of American, was at his best in this debate. He was the last speaker, and as he went on to rear the firm and graceful and original and harmonious structure of his argument, even his adversaries and the august and impassive Justices of that greatest court of justice on the face of the earth were moved to admiration. It was thought that there was nothing new to say against the tax, that all argument had been exhausted. But Mr. Choate, fixing his deep, shrewd mind upon the Constitution, found new and plausible meanings there, and made his adversaries feel like Socrates, who was so spellbound by the rhetoric and plausibility of the Sophist Protagoras that he could scarce collect himself for a renewed search for the truth.

"Mr. Choate began by deploring the communistic tendency of the tax. He told how he was riding with ex-President Hayes at the funeral of Gen. Sherman five years ago, and how Hayes had said to him: 'You will probably see the day when at the death of any man of large wealth the State will take for itself all above a certain prescribed limit of his fortune and divide it or apply it to the equal uses of all the people.' Mr. Choate then thought that this was as the wanderings of a dreaming man. But, he said, he would not have thought so had he known that within five years he 'should be standing before this tribunal to dispute the validity of an alleged act of Congress, defended by the authorized legal representatives of the Federal Government upon the plea that it was a tax levied only upon classes and extremely rich men.'

"Further in the same direction, Mr. Choate said, it was not only an assault upon the rich, but an assault of the rest of the United States upon the four States, Massachusetts, New York, Pennsylvania and New Jersey, which paid four-fifths of the war-time income tax and would pay nine-tenths of the present tax, although they had less than one-fourth the representation in the lower house of Congress, where all tax measures must originate. He asked if those two most distinguished men in the Constitutional Convention, Washington and Franklin, would not have rushed forward to erase their signatures from the Constitution had they foreseen that that document would be brought forward to justify a raid by a combination of States upon the strong-boxes of four other States, wealthier, stronger, richer.

"After this general denunciation Mr. Choate laid down the principles of his argument. It may be concisely stated in this way: The Constitution divides taxes into direct taxes and duties, imposts and excises, which three may be called indirect taxes. Direct taxes must be levied according to population, according to the census, since they are taxes directly upon persons. Indirect taxes, which are taxes upon commodities or occupations, must be levied with uniformity, so that all who use the taxed commodities or follow the taxed occupations shall bear the burden alike. Such, he insisted, were the plain, clear provisions of the Constitution as to the manner of taxation.

"As to the matter of taxation, he contended that the Constitution was no less clear. He held that a tax upon real estate or upon personal property or upon the proceeds of them must, in fact and in the Constitution, be a direct tax. With this established to his satisfaction the conclusion was inevitable that the present income tax was unconstitutional because it levied direct taxes— that is, taxes upon the proceeds of real and personal property without regard or pretense of regard to the census of population.

"He admitted that the tax upon incomes derived from labor was an indirect tax, an excise, but he held that it was, under this law, laid without regard to the constitutional command as to uniformity. And in support of this contention he cited specifically the various persons and companies excluded from the tax.

"The mere statement of his propositions shows how powerful they are if true. Now let us see how he supported these propositions. Let us see the mighty weapon he forged with the hope of giving the income tax a mortal wound. First, let us hear him upon the constitutional provisions for taxation. He found that the Constitution provided in article 1, section 2, that 'Congress shall have power to lay and collect taxes, duties, imposts and excises,' but that 'all duties, imposts and excises shall be uniform throughout the United States.' He insisted that the omission of the word 'taxes' from the second clause was not a slip of the pen, but was deliberate; that the word 'taxes' was intended to mean direct taxes as distinguished from duties, imposts and excises, which are indirect taxes. Then he found that in article 1, sections 2 and 8, it was distinctly provided that direct taxes should only be levied under a census of the population—that is, that representation and direct taxes should go hand in hand.

"So much for the provisions of the Constitution as interpreted by Mr. Choate. And now he goes on to show what are direct taxes. In doing this he freed all who own stocks, bonds, mortgages, all who get their incomes from houses and lands, from the necessity of paying the tax. He insisted in the first place that so far as real estate was concerned no one had ever denied that a tax upon real estate was a direct tax. Then he attacked the contention of the other side that a tax upon an income was not a tax upon the specific sources of that income. He said that a tax upon the rent of real estate is a tax upon real estate itself, and that money got from rent did not lose its specific name of rentals simply because it was in the pockets of a man, mixed with other money. 'I say,' he declared, 'that a tax on land yielding income, by whatever name, is in reality, in effect and substance a tax upon the rental. Would any free people, if they had prohibited a land tax, submit to a tax on rentals?'

"He said that the Attorney-General was urging an unsound argument when he urged that though you cannot tax rent, you can tax the money in the owner's pocket received from rent. And he went on to quote opinion after opinion of the Supreme Court that the name does not decide the nature of the real thing.

"With the status of a real estate tax thus established, he went on to say that what is true of real property is true of personal property also. 'I own a house today and sell it tomorrow, and take as its consideration a mortgage upon the same property for its full value. Is a tax upon the house one kind of tax and a tax upon the proceeds of the house another? It cannot be. A tax upon personality has all the elements of a direct tax, exactly as a tax upon real estate. It is directly imposed; it is presently paid; it is ultimately borne by the party owning it. There is no chance for him to escape from the tax but to run away.'

"Mr. Choate now outlined the history of the compromises by which the makers of the Constitution agreed upon the two systems—the uniform indirect tax and the direct tax by apportionment by the census. His reading of history was that the rich seaboard States gave up to the Union the right to levy customs duties and to regulate interstate commerce, rights which had been their chief sources of revenue. In return for this the smaller and poorer States agreed to the inequality of the apportionment system of direct taxation.

"He told the story of those days and quoted statements from makers of the Constitution to show that this inequality was perfectly understood and that with this understanding the bargain of Federal union was struck. Now, he said, the weaker and smaller States were trying to repudiate the bargain. He said that this principle of direct taxation according to representation was the only thing that was affirmed twice in the Constitution. This was done, he said, so that 'when a man came from a poor State to put a direct tax upon Massachusetts or New York or Pennsylvania, however poor his State might be, however small might be its population, it should bear just that proportion of the tax.'

"Mr. Choate now took up former decisions of the Supreme Court upon income taxes, and asserted that his particular strictures upon such taxes had never been before the Supreme Court, had never been decided. In all other cases, he said, the law had been attacked upon different grounds, and therefore the court could decide for him without reversing itself, because all other decisions had been limited decisions, setting forth that particular objections to income taxes were not well founded. He reviewed each of the five cases under previous income tax laws and found that the court had never touched upon the points he had raised.

"Mr. Choate had now destroyed to his satisfaction that part of the income tax law which assessed incomes derived from real estate and personal property. He maintained that he had shown that under the Constitution these were direct taxes, and could only be legal if laid by the census without distinction. He also felt that he had shown that the Supreme Court was not in any way hampered by any previous decision for an income tax.

"And now began his assault upon the part of the in-

come tax law which even he admitted provided for indirect taxes. He had already shown that the Constitution
provided explicitly that such taxes must be laid uniformly.
He asserted that under this law they were not laid uniformly, but with ridiculous and scandalous exemptions.
Four thousand dollars, the income exempted, was, he
said, the interest upon $133,000 at 3%. He scouted the
idea that this was a just exemption. He maintained
that this was luxury, and that $1,000 was the highest
possible just exemption. The exemption of individual
incomes of $4,000 and the taxing of corporation incomes
of the same amount was a further violation of the principle of uniformity. 'Could Your Honors,' he said, bas-
ing his satire upon his proposition that this tax was of
the nature of a duty, 'justify an act that a given brand
of tea should pay a duty of ten cents if imported by an
individual, or twenty cents if imported by a corporation,
and no duty at all if imported by a mutual association?'

"And now he was laughing at the exemption of rich
church and college corporations, was deriding the exemption of mutual associations, which go free on the plea
that they are benevolent institutions. He could not
see why citizens of Nebraska should be practically taxed
to support Trinity Church or Harvard College. As for
the mutual associations, their total deposits were near
two thousand millions, and greater than the total deposits
of the State and national banks. He was mightily amused
that the Mutual Life, with $204,000,000 of accumula-
tions, and the Equitable, with $185,000,000, should get
out of $200,000 and $180,000 income tax annually because they were benevolent institutions, but he failed to
see where the constitutional command that there must
be uniformity was obeyed.

"Most of the widows and orphans, most of the helpless, he said, had their small capital invested in corporations, and the income tax robbed them. 'We speak for
them,' he said. 'In striking at the corporations, in attempting to confiscate their property, you injure, not the
wealthy—they can now stand it—but the widow and
the orphan.'

"Such was the argument of Mr. Choate. He paid
small attention to the arguments from public policy,
from political economy, with which his adversaries dealt
so admirably. He kept close to the Constitution and
addressed himself to the interpreting of constitutional
principles. And when he sat down every one there present felt that the best that could be said had been said,
that the income tax had had its worst blow. If it with-
stood that splendid assault of close-armored, close-ranked
arguments, there was no chance for its overthrow."

Of Mr. Southmayd's part in the income-tax case, Mr.
Choate spoke most generously in his address on Mr.
Southmayd before the Bar Association of the City of
New York on May 14, 1912: "This Bar Association,"
he said, "has never had or lost a member who reflected
upon it greater honor than Mr. Southmayd. If Mr.
Evarts were alive today I am sure that he would join
with me in declaring that much of our professional success and repute was due to his support, his assistance,
his inspiration.

"For myself, I can give no better illustration of this
than in the celebrated Income Tax case, in which was
accomplished what was at the time regarded, at home
and abroad, as the almost impossible achievement of
overthrowing, in the Supreme Court, the entire scheme

of an Income Tax embodied in an act of Congress. I might almost say with entire truth that it was South-mayd, who never went near the Court, who won the case. He was then seventy years old; he had retired from practice ten years before, and all that time he had refrained from any legal labor. In fact, as he claimed, he had ceased to be an attorney at law, and when he had occasion to put his name to a brief, he always signed Charles F. Southmayd in person.

"What he regarded as the iniquity of the Income Tax aroused all his old-time energy. By this time he had an ample income of his own which was affected, and he had a strong idea of the right of property being at the foundation of civilized government. Other men have five senses, but he had a sixth—the sense of property— very keen and very powerful; and he also had an abiding allegiance to the Constitution under which the country had so long prospered, and an abhorrence of any violation of it. So, when he heard that I was to be in the case, he volunteered to prepare a brief, which proved, when completed, to be the keystone of the whole argument, and, indeed, of the decision which overthrew the Act of Congress. The Constitution had provided that direct taxes should be apportioned among the states according to their respective numbers, but this Act had levied all taxes upon income, from whatever source derived, indiscriminately upon all alike, without such apportionment.

"To his clear mind, whatever else might be disputed, a tax on land was certainly a direct tax within the meaning of the Constitution, and a tax upon the income of land could by no possibility be distinguished from a tax on the land itself, for it was a tax on the land from which the rent was derived, and was therefore necessarily a direct tax; a tax upon the income of accumulated personal property could not be distinguished in principle from the tax on rents;—and these all being found to be direct taxes, and therefore unconstitutionally levied, the Court in annulling them must find that Congress without them would not have enacted the rest of the tax, and therefore must declare the whole Act void.

"This was the whole argument in a nutshell, and it all rested upon his first proposition, which was absolutely unanswerable then and is unanswerable now, and can never be answered, except by an amendment of the Constitution, which I, for one, hope will never be carried through, because it will throw almost the whole burden of every Federal Income Tax upon a very few of the larger States. However that may be, it was his masterful brief that drove the entering wedge which by its cleavage demolished the Act, while the rest of us who appeared in Court, and argued the cause to its final conclusions, on the foundation which he had laid, won an undue share of the glory. I have heard from the Clerk's office that all the judges called for extra copies of his brief, but for none of the others."

Mr. Choate made his first argument on the income tax on the 13th of March. Intervals of repose and self-congratulation after his more strenuous efforts were not at all part of his programme. He seems to have rested himself habitually by doing the next thing, and doing it as hard as was consistent with the tranquillity of his temperament. Out of his scrap-book it is possible to get an idea of the variety of his activities in this year of '95. On March 15 we find him speaking for the New

York Kindergarten Association before the Chamber of Commerce. In May he had a second turn at the income tax, and in June he had his fourth go with Mr. Sage in the Laidlaw case, and a week later appeared for Executor Barling in an application by Mrs. Hetty Green to get rid of him. On June 25 he spoke in Boston at the dinner given to Professor Langdell of the Harvard Law School, a very considerable occasion, and doubtless made other discourse at the Harvard commencement. After that letters dated from Stockbridge imply that his vacation had begun. On the 22d of August he was a speaker at Professor Norton's annual Ashfield dinner in behalf of Sanderson Academy. Ashfield is in the Berkshires, and no doubt Mr. Choate went over there to contribute entertainment and edification as a neighborly act. In September law labors had come around again, and on the 30th he was the lawyer for the American Tobacco Company to defend it against the disposition of the government to dissolve it as a trust. In October he was as full of politics as his other engagements allowed—fighting Tammany as usual, speaking as the representative of the Committee of Fifty, helping to elect Governor Morton and Mayor Strong, and having withal a lot of fun as usual, especially with the Goo Goos (Good Government Club), whom he helped to get their emblem on the ballot, and made fun of between times, and went to the dinner at which they celebrated what they had done. Immediately after election one finds traces that he is in increased disfavor with the Irish and the object of verbal assaults by Patrick Egan, but that would probably not have taken up any of his time. On the 10th of November he spoke as the representative of the Municipal Art Society at the unveiling of Simmons's decorations in the new court-house. Later in the month he appeared

for the Milk Producers' Association before the Interstate Commerce Commissioners in a dispute with the
Erie Railroad, but that was in the line of business. It
was not in the line of business that he spoke at the St.
Andrew's dinner on the 30th of November, nor yet that,
"by request of Miss Florence Fairview," he represented
the United House-Smiths at a conference with the Iron
League, nor yet that he spoke on December 22 before
the Board of Estimate on the need of compelling charitable institutions where the city paid children's board to
put the children out into families as soon as they could,
and not keep them in institutions until they become in-
stitutionalized. In that effort he opposed Commodore
Gerry, who wanted the Children's Society to attend to
all that, but Mr. Choate would not agree, though he
was a director in the Commodore's society. Finally, on
December 27, came the hearing on Lord Dunraven's
charges that the Yankee winner hadn't played fair in
the yacht-race.

This list of his labors, very far from being complete,
only includes a part of those that were notorious enough
to be news for the papers, but it may give some idea of
the variety of the things he did. But, as said, after commencement he went to Stockbridge. From there he
writes, on July 15, to his daughter:

"Stockbridge,
Monday, 15 July, 1895.

"DEAREST MABEL:—
"I received your telegram early this morning and replied that Effie was better and that you must not change
your plans on her account. Poor thing! she is still very
ill as you may suppose. * * *
"This morning the troop of U. S. Artillery so long
heralded passed through town on their way to Bear Town

for a two months' camp for practice and drill. Of course
the whole town including all the clergymen were out to
meet so novel a sight. The Stockbridge Band tendered
them a complimentary escort, to supplement their single
bugle. They halted in front of the Hotel and Mr. Plumb
regaled them in the street with pies and Mr. Clark afterwards with cigars (bad of course), so that when the bugle
sounded for the advance each soldier started with a long
nine in his mouth. * * *"

To the Same

"Stockbridge, Mass.
16 July 1895.

" * * * A signal event happened yesterday—Prof. Rood
was seen taking his first lesson on the bicycle on the little
stretch of road between his house and Mercer's Cottage.
It seemed to be a great struggle, but he will doubtless
try again and succeed so that you will have another companion in your excursions, and who knows but that before you get home I may have been inspired to learn.
* * *"

Just as a happy nation has no history, so the happiest
periods of Mr. Choate's life left no record. When he
was at home with his family he did not write letters to
them. We hear from him again when he has got back
to town, and the accents are familiar:

To His Wife

"The Century Association
New York, 5 Octr. 1895.

"There is no telling how lonesome I have been since
Mabel left, but then I have been very busy and shall
be for a week, working up a new case on a subject wholly

new to me, and so, very interesting, to be argued at Washington on the 21st they say, but likely enough to be postponed until the Court is filled by the appointment of a new Judge in Justice Jackson's place. But I have to be ready all the same, and that accounts for my having to stay here when I really ought to be with you in Stockbridge.

"I have moved to the Union League where I have got for a wonder a big square room and am very comfortable indeed. I tried in vain for a room both at the Metropolitan and the University. I dine here at the Century where I almost always find some good fellow to sit with. Last night it was Dick —— who had a great deal to say about ——, and is not at all reconciled to her adventurous course. It seems that he did go with her to the altar and left her there, not being willing to give her away, and so that part of the service was omitted as it may be without harm. He says —— will not recognize —— in any way, and that he himself has never seen him except on the day of the wedding. I have had several interviews with the eight-tongued one at Madison Ave. He is now a theosophist, doesn't care whether he lives or dies, because he believes in re-incarnation, and that if he dies he will soon come back, as he knows he has been here several times before, in various shapes, although he can't remember it. He is writing a new criminological romance intended to illustrate the perpetual conflict between environment and heredity and is altogether a most amusing character. * * * J. H. C."

To the Same

"New York, 7 October, 1895.
" * * * All the anti-Tammany forces have united on Mr. Beaman for a Judge of the Supreme Court, and have

persuaded him that the use of his name is necessary for another triumph and so he has consented to run, and I'm afraid he will be elected much to our loss. He would probably like the life, have less work, and get three or four months vacation every year, but couldn't run to Blowmedown * every few days throughout the year as he does now.

"Mr. Carter has just arrived here looking very old and tired I thought, but perhaps he had been in a Goo-Goo Conference at the City Club. * * *

J. H. C."

"Union League Club, New York.
Monday 2:30 P. M. Oct. 14, 1895.

"MY DEAREST EFFIE:—

"I am just off for Washington, on the very finest day you ever saw, and although I have nothing else to say I write to tell you how very, very dear you are, and how I insist upon your getting better and better every day, and how everybody I meet is interested in your welfare. Everybody I talk to wants to know all about you, whether they ever saw you or not.

"I have just heard that my case which was to be argued next Monday, and which for that reason has been pressing me so, will probably be adjourned by the Court, and if that should turn out to be so, and no other bugbear turns up, I may very possibly get next Saturday and Sunday with you in Stockbridge, which I very much wish, for I miss my visits to you so much and I do want another forenoon on the Lake and another long ride over the hills.

"It poured all the way till I got to New York, and I

* His country place.

imagined the dear L. L. C.* riding drearily home in the wet and the dark.

"I met Mr. Rhinelander and one of his sons this morning. I couldn't tell which—but it was the other one—who was not at Daisy Wells's wedding and they asked most kindly for you. They said Tom's wife *and son* were prospering well now.

Ever your loving, PAPA."

"Tell Mama my new trousers came in time, so that she need feel no shame of me, and that I will drink no water so that she need have no fear for me."

To His Wife

"New York, 16 Octr. 1895.

"MY DEAREST,

"This has been just such a day as it was 34 years ago and on my way from Washington in the Limited I have recalled all the events of that great red letter day of our lives and don't really see how we could have done better. You have been to me all and more than all that I hoped, and I haven't begun to be tired, as Suzette feared Carl might after four weeks. * * *

"I had quite a compliment on the street. As I was crossing the Avenue near the Capitol a very good looking man who was spinning by on a bicycle suddenly stopped and jumped off, and said 'Isn't this Mr. Choate?' I said 'Yes.' 'Well,' he went on, 'I'm a lawyer and I only stopped to pay my respects, recognizing you by your photographs, and I wanted to say that I esteem you just as much as all the rest of the lawyers in the coun-

* "Lone Lorn Critter," one of his names for Mrs. Choate when she seemed overanxious about anything.

try do,' and upon that he remounted and was off again before I could even find out who he was. * * *

J. H. C."

Late in 1895 came the Venezuela sensation, when Mr. Cleveland and Mr. Olney stirred up the British lion. How Mr. Choate felt about it is discernible in his remarks at the New England dinner in New York on Christmas eve, when he rose, after Senator Morgan had spoken an hour and a half, to respond to the toast, "The Constitution and the *Mayflower*." A newspaper of the day says he quoted an old prophecy and said:

"I can give but one translation, and that is that he, whoever he may be, that creates or provokes an unjust or unnecessary war is no true descendant of the Pilgrims and the Puritans. Our Pilgrim fathers did believe in war, but only on one condition. They consented to it in the constitution, in the cabin of the *Mayflower*, when they wrote and subscribed their names that for the glory of God and the furtherance of the Christian faith and the honor of their country they bound themselves to submission and obedience to just and equal laws. And how true they and their children were in this very matter of peace and war was shown by the fact that they never encouraged, they never favored any war unless it was for the glory of God, for the furtherance of the Christian faith, and for the honor of their country. And it was in that spirit that the children of the Pilgrims and the Puritans have been parties to two great wars—the war of the Revolution, which secured the independence of their country against British aggression, which had become intolerable, and the war for the union, when they

JOSEPH HODGES CHOATE AT FIFTY YEARS OF AGE.
From a photograph by Sarony.

gave their fortunes, their lives and their children for the support of the government which their fathers had founded. But now we are confronted with a new condition. (That is a quotation.) And how shall we meet it? In what spirit? I sit at the feet of a great master, and I will tell you. Let me read to you what John Bright says, one of the truest friends that America ever had; what he says in a similar emergency which threatened his own country. Apply it, gentlemen, to the subject and the hour. Substitute America for Europe and for Britain in his utterances, and you have all I have to say on the present emergency. He says:

" 'It becomes a great state like this to set always to the world a great and noble example. We must always remember that the greatest of British interests is the interest of peace. Five years hence, if this matter be settled and we do not interfere, we shall be delighted that we did not interfere. Five years hence, if we do interfere, we shall lament for the dead whose blood has been sacrificed, for the treasure that has been wasted, and for the added discord that we have brought to Europe, and it may be for the humiliation of our statesmanship. Let us try to be just to all nations as far as we can, getting rid of the jealousies that have disturbed them. Let us believe that whether it be the United States on the other side of the Atlantic or the great empire of Russia in the east of Europe, that there are good and great and noble men in those countries.' "

Mr. Choate's last notable job of this busy year was to appear (December 27) for the New York Yacht Club at the investigation of the charges of Lord Dunraven, who brought over *Valkyrie III*, and sailed her for the

America's cup. Lord Dunraven had imbibed the unpleasant suspicion that ballast had been surreptitiously introduced into the American contesting yacht, *Defender*, and that that boat had been more deeply immersed on the 7th of September, when she sailed the race, and therefore had a longer water-line, than on the 6th of September, when she was measured. Mr. Choate examined Lord Dunraven as a witness. Whether his lordship was ever convinced that his suspicions were unfounded does not appear, but certainly most other persons were so persuaded, especially after the newspapers had published their reports of the questions Mr. Choate put to him, and his replies.

Moving pictures had not become a habit in 1895, but here are some reporters' stories that go a little of the ways to show Mr. Choate in action about that time. One is from the New York *Press* of December 20, 1895, whose representative says:

"It has afforded me considerable amusement to notice the attitudes assumed by prominent men riding in the elevated cars from home to business and back again. A good deal of character pops out now and then. Joe Choate drops into the northeast corner of the first car and curls himself up as if he were to settle there for life and cared for no creature in the world, not thinking of himself or of his appearance. He sees no one in the car. His mind is elsewhere."

(He once confessed to choosing the corner seat "so as not to be bored on more than one side at once.")

Five months later, in May. 1896, the *Mail and Express* had a similar tale:

"I saw Mr. Joseph H. Choate in an elevated car the other day, a day full of perspirations and prostrations, and he was more comforting to look at than the finest sherry cobbler ever designed by a master's hand. There was in his manner and appearance none of that smouldering indignation which you can trace in the countenances of most of the persons who arise in the morning early and mow themselves with their own scythes. I am told that Mr. Choate shaves himself with a Toledo rapier, and bathes his face in water specially imported from the north side of the oldest well in Topsfield, Mass. The guard on the car assured me that the company ought not to charge anything for transporting Mr. Choate. 'He cools a whole car,' said this admirer; 'he beats an electric fan all to pieces.' Hundreds of persons board the train at Fiftieth Street every morning solely for the purpose of making themselves comparatively comfortable by looking at Mr. Choate."

A third story, origin not given, and hardly of a dignity to find a place in a biography, still discloses in an amusing way how Mr. Choate in the real heat of action maintained his energies with least obstruction to the processes of active thought:

"The colored gentlemen who stand in an imposing row behind the long lunch counter in Nash & Crook's restaurant and wear white jackets the year round, regardless of the condition of the thermometer, were on the *qui vive* for an extensive order and a liberal fee when an elegantly attired gentleman in a light spring top coat and a shining silk hat rushed breathlessly into the restaurant recently with his arms full of legal papers and threw himself on to a bracket (?) with a famished look in his eyes.

"They of the white jacket made a rush for his section

of the counter, and the lucky one who got there first had hardly begun to polish the marble with expectant empressement when the gentleman said:

"'Hi! Give me a cup of coffee, quick!'

"'Cert'ly, Sah! What else?' responded the ebony gentleman, with a slight diminution of enthusiasm.

"'Nothing else,' retorted the customer, with an asperity that has made Judges quail on the bench before now.

"Before the waiter brought the coffee the gentleman left the bracket and rushed over to the oyster-stand where he seized a handful of crackers from the dish on the counter, and then swept back to his stool. Here he seized the coffee cup, and breaking the crackers into it, proceeded to bolt them with a spoon. The long row of waiters stood aghast, and watched him in horrified silence.

"'Golly!' said he, who had been fortunate enough to get the order at last, 'I'm ec'nom'cal myse'f, but I'm hanged 'f I'm ec'nom'cal as dat. Ten cents foh a lunch! Great Moses!'

"'Guess he muss have been stuck in the Marine Bank,' suggested another.

"'Or else loss his change in de bottom of a street car,' hazarded a third.

"But the object of their comments rapidly finished the contents of the cup without hearing their remarks, threw his check and a dime onto the cashier's desk, purchased two twenty-five cent cigars at the establishment of Mr. Michael Kelly in the corner, and hurled himself and his legal papers into the street.

"'Say!' said one of the gentlemen of the white jacket to Mr. Kelly after he had left, 'better see 'f that hawf dollaw's any good 'fore you try to pass it.'

" 'Don't you know who that was?' was the response. 'That was the Hon. Joseph H. Choate.'

" 'Dat so?' inquired the bewildered waiter. 'I fought he had all the money he wants. Gorra-mighty, bet 'f I was him I'd have quail on toast!'

" 'Now see how easy a man can get a reputation for being close,' observed Mr. Kelly, philosophically, when the waiter had returned to his dishes. 'Mr. Choate is one of the most liberal men with his money in this city, and because he runs in to get a cup of coffee to stay his stomach, without spoiling his dinner, those black rascals think he's trying to save money.'

"And Mr. Choate, in the dim recesses of the Surrogate's Court, continued to harass ex-Senator Roscoe Conkling with a running fire of sarcasm, unaware that his fair fame had been blighted forever."

To His Wife

"The Arlington, Washington, Jan. 14, 1896.

" * * * One of my three cases here came on today and is to be continued tomorrow, but the Irrigation Case seems hardly likely to be reached until next week. But I have so much to do in preparing for it and the Stanford case that I must stay here until they are argued. They are too important to leave and you know how impossible it is for me to escape from pursuers in New York. Even here the reporters are if possible more saucy than in New York. Last night I went to bed, which I have always believed to be a safe refuge you know, and at midnight there was a cry heard and a knock on the door— two California reporters who must see the Attorney General's brief in the Stanford case, of which they had heard I had a copy. * * *

J. H. C."

Of the irrigation cases, the Washington correspondent of *The Tribune* said (January 17):

"Joseph H. Choate, the well known lawyer of New York, is at the Arlington. Mr. Choate has several cases to argue before the United States Supreme Court, the most notable of which probably are the California irrigation cases, in which ex-President Harrison and Judge John F. Dillon are also concerned. The point of constitutional law involved is one of general interest, while the subject matter of the suits is of the most vital importance to the people of California. Under what is known as the Wright act, irrigation districts are created and these issue bonds as municipal corporations, impose irrigation taxes, and with the money thus obtained construct and maintain waterworks for the purpose of reclaiming the arid lands. The law has been upheld by the California Supreme Court, but in the United States Supreme Court after one hearing it was disposed of. The problem which causes the most trouble can be stated in a few words but the most profound lawyers in the country have given the deepest thought to the subject and have reached no certain conclusion. The question is, does the delegation of such powers to a district for the purposes of building waterworks constitute a delegation of sovereignty. If it does, the law is void. Millions of dollars' worth of property, including vast amounts invested in bonds of districts already established, which are held in all parts of the country, is involved, and the 'Treager case' will rank with the Dartmouth College case and the Wheeling Bridge case in point of importance and national interest."

As to the Stanford case, *The Associated Press* despatch, dated Washington, January 28, reads:

"Argument was heard today by the Supreme Court of the United States in the famous suit brought by the United States against the late Senator Stanford, of California, as a stockholder in the Central Pacific Railroad Company, to establish his liability for the debts of that corporation to the Government. The importance of the suit, with its far-reaching consequences if the contention of the Government should be sustained, and the popular interest of the case, attracted a large attendance to the court. Among the auditors was Mrs. Stanford, to whom the determination of the litigation means so much. Should it be adverse, the result would beggar her, and render it impossible to continue the work of the Leland Stanford, Jr., University at Palo Alto. The argument was opened by Assistant Attorney-General Dickinson, and will be closed by Solicitor-General Conrad. Mrs. Stanford was represented by Joseph H. Choate.

"The suit was originally begun in the Circuit Court of the United States for the Southern District of California, the demand being for $15,237,000. Both in that court and in the Circuit Court of Appeals the Government was defeated, and the case comes to the Supreme Court of the United States by appeal from the judgment of the Court of Appeals against the United States."

To His Wife

"Washington, D. C. 16 Jany. 1896.
" * * * Almost everybody in Washington is decidedly Jingo—apparently upon the idea of standing by the President against a foreign power no matter what he says or does. The Tuckermans and Wards, however stand firm, but Emily says it isn't safe now inviting a miscellaneous company to dinner without knowing their

opinions beforehand, because the Jingoes are so loud and angry in their denunciations of all who don't fall into line.

"I enclose a page from the *Congressional Record* containing a speech of Senator Vest of Missouri delivered in the Senate last week in which he shows up the Supreme Court and me in connexion with it in first rate style. You will find it good reading, but it's a pity that Senators can't find some better use for their time. * * * "

So apparently thought the Washington correspondent of the Boston *Advertiser*, who said on January 18:

"J. H. Choate, the New York lawyer, who gained much fame in arguing the unconstitutionality of the income tax and who was the subject of an attack for so doing by Senator Vest in his recent speech, is in town. The rumor that he has come on to arrange a duel with the grey-haired Missourian is untrue."

To His Wife

"Washington, Jan. 18, 1896.
"I meet a good many people, but you would be surprised to see how little they are disturbed by the President's antics. The official atmosphere seems to overwhelm the average man."

(January 20.) "Yesterday I had a pleasant lunch at Judge Field's, with Judge Brewer, Henry Field and Senator Perkins of California, one of those accidental Senators who began life by running away from home in Kennebunk, going several voyages before the mast, landing in California at a lucky moment, climbing to the

Governorship & then going to the Senate. In the evening I dined at the Williams's. * * * Admiral Walker was there, and Genl. Foster who went to China and negotiated for them the peace treaty with Japan, for which he is said to have received a fee of $100,000. He gave me a most interesting account of going to Pekin to expound the Treaty to the Grand Council. Dr. T. DeWitt Talmage is here, as boisterous as ever. Also Mr. Coudert in search of the Venezuela Boundary. Everybody here is still wild."

General Foster, whom he speaks of, was the father-in-law, and reputed tutor in diplomacy, of Mr. Lansing, secretary of state for President Wilson.

(January 22.) "I am truly sorry at the prospect of being kept here so long, but now fear that I shall be kept here all next week, for after the Irrigation and the Stanford cases, Mr. Rowe is to come down and cram me up for the summing up of the *milk* case which is set down to be argued here next week.

"The bores are beginning to find me out. I have just had a crazy lawyer down from New York who talked me nearly to pieces and I only said 'Yes! Yes! Uh! Ah!' which was certainly easy. 'Squire' Smalley is here getting up his letters for the London *Times*. He thinks he finds a great change of feeling among all the officials here, and that they are looking for some hole to creep out of."

(January 25.) " * * * You cannot imagine how lonely I was yesterday to have to spend my birthday alone. However, I was frightfully busy and at last before the day closed began my own argument in the Irrigation cases which will be finished on Monday afternoon when the Stanford case will be taken up to be finished on Wednesday. You will appreciate what a relief it will be to get rid of two such loads together. One gets so tired of carrying the details in one's head, which makes it almost impossible to think of anything else. After that my milk case will detain me a day or two and I shall come on Saturday morning. * * * One ought to have a double head to carry these two cases together. Last evening my twin and I celebrated our birthday by going to the theatre together to see 'Madame Sans Gêne,' and found it very interesting. Tonight I am to dine again at the Wolcotts' to meet those jingling jingoes, Cabot Lodge and Theodore Roosevelt, both of whom I think would like very much *the fun* of a war with England. * * *

J. H. C."

"The Arlington, Washington, D. C.
26 Jan. 1896.

"DEAR MABEL.

" * * * Last night at the Wolcotts' I met Speaker Reed and Mrs. Reed who evidently have a strong hope and expectation of taking the places of Mr. and Mrs. Cleveland. Mr. & Mrs. Roosevelt were there too. They are great devotees of Mr. Reed. Roosevelt says that Platt is after his scalp and is trying to get the Police Commissioners legislated out of office. What a shame that such a man as Platt should have so much power!

"I keep receiving a great many more invitations to dinner than I can possibly attend to and think I must get a double to do that part of the work for me."

To His Wife

"Washington, D. C. 28 Jany. 1896.

"I can not tell you how great a sense of relief is coming over me, at the prospect of getting rid in one hour more tomorrow of the Stanford case, having concluded the Irrigation case yesterday. I have been brooding over them so long that my brain has hardly been able to hold any other thing. The milk case will be just nothing at all.

"I have just telegraphed you to send me some more visiting cards. Etiquette rules everything here, and I find it necessary to make any quantity of calls.

"Yesterday I made the round of the Justices' wives and called on Mrs. Cleveland who seemed to have a great crowd. * * *

                                            J. H. C."

282882

He got back to New York to more work and more dinners—the Harvard Club dinner on February 7, the Ohio Club dinner on February 8; to an address to the Consumers' League, on February 12, to help the shopgirls; and so on, about as usual.

On April 11 the Raines Law case began, in which Mr. Choate, as counsel for the brewers and maltsters, attacked the Raines Law as unconstitutional. Public memory may be growing faint as to the details of the regulation of the sale of intoxicants while there were still intoxicants sold, but the Raines Law had to do with the regulation of saloons and of licenses, and though it was not a particularly good law, Mr. Choate failed to upset it.

On April 13 he represented New York at the semi-centennial jubilation of the Pennsylvania Railroad in Philadelphia. He made a very amusing speech, but duly enriched with matter fit for thought, as all his speeches were. The next day the Republican Club in New York gave him a dinner, and of course he spoke at that.

To His Daughter Josephine

"52 Wall St.
Tuesday morning, June 9, 1896.

"MY DARLING EFFIE:—

"I must write you the very first thing before crowds of people come in (as they always do) and interrupt the pleasantest thing I have to do today. First, let me say how delighted I am to feel that you are out of this furnace heated city, and at least within hearing of the cool breezes of Berkshire, for today is one of the worst of those hot, moist, sticky and damp, unpleasant days which wear everybody out, and which you particularly found so wilting, and this in spite of several thunder showers which began while I was at dinner and lasted till after their music had put me to sleep. The house I found very desolate and forlorn. Think how much was gone—you, and Mama and Mabel and Polly and Dinah, to say nothing of the innumerable 'things' which have disappeared from sight, and which ordinarily make the house sightly and comfortable. Where have they all gone? However, Emma and Matilda were delighted to hear that you had got to Stockbridge so comfortably and are immensely interested in your welfare. I had to tie two knots in my handkerchief coming down, by dint of which I remembered to mail Dr. Kinnicutt's letter, and then to go

to the Metropolitan Club and order Mabel's bicycle to
be packed and sent to Stockbridge, which will be done
today by Adams Express. * * *
                                                    PAPA."

To His Wife

"New York, 22 June 1896.
"On my return from Court this afternoon I received
the very shocking news of the sudden death of our friend
Genl. Bristow, who breathed his last at noon today. * * *
I had known him so well and been with him in so many
things, that his death is more of a shock to me than that
of any other man would be except one of our brothers or
Mr. Carter. * * * He was one of our noblest men, and
it will not be easy to find his peer. * * *
                                                 J. H. C."

Josephine Choate died at Stockbridge on July 20,
after an illness lasting nearly two years.

To His Wife

"New York, Oct. 7, 1896.
"MY DEAREST ONE,
"How fearfully lonely you must feel just now, with
not one of us at hand to cheer or to jeer you. It makes
one miss our darling lost ones more and more. I have
been irresistibly drawn toward Woodlawn since I found
myself in New York, and today after breakfast I went
to the depot intending to visit that sacred spot, but no
study of the time table enabled me to see any way in
which I could go and return before the meeting of our
Board. But I shall certainly go some time tomorrow.
My case that I intended or was ready to argue here on
Friday has 'gone off' till November—another instance

of my favorite theory that if I get ready all along the line, at least half of my adversaries will be sure to back down. This will enable me to come up by the nine o'clock train on Friday after registering, and so I shall have at least a full week again in Stockbridge.

"The meeting of our Board of Trustees was a successful one. Every Trustee was present except President Cleveland, and Judge Endicott who is reported as in a very bad state. Some days he appears well enough, but on others he fails to recognize his best friends. The question of dissolving the Trust* and distributing the money which Mr. Peabody provided might be done by consent of two-thirds of the Trustees after thirty years, was indefinitely postponed. We all thought that to distribute the money in the South as matters now stand would be little better than throwing it away. Next year I hope you will be able to attend the meeting with me as you have never yet had a chance to do. Members from the South bring their wives and daughters along and make it quite interesting. Twenty-one will dine together tonight without me or Mr. Morgan or Mr. Evarts who for the first time said he couldn't attend, for no particular reason, but I suppose it is quite out of the question now for him to sit so long. Mary was in charge of him all day; that is, she brought him in the morning and came and waited for him in the afternoon, and he seemed to me to have declined somewhat since Spring.

"I suppose that Mabel got off yesterday, and trust she will sleep long and well in Newport. We must look well after her now.

"With much love to dear Kitty,
            Ever your devoted,   J. H. C."

* The (George) Peabody Trust for education in the South.

To the Same

"Washington, 20 Oct. 1896.

"At this Arlington you do see all sorts and conditions of men. Today at the lunch table next me sat two refined looking Chinese in their pigtails and blue silks eating oysters with a fork and chicken livers and rice like any Christians. On inquiry they proved to be gentlemen sent over here by the Chinese Government to inspect our shipping, and to learn and report about that.
* * *   J. H. C."

"The Century, 7 W. 43rd St.
21 Oct. 1896.

"Dear Mabel,

" * * * I have been for the first time today in the new Bar Association Building which is a perfect marvel of beauty and comfort—I was indeed very proud to see my portrait on its walls, and must take you there to see the Library at the first opportunity.   Papa."

To His Wife

"Union League Club.
New York, 3 Nov. 1896.

"This is going to be a tremendous night in New York —everybody is highly excited and apparently determined to sit it out until McKinley is elected. New York City is the only place heard from as yet, and that of course gives a large majority for McKinley. * * *

"As I write, pandemonium is all about—horns, trumpet, and bon-fires outside, and the crowd of members within cheering lustily at the returns. I hardly think however that anything decisive will come till very late in the night. * * *   J. H. C."

"The Arlington, Washington, D. C.
8 Nov. 1896.

"MY VERY DEAREST MABEL.

" * * * Since I arrived here I have been hard at work
all the time getting ready for the Bell Telephone argument by boiling down all that I have been brooding over
for two months into an argument not to exceed two hours,
which is always a difficult thing. * * *

"People here are already beginning to look for the
departure of Cleveland and the coming of McKinley,
which is expected to bring a decidedly Western flavor
into Washington life, but I feel very sure that Mr. &
Mrs. Cleveland are joyfully counting off the 120 days
which will bring freedom to them. * * *
                                            PAPA."

To His Wife

"New York, 16 November 1896.

" * * * All Boston is now divided into two hostile
camps—the Bacchantes and the Anti Bacchantes. Yesterday there was a private view of the creature* in the
Courtyard of the Library. The Trustees had accepted
it from McKim, when the Art Commission intervened,
and forbade its being exhibited, but relented so far as
to allow it to be set up for one day—Sunday—on condition that after that it should be instantly removed.
Jo and I went with the rest of the Elite to see it, but could
find no harm in it. It is a very lively creation, shrouded
quite enough by a dozen jets of spray playing over it.
The fuss they are making about it seems supremely silly,
but the wise men of Boston are about equally divided.
                                            J. H. C."

* MacMonnies's statue, now in the Metropolitan Museum in New York.

To the Same

"New York, Nov. 20, 1896.

" * * * Today in a horse car a young clergyman approached me most deferentially and addressed me as Bishop Potter, and seemed much disappointed when I had to answer 'Nolo episcopari.' He thought the resemblance was marvellous. * * *

"I am bothered just now with getting up an address for the ovation to Dr. Storrs at the Academy of Music on Tuesday evening. As he has been the victim of constant fêtes and glorifications for the last ten years it is not very easy to put a fresh face on it, but he is such a dear that I am glad to do it as a labor of love. * * *

J. H. C."

"The Arlington, Washington, D. C.
3 Decr. 1896.

"MY DEAREST MABEL.

"I have just come out of an entire day's session of the Court which ended my great case (Bell Telephone), and of course take great delight in writing to you as a rest and contrast. I have now got rid of the whole load which I have been carrying all the fall, and shall have easy times. I have a case for Monday here of very easy character about the New York Indians, for which I shall have to come down I suppose on Sunday afternoon.

"Last night I dined with Emily* and her mother, who were both I think pretty tired from moving down, and yet they were both very bright and cordial. Emily is bent upon my packing you and Mama both off to the Sunny South—Jekyl Island—or some such place, where

* Miss Tuckerman.

you can be out of doors all the time and out of the way of all bores and trouble. What do you say to that? Of course I should go with you and visit you from time to time. They were both much excited about the Senatorship as though it might possibly materialize, but I told Emily that I should probably go into the Senate about the same time that she does, and we can have a good time together there. * * *"

To His Wife

"Washington, D. C. 6 Dec. 1896.

"Thanks to a couple of quiet days I have easily got ready for the New York Indians tomorrow, and shall take great satisfaction in presenting their case to the Supreme Court. The Government took away their lands more than thirty seven years ago since which they have been applicants to Congress for compensation, and after being kicked to and fro there for more than three decades their case was sent to the Court of Claims. They following the example of Congress again kicked them out, and now we are in the Supreme Court—the last ditch—and expect to win. * * *

J. H. C."

One of Mr. Choate's supplementary exercises in the last weeks of 1896 and the first two weeks of 1897 was to run for United States Senator from New York. The Legislature at Albany was Republican and would elect a Senator to succeed David B. Hill. The question came to be whether it would choose Thomas Platt or some one else, and the Republicans who wanted some one else selected Mr. Choate to be that man. The Union League Club came out strong for him and appointed a committee, including its most influential members, to try to get him elected. There was a big meeting in support of him at Carnegie Hall on December 23, 1896. There was a very active movement in support of him in Brooklyn; and an imposing committee there to support his candidacy. For two or three weeks the campaign was the leading topic in the papers. The claim for Mr. Choate was that he was infinitely more fit to be Senator than Mr. Platt. The claim for Mr. Platt was that he understood the business of politics better than Mr. Choate did. A quotation from *Puck*, of January, 1897, doubtless written by Bunner, puts the case fairly well as the Choate men saw it. It says:

"Do the people of the state of New York ever reflect, we wonder, that their general intelligence and moral status may reasonably be inferred from the kind of men they send to speak for them in the United States Senate? At present their state is reputed throughout the country to be one wholly given over to the most corrupt form of boss rule—a state where the best citizenship is of a low order and where the opportunities for official stealings are the most magnificent known. And if they feel resentful of this view and inclined to wonder at it, they have only to consider the two men who now represent them in the Senate, and the character of the man who seems to have the better chance of succeeding one of them. For Senator Murphy they can offer no excuse. As a ward-heeler he attained the highest efficiency possible to him. As a Senator he is an illiterate nonentity, incapable of anything save to show what boss rule may do for a state. Of Senator Hill—Charity invoking her favorite *De mortuis nil nisi bonum*—we feel constrained to say nothing. But, unfit as he was for the position of Senator, he was not so preposterous as Thomas C. Platt would be. Mr. Hill often displayed a commendable interest in the questions of the day.

"Mr. Platt is unique and remarkable for having never, by spoken or written word, declared the shadow of an opinion concerning any of the vital issues of the time. He has singly and unswervingly devoted himself to the manipulation of Legislatures by corrupt means, and to the doling out of spoils. As far back as 1878 we find him attacking President Hayes for treachery to the New York State machine, and never since then has he opened his head except upon the one subject of patronage. Sent to the Senate, himself, in 1881, he promptly resigned, not from any high conviction that he could not acceptably serve the people of this state as a Senator, but because he was denied the spoils of office for which he had worked."

What there was to be said for Mr. Platt was best said in *The Sun*. To the question put by the Utica *Press*, "Let any reader answer, honor bright, which is the abler man, Mr. Choate or Mr. Platt," it replied:

"To this public history has made the answer easy. Regarding uprightness Mr. Choate's word is equally good with Mr. Platt's, and they pay their debts with equal promptitude; at least we have never heard to the contrary.

"Regarding ability, while both Mr. Choate and Mr. Platt possess a very high order of it, comparison has to be forced, their qualities being so dissimilar. Mr. Choate has been trained in the law, which is his livelihood, to a high point of perfection; Mr. Platt has been trained in politics, which is not his livelihood, to a high point of perfection. Each is a topsawyer in his respective walk, although Mr. Platt's regular vocation has probably made him the more expert in the ways of business. Mr. Choate's intellectual machinery, which has enjoyed far greater opportunities for display, may be more complicated, more voluminous, and more brilliant in its manifestations than Mr. Platt's; but as to the more commanding and more vital quality of judgment, we must think that Mr. Platt's is generally sounder and more valuable to his friends in council than Mr. Choate's.

"When it comes to moral stamina, the persistence and energy with which one maintains and advances his purposes, Mr. Choate has shown himself to be truly a hero on the ground where he has been tried, while on the larger and far more perplexing and difficult field of public affairs where Mr. Platt has been tried, the latter has shown himself to be an indomitable, unyielding, and veritable tiger. In the matter of experience, Mr. Platt is very highly trained, as Mr. Choate is not at all, to perceive public sentiment, to deal with it, and to respect it in his dealings. He enjoys an overwhelming advantage over Mr. Choate in political skill and practice, and his eminent and invaluable achievements in politics, in State and nation, are facts with which Mr. Choate's record provides next to nothing for comparison.

"Putting together the equipments of these two eminent New Yorkers, unemotional and impartial opinion will conclude that Mr. Platt is an abler and fitter man for Senator, particularly for a Republican Senator, than Mr. Choate."

Mr. Platt controlled the Legislature, and it voted just as he said. What happened in Albany is succinctly disclosed in a paragraph in *The Tribune*:

"Albany, N. Y. Jan. 14. Thomas C. Platt has named himself for United States Senator. In 1881 it might have been said with truth that a majority of the Republican members of the Legislature selected him as their candidate for Senator, but in 1897 the process was reversed. Mr. Platt instructed the Republican Senators and Assemblymen to select him, and they obeyed his orders. There never has been in Albany a Legislature more completely under the domination of a political machine. * * *

"Of the 149 votes cast, Mr. Platt received 142—110 Assemblymen and 32 Senators."

Mr. Choate said that he only expected to get one vote and that it gratified him very much that he got seven. Judging from the records in his scrap-books he went on as though nothing had happened, and of course nothing very much had happened so far as he was concerned.

One of his greater cases in the first half of the year was the defense of the American Tobacco Company against the disposition of the federal law officers to dissolve it as a trust. About this trial and Mr. Choate's appearance in it, the *Mail and Express* of June 26 said:

"Circumstances combine to give importance to the trial of what the public has been wont to call the Tobacco Trust, which has been going on now for three weeks in the Court of General Sessions. For the first time in the history of the commonwealth the State has essayed to press home on a legitimate corporation a criminal charge based on business methods that, whether legitimate or not, are not at all unknown to trade. And it has brought to book the officers of one of the most powerful corporations in the country. The American Tobacco Company stands behind the defendants with a capitalization of $35,000,000 and the prestige of what is almost a monopoly of the cigarette output of the United States. Its yearly production of cigarettes is about four billions, and nine out of every ten men who affect this attenuated culture of the weed are in some sense interested in its fate, for nine out of ten men smoke only their brands.

"It is charged that the defendants were not content with the natural results of the economies incident to the combination of independent companies, but that they conspired to rid the field of a rival by compelling the jobber to handle only their products, and, when he admitted to his counters other goods, withdrew their consignments from him. They restricted trade, in the language of the indictment. To repel this charge the American Tobacco Company has retained the ablest members of the New York bar. To prove it beyond cavil the District Attorney himself has conducted the case, and has given it a degree of personal attention that indicates the quality of his determination and expectation.

"And that is where the personal interest of the trial comes in, for it brings face to face, in a criminal litigation, the young District Attorney, still new to this branch of the law, and Joseph H. Choate, who is feared of all men, and whose argument against the income tax before the highest tribunal established his supremacy among American advocates. It is more like a baptism of fire than a graduated and orderly introduction to the criminal bar. Without much preliminary skirmishing even with field pieces, Mr. Olcott has had to march right up against the heaviest siege guns.

"The thundering of those pieces has sounded pretty constantly for the last fortnight. Mr. Choate may be likened to a dynamite gun of great range and kicking power. * * *

"There are few more striking faces than Mr. Choate's. Youthful in its expression, but marked with lines of power, the thick curly hair that surmounts it and the quizzical brown eyes that light it, half belie the strongly chiseled chin, the firmly set mouth, the bold and resolute nose. The head is round and massive, and it is finely, if jauntily, posed on an erect and active figure of more than the middle height. When Mr. Choate lowers his chin and compresses his lips and glooms under knitted brows with those deep brown eyes, he presents as disconcerting an apparition as ever confronted a witness.

"Not until Monday morning will the senior counsel for the defense find his full opportunity. His summing up, it goes without saying, will attract a crowd to Part IV of the General Sessions. He has not a large voice, but there is not a clearer voice in the American forum, and none that is used with more skill. A singing teacher would classify it probably as a robust tenor. When the speaker exerts himself his whole body becomes merely a resonant organ, and his words ring above the words of others as music will above mere voices. There is a whole range of inflections and suggestion in that voice that is terra incognita to other speakers. New meanings and qualifications are expressed by its lightest shadings. That is Joseph H. Choate, attorney to the Committee of Seventy, that prosecuted the Tweed ring twenty-five years ago.

"Twenty-five years is a quarter of a century, but Mr. Choate looks as if he had just grown up."

In June Mrs. Choate had gone to Stockbridge, and there are letters again:

To His Wife

"New York, 16 June 1897.

"*My best day*—my dearest one, and the one for which I shall always be more grateful than for all others—and today it is *sixty* times as good as it ever was before. And what a shame that we can never seem to be able to spend it together! Isn't it most time for us to defy all the rest of mankind and just devote ourselves to ourselves and each other. * * *

"These low papers—*The World* and *The Journal*—are caricaturing me in the vilest way as the Champion of the Tobacco Trust. You could hardly imagine how ugly they make me, and since I proposed to have the proprietor, manager and reporter of *The Journal* indicted for tampering with our jury, its abuse is most villainous of course. * * *

                                          J. H. C."

To the Same

"New York, 16 June 1897.
Union League Club.

" * * * Mr. Root and I have been fighting hard all day in Court and dining together at the Club tonight. He desires to be remembered to both you and Mabel. * * *

                                          J. H. C."

To the Same

"New York, 19 June 1897.

" * * * Last night for almost the first time since our return I had a quiet evening to myself and read the first volume of Sally Gibbons' life of her mother. I think she has done it amazingly well. At any rate I found the book intensely interesting because it brings most vividly to mind some of my early experiences in New York which I had well nigh forgotten. * * *

J. H. C."

To His Son

"50 West 47th Street,
Sunday evening, June 20, '97.

"DEAR JO:—

"While your examinations were going on, I suppose your Class Day* and Commencement parts stared you in the face and annoyed you very much—but now that those are over, you will have plain sailing. Of course for a few days before such performances those who are to take part in them are more or less apprehensive. I remember that even Mr. Lowell was in a terrible funk the day before he had to read his great oration in Sanders Theatre on the 250th year celebration, and told his daughter that it was good for nothing and he couldn't possibly go through with it. And in spite of my long experience I am always more or less troubled in spirit for a day or two before an 'occasional' speech, but it always comes out all right.

"If your poem were ten times as good as it is of course you wouldn't be satisfied with it. Nobody ever is, and so you have only to go ahead and make the best of it.

"You must have got pretty tired by this time, and so I should take all the rest and sleep I could between now and Thursday and not try to lie awake nights about it, and pray be careful about eating and drinking, especially if there are any farewell suppers in the meantime.

* He was class poet.

"Henry Ward Beecher used to say that nine hours sleep the night before was his best preparation for a speech.

"You see I am thinking of you all the time, and do not doubt of your acquitting yourself well.
                                                    PAPA."

One of the incidents of the summer was the visit of President McKinley and a party to Stockbridge, where they were welcomed and entertained, and stopped to see, among other people, Mr. and Mrs. Choate. The newspaper account of their call gives this description of Mr. Choate's house:

"The Choate house is of light-colored brick and rises three stories above the lawn. It is on the top of a steep slope of the hills that rise above Stockbridge village. The party drove in, and all got down from the carriages and went indoors, where a party of some thirty friends had been bidden to meet the guests. The interior of the house is charming. There is a great hall running through from the front door to the veranda beyond, and the windows afford a charming outlook. On the right of the hall and near the door, stairs rise entirely out of sight from the hall. On the further side is the dining-room, finished in mahogany, and the hall in old English oak, and both handsomely furnished. The fireplace and mantel in the hall are of dark brown stone. The parlor opens on the left, and is finished and furnished in light colors. Beyond it, and yet opening from the hall, is the library, a large room with a bay window and finished in dark wood. It was in this room that the President signed for himself and his wife in the 'Guest Book.'"

There was an election again in the fall. There had been a great Republican triumph the previous year in the election of McKinley. It was followed in 1897 by a spectacular Tammany success in New York in the election of Robert Van Wyck as mayor. It is of that Mr. Choate speaks when he writes to his wife on November 4:

" * * * Of course we have not yet been able to think of anything but the election and its frightful results. It seems to have brought us into great contempt with foreign nations as well as with the rest of the country. Everybody here seems to be very mad with everybody else, but the chief vengeance from all quarters is visited on Platt. As long as such a man commands success he has many followers, but such an absolute and total failure as this must go far to destroy him. Poor Mr. Southmayd couldn't make up his mind how to vote, and so didn't vote at all. He couldn't take the responsibility of voting for Seth Low and wouldn't vote for any of the others.

"The idea of Van Wyck and Tammany apparently is to keep everything 'open' so that we may expect all forms of vice to be freely cultivated and exhibited without restraint. A specimen of it was given on Election night, when the worst characters in town of both sexes paraded the streets and parks in the most shameless way, singing 'To Hell with reform!'—the refrain of the new District Attorney who by the way ran ahead of his ticket—no doubt for that very thing. * * * "

On February 4, 1898, he was the guest of honor of the Bar Association of Chicago at a great dinner given at the Palmer House in that city, and replied to the toast,

"Our Profession," in a discourse well worth quoting here in full, which is included in the volume of his "American Addresses."

Another notable address to lawyers made in that same year was his speech on August 18, in Saratoga to the American Bar Association, on Trial by Jury. That address also will be found in the volume of his "American Addresses."

Still another address of special interest to lawyers he made this year on October 15 at the unveiling of French's statue of Rufus Choate in the court-house at Boston. He put it first in the book of his "American Addresses," and it is likely to rank as the best of them all. He loved Rufus Choate as a relative who had been kind to him in his youth and, as he said, smoothed his first steps and paved his way to fortune; and as a lawyer, a citizen and a man he greatly admired him. His own character will be better understood if one has read what he found to say about his illustrious cousin who contributed so much to inspire and shape it.

"I deem it a very great honor," he said, "to have been invited by the Suffolk Bar Association to take part on this occasion in honor of him who still stands as one of the most brilliant ornaments of the American Bar in its annals of two centuries. Bearing his name and lineage, and owing to him, as I do, more than to any other man or men—to his example and inspiration, to his sympathy and helping hand—whatever success has attended my own professional efforts, I could not refuse the invitation to come here to-day to the dedication of his statue, which shall stand for centuries to come, and convey to the generations who knew him not some idea of the figure and the features of Rufus Choate. Neither bronze nor marble

can do him justice. Not Rembrandt himself could reproduce the man as we knew and loved him—for until
he lay upon his death-bed he was all action, the 'noble,
divine, godlike action' of the orator—and the still life
of art could never really represent him as he was.

"I am authorized, at the outset, to express for the
surviving children of Mr. Choate their deep sense of
gratitude to the generous donor of this statue of their
honored father, and their complete appreciation of the
sentiment which has inspired the city and the court to
accept it as a public treasure, and to give it a permanent
home at the very gates of the Temple of Justice, at whose
shrine he worshipped. They desire also to express
publicly on this occasion their admiration of the statue
itself, as a work of art, and a faithful portrait, in form
and feature, of the living man as he abides in their loving
memory. The City of Boston is certainly indebted to
Mr. French for his signal skill in thus adding a central
figure to that group of great orators whom its elder citizens once heard with delight—Webster, Choate, Everett,
Mann, Sumner and Garrison. In life, they divided the
sentiments and applause of her people. In death, they
share the honors of her Pantheon.

"It is forty years since he strode these ancient streets
with majestic step—forty years since the marvellous
music of his voice was heard by the living ear—and those
of us who, as students and youthful disciples, followed
his footsteps, and listened to his eloquence, and almost
worshipped his presence, whose ideal and idol he was,
are already many years older than he lived to be; but
there must be a few still living, and present here to-day,
who were in the admiring crowds that hung with rapture
on his lips—in the courts of justice, in the densely packed

assembly, in the Senate, in the Constitutional Convention, or in Faneuil Hall consecrated to Freedom—and who can still recall, among life's most cherished memories, the tones of that matchless voice, that pallid face illuminated with rare intelligence, the flashing glance of his dark eye, and the light of his bewitching smile. But, in a decade or two more, these lingering witnesses of his glory and his triumphs will have passed on, and to the next generation he will be but a name and a statue, enshrined in fame's temple with Cicero and Burke, with Otis and Hamilton and Webster, with Pinkney and Wirt, whose words and thoughts he loved to study and to master.

"Many a noted orator, many a great lawyer, has been lost in oblivion in forty years after the grave closed over him, but I venture to believe that the Bar of Suffolk, aye, the whole Bar of America, and the people of Massachusetts, have kept the memory of no other man alive and green so long, so vividly and so lovingly, as that of Rufus Choate. Many of his characteristic utterances have become proverbial, and the flashes of his wit, the play of his fancy and the gorgeous pictures of his imagination are the constant themes of reminiscence, wherever American lawyers assemble for social converse. What Mr. Dana so well said over his bier is still true to-day: 'When as lawyers we meet together in tedious hours and seek to entertain ourselves, we find we do better with anecdotes of Mr. Choate, than on our own original resources.' The admirable biography of Professor Brown, and his arguments, so far as they have been preserved, are text books in the profession—and so the influence of his genius, character and conduct is still potent and far reaching in the land.

"You will not expect me, upon such an occasion, to enter upon any narrative of his illustrious career, so familiar to you all, or to undertake any analysis of those remarkable powers which made it possible. All that has been done already by many appreciative admirers, and has become a part of American literature. I can only attempt, in a most imperfect manner, to present a few of the leading traits of that marvellous personality, which we hope that this striking statue will help to transmit to the students, lawyers and citizens who, in the coming years, shall throng these portals.

"How it was that such an exotic nature, so ardent and tropical in all its manifestations, so truly southern and Italian in its impulses, and at the same time so robust and sturdy in its strength, could have been produced upon the bleak and barren soil of our northern cape, and nurtured under the chilling blasts of its east winds, is a mystery insoluble. Truly, 'this is the Lord's doing, and it is marvellous in our eyes.' In one of his speeches in the Senate, he draws the distinction between 'the cool and slow New England men, and the mercurial children of the sun, who sat down side by side in the presence of Washington, to form our more perfect union.' If ever there was a mercurial child of the sun, it was himself most happily described. I am one of those who believe that the stuff that a man is made of has more to do with his career than any education or environment. The greatness that is achieved, or is thrust upon some men, dwindles before that of him who is born great. His horoscope was propitious. The stars in their courses fought for him. The birthmark of genius, distinct and ineffaceable, was on his brow. He came of a long line of pious and devout ancestors, whose living was as plain as their thinking was high. It was from father and mother that he derived the flame of intellect, the glow of spirit and the beauty of temperament that were so unique.

"And his nurture to manhood was worthy of the child. It was 'the nurture and admonition of the Lord.' From that rough pine cradle, which is still preserved in the room where he was born, to his premature grave at the age of fifty-nine, it was one long course of training and discipline of mind and character, without pause or rest. It began with that well-thumbed and dog's-eared Bible from Hog Island, its leaves actually worn away by the pious hands that had turned them, read daily in the family from January to December, in at Genesis and out at Revelations every two years; and when a new child was born in the household, the only celebration, the only festivity, was to turn back to the first chapter, and read once more how 'in the beginning God created the heaven and the earth,' and all that in them is. This Book, so early absorbed and never forgotten, saturated his mind and spirit more than any other, more than all other books combined. It was at his tongue's end, at his fingers' ends—always close at hand until those last languid hours at Halifax, when it solaced his dying meditations. You can hardly find speech, argument or lecture of his, from first to last, that is not sprinkled and studded with biblical ideas and pictures, and biblical words and phrases. To him the book of Job was a sublime poem. He knew the Psalms by heart, and dearly loved the prophets, and above all Isaiah, upon whose gorgeous imagery he made copious drafts. He pondered every word, read with most subtle keenness, and applied with happiest effect. One day coming into the Crawford House, cold and shivering—and you remember how he could shiver—he caught sight of the blaze in the great fireplace, and was instantly warm before the rays could reach him, exclaiming, 'Do you remember that verse in Isaiah, 'Aha! I am warm. I have *seen* the fire'? and so his daily conversation was marked.

"And upon this solid rock of the Scriptures he built a magnificent structure of knowledge and acquirement, to which few men in America have ever attained. History, philosophy, poetry, fiction, all came as grist to his mental mill. But with him, time was too precious to read any trash; he could winnow the wheat from the chaff at sight, almost by touch. He sought knowledge, ideas, for their own sake, and for the language in which they were conveyed. I have heard a most learned jurist gloat over the purchase of the last sensational novel, and have seen a most distinguished bishop greedily devouring the stories of Gaboriau one after another, but Mr. Choate seemed to need no such counter-irritant or blister, to draw the pain from his hurt mind. Business, company, family, sickness—nothing could rob him of his one hour each day in the company of illustrious writers of all ages. How his whole course of thought was tinged and embellished with the reflected light of the great Greek orators, historians and poets; how Roman history, fresh in his mind as the events of yesterday, supplied him with illustrations and supports for his own glowing thoughts and arguments, all of you who have either heard him or read him know.

"But it was to the great domain of English literature that he daily turned for fireside companions, and really kindred spirits. As he said in a letter to Sumner, with whom his literary fraternity was at one time very close: 'Mind that Burke is the fourth Englishman—Shakespeare, Bacon, Milton, Burke': and then in one of those dashing outbursts of playful extravagance, which were so characteristic of him, fearing that Sumner, in his proposed review, might fail to do full justice to the great ideal of both, he adds: 'Out of Burke might be cut 50 Mackintoshes, 175 Macaulays, 40 Jeffreys and 250 Sir Robert Peels, and leave him greater than Pitt and Fox together.' In the constant company of these great thinkers and writers he revelled, and made their thoughts his own; and his insatiable memory seemed to store up all things committed to it, as the books not in daily use are stacked away in your public library, so that at any moment, with notice or without, he could lay his hand straightway upon them. What was once imbedded in the gray matter of his brain did not lie buried there, as with most of us, but grew and flourished and bore fruit. What he once read he seemed never to forget.

"This love of study became a ruling passion in his earliest youth. To it he sacrificed all that the youth of our day—even the best of them—consider indispensable, and especially the culture and training of the body; and when we recall his pale face, worn and lined as it was in his later years, one of his most pathetic utterances is found in a letter to his son at school: 'I hope that you are well and studious, and among the best scholars. If this is so, I am willing you should play every day till the blood is ready to burst from your cheeks. Love the studies that will make you wise, useful and happy when there shall be no blood at all to be seen in your cheeks or lips.' He never rested from his delightful labors— and that is the pity of it—he took no vacations. Except for one short trip to Europe, when warned of a possible breakdown in 1850, an occasional day at Essex, a three days' journey to the White Mountains was all that he allowed himself. Returning from such an outing in the summer of 1854, on which it was my great privilege to accompany him, he said: 'That is my entire holiday for this year.' So that when he told Judge Warren so playfully that 'The lawyer's vacation is the space between the question put to witness and his answer,' it was of himself almost literally true. Would that he had realized his constant dream of an ideal cottage in the old walnut grove in Essex, where he might spend whole summers with his books, his children and his thoughts.

"His splendid and blazing intellect, fed and enriched by constant study of the best thoughts of the great minds of the race, his all-persuasive eloquence, his teeming and radiant imagination, whirling his hearers along with it, and sometimes overpowering himself, his brilliant and sportive fancy, lighting up the most arid subjects with the glow of sunrise, his prodigious and never-failing memory, and his playful wit, always bursting forth with irresistible impulse, have been the subject of scores of essays and criticisms, all struggling with the vain effort to describe and crystallize the fascinating and magical charm of his speech and his influence.

"But the occasion and the place remind me that here to-day we have chiefly to do with him as the lawyer and the advocate, and all that I shall presume very briefly to suggest is, what this statue will mean to the coming generations of lawyers and citizens.

"And first, and far above his splendid talents and his triumphant eloquence, I would place the character of the man—pure, honest, delivered absolutely from all the temptations of sordid and mercenary things, aspiring daily to what was higher and better, loathing all that was vulgar and of low repute, simple as a child, and tender and sympathetic as a woman. Emerson most truly says that character is far above intellect, and this man's character surpassed even his exalted intellect, and, controlling all his great endowments, made the consummate beauty of his life. I know of no greater tribute ever paid to a successful lawyer, than that which he received from Chief Justice Shaw—himself an august and serene personality, absolutely familiar with his daily walk and conversation—in his account of the effort that was made to induce Mr. Choate to give up his active and exhausting practice, and to take the place of professor in the Harvard Law School, made vacant by the death of Mr. Justice Story—an effort of which the Chief Justice, as a member of the corporation of Harvard, was the principal promoter. After referring to him, then, in 1847, as 'the leader of the Bar in every department of forensic eloquence,' and dwelling upon the great advantages which would accrue to the school from the profound legal learning which he possessed, he said: 'In the case of Mr. Choate, it was considered quite indispensable that he should reside in Cambridge, on account of the influence which his genial manners, his habitual presence, and the *force of his character*, would be likely to exert over the young men, drawn from every part of the United States to listen to his instructions.'

"What richer tribute could there be to personal and professional worth, than such words from such lips? He was the fit man to mould the characters of the youth, not of the city or the State only, but of the whole nation. So let the statue stand as notice to all who seek to enter here, that the first requisite of all true renown in our noble profession—renown not for a day or a life only, but for generations—is Character.

"And next I would point to it as a monument to self-discipline; and here he was indeed without a rival. You may search the biographies of all the great lawyers of the world, and you will find none that surpassed, I think none that approached him, in this rare quality and power. The advocate who would control others must first, last and always control himself. 'Every educated man,' he once said, 'should remember that "great parts are a great trust,"' and, conscious of his talents and powers, he surely never forgot that. You may be certain that after his distinguished college career at Dartmouth— first always where there was none second—after all that the law school, and a year spent under the tuition of William Wirt, then at the zenith of his fame, could lend to his equipment, and after the five years of patient study in his office at Danvers, where he was the only lawyer, he brought to the subsequent actual practice of his profession an outfit of learning, of skill and research, which most of us would have thought sufficient for a lifetime; but with him it was only the beginning. His power of labor was inexhaustible, and down to the last hour of his professional life he never relaxed the most acute and searching study, not of the case in hand only, but of the whole body of the law, and of everything in history, poetry, philosophy and literature that could lend anything of strength or lustre to the performance of his professional duties. His hand, his head, his heart, his imagination were never out of training.

"Think of a man already walking the giddy heights of assured success, already a Senator of the United States from Massachusetts, or even years afterwards, when the

end of his professional labors was already in sight, schooling himself to daily tasks in law, in rhetoric, in oratory,
seeking always for the actual truth, and for the 'best
language' in which to embody it—the 'precisely one
right word' by which to utter it—think of such a man,
with all his ardent taste for the beautiful in every domain
of human life, going through the grinding work of taking
each successive volume of the Massachusetts Reports,
as they came out, down to the last year of his practice,
and making a brief in every case in which he had not
been himself engaged, with new researches to see how
he might have presented it, and thus to keep up with
the procession of the law. Verily, 'all things are full of
labor; man cannot utter it: the eye is not satisfied with
seeing, nor the ear filled with hearing.'

"So let no man seek to follow in his footsteps, unless
he is ready to demonstrate, in his own person, that infinite work is the only touchstone of the highest standing in the law, and that the sluggard and the slothful
who enter here must leave all hope behind.

"Again we hail this statue, which shall stand here
as long as bronze shall endure, as the fit representative
of one who was the perfect embodiment of absolute loyalty to his profession, in the highest and largest and
noblest sense; and, if I might presume to speak for the
whole American Bar, I would say that in its universal
judgment he stands in this regard pre-eminent, yes, foremost still. Truly, he did that pious homage to the Law
which Hooker exacted for her from all things in Heaven
and Earth, and was governed by that ever-present sense
of debt and duty to the profession of which Lord Bacon
spoke. He entered her Courts as a High Priest, arrayed
and equipped for the most sacred offices of the Temple.

He belonged to the heroic age of the Bar, and, after the retirement of Webster, he was chief among its heroes. He was the centre of a group of lawyers and advocates, the ablest and the strongest we have known, by whose aid the chief tribunal of this ancient commonwealth administered justice so as to give law to the whole country. Such tributes as Loring and Curtis and Dana lavished upon his grave can never wither. Each one of them had been his constant antagonist in the great arena, and each could say with authority:

—'*experto credite quantus*
In clypeum assurgat, quo turbine torqueat hastam.'

"One after the other, they portrayed in words not to be forgotten his fidelity to the Court, to the client and to the law, his profound learning, his invincible logic, his rare scholarship and his persuasive eloquence, his uniform deference to the Court and to his adversaries— and more and better than all these—what those specially interested in his memory cherish as a priceless treasure— his marvellous sweetness of temper, which neither triumph nor defeat nor disease could ruffle, his great and tender and sympathetic heart, which made them, and the whole bench and bar, love him in life, and love him still.

"He magnified his calling with all the might of his indomitable powers. Following the law as a profession, or, as Judge Sprague so justly said, 'as a science, and also as an art,' he aimed always at perfection for its own sake, and no thought of money, or of any mercenary consideration, ever touched his generous and aspiring spirit, or chilled or stimulated his ardor. He espoused the cause of the poorest client, about the most meagre subject of controversy, with the same fidelity and enthu-

siasm as when millions were at stake, and sovereign States
the combatants. No love of money ever planted the
least root of evil in his soul; and this should not fail to
be said in remembrance of him, in days when money
rules the world.

"His theory of advocacy was the only possible theory
consistent with the sound and wholesome administration
of justice—that, with all loyalty to truth and honor,
he must devote his best talents and attainments, all that
he was, and all that he could, to the support and en-
forcement of the cause committed to his trust. It is
right here to repeat the words of Mr. Justice Curtis,
speaking for himself and for the whole Bar, that 'Great
injustice would be done to this great and eloquent advocate, by attributing to him any want of loyalty to
truth, or any deference to wrong, because he employed
all his great powers and attainments, and used to the
utmost his consummate skill and eloquence, in exhibiting and enforcing the comparative merits of one side of
the cases in which he acted. In doing so he but did his
duty. If other people did theirs, the administration of
justice was secure.'

"His name will ever be identified with trial by jury,
the department of the profession in which he was absolutely supreme. He cherished with tenacious affection
and interest its origin, its history and its great fundamental maxims—that the citizen charged with crime
shall be presumed innocent until his guilt shall be established beyond all reasonable doubt; that no man shall
be deprived by the law of property or reputation until
his right to retain is disproved by a clear preponderance
of evidence to the satisfaction of all the twelve; that
every suitor shall be confronted with the proofs by which

he shall stand or fall; that only after a fair hearing, with full right of cross-examination, and the observance of the vital rules of evidence, shall he forfeit life, liberty or property, and then only by the judgment of his peers.

"Regarding these cardinal principles of Anglo-Saxon justice and policy as essential to the maintenance of liberty and of civil society, he stood as their champion

"'with spear in rest and heart on flame,'

sheathed in the panoply of genius.

"To-day, when we have seen a great sister republic on the verge of collapse for the violation of these first canons of Freedom,* we may justly honor such a champion.

"But he displayed his undying loyalty to the profession on a still higher and grander scale, when he viewed and presented it as one of the great and indispensable departments of Government, as an instrumentality for the well-being and conservation of the State. 'Pro clientibus saepe; pro lege, pro republica semper.'

"I regard the magnificent argument which he made on the judicial tenure in the Constitutional Convention of 1853 as the greatest single service which he ever rendered to the profession, and to the Commonwealth, of which he was so proud. You will observe, if you read it, that it differs radically in kind, rather than in degree from all his other speeches, arguments and addresses.

"Discarding all ornament, restraining with careful guard all tendency to flights of rhetoric, in clear and pellucid language, plain and unadorned, laying bare the very nerve of his thought, as if he were addressing,

* France in the Dreyfus case.

as no doubt he meant to address and convince, not alone his fellow delegates assembled in the convention, but the fishermen of Essex, the manufacturers of Worcester and Hampden, and the farmers of Berkshire—all the men and women of the Commonwealth, of that day and of all days to come—he pleads for the continuance of an appointed judiciary, and for the judicial tenure during good behavior, as the only safe foundations of justice and liberty.

"He draws the picture of 'a good judge profoundly learned in all the learning of the law'; 'not merely upright and well intentioned'; 'but the man who will not respect persons in judgment'; standing only for justice, 'though the thunder should light upon his brow,' while he holds the balance even, to protect the humblest and most odious individual against all the powers and the people of the Commonwealth; and 'possessing at all times the perfect confidence of the community, that he bear not the sword in vain.' He stands for the existing system which has been devised and handed down by the Founders of the State, and appeals to its uniform success in producing just that kind of a judge; to the experience and example of England since 1688; to the Federal system which had furnished to the people of the Union such illustrious magistrates; and finally to the noble line of great and good judges who had from the beginning presided in your courts. He then takes up and disposes of all objections and arguments drawn from other States, which had adopted an elective judiciary and shortened terms, and conclusively demonstrates that to abide by the existing constitution of your judicial system was the only way to secure to Massachusetts forever 'a government of laws and not of men.'

"It was on one of the red-letter days of my youth that I listened to that matchless argument, and, when it ended, and the last echoes of his voice died away, as he retired from the old Hall of the House of Representatives, leaning heavily upon the arm of Henry Wilson, all crumpled, dishevelled and exhausted, I said to myself that some virtue had gone out of him—indeed some virtue did go out of him with every great effort—but that day it went to dignify and ennoble our profession, and to enrich and sustain the very marrow of the Commonwealth. If ever again the question should be raised within her borders, let that argument be read in every assembly, every church and every school-house. Let all the people hear it. It is as potent and unanswerable to-day, and will be for centuries to come, as it was nearly half a century ago when it fell from his lips. Cling to your ancient system, which has made your Courts models of jurisprudence to all the world until this hour. Cling to it, and freedom shall reign here until the sunlight shall melt this bronze, and justice shall be done in Massachusetts, though the skies fall.

"And now, in conclusion, let me speak of his patriotism. I have always believed that Mr. Webster, more than any other one man, was entitled to the credit of that grand and universal outburst of devotion, with which the whole North sprang to arms in defense of the Constitution and the Union, many years after his death, when the first shot at Fort Sumter, like a fire bell in the night, roused them from their slumber, and convinced them that the great citadel of their liberties was in actual danger. Differ as we may and must as to his final course in declining years, the one great fact can never be blotted out, that the great work of his grand and noble life was the defense of the Constitution—so that he came to be known of all men as its one Defender—that for thirty years he preached to the listening nation the crusade of nationality, and fired New England and the whole North with its spirit. He inspired them to believe that to uphold and preserve the Union, against every foe, was the first duty of the citizen; that if the Union was saved, all was saved; that if that was lost, all was lost. He moulded better even than he knew. It was his great brain that designed, his flaming heart that forged, his sublime eloquence that welded the sword, which was at last, when he was dust, to consummate his life's work, and make Liberty and Union one and inseparable forever.

"And so, in large measure, it was with Mr. Choate. His glowing heart went out to his country with the passionate ardor of a lover. He believed that the first duty of the lawyer, orator, scholar was to her. His best thoughts, his noblest words were always for her. Seven of the best years of his life, in the Senate and House of Representatives, at the greatest personal sacrifice, he gave absolutely to her service. On every important question that arose, he made, with infinite study and research, one of the great speeches of the debate. He commanded the affectionate regard of his fellows, and of the watchful and listening nation. He was a profound and constant student of her history, and revelled in tracing her growth and progress from Plymouth Rock and Salem Harbor, until she filled the continent from sea to sea. He loved to trace the advance of the Puritan spirit, with which he was himself deeply imbued, from Winthrop and Endicott and Carver and Standish, through all the heroic periods and events of colonial and revolutionary and national life, until, in his own last years, it dominated and guided all of Free America. He knew full well, and displayed in his many splendid speeches and addresses, that one unerring purpose of freedom and of Union ran through her whole history; that there was no accident in it all; that all the generations, from the *Mayflower* down, marched to one measure and followed one flag; that all the struggles, all the self-sacrifice, all the prayers and the tears, all the fear of God, all the soul-trials, all the yearnings for national life, of more than two centuries, had contributed to make the country that he served and loved. He, too, preached, in season and out of season, the gospel of Nationality. He was the faithful disciple of Webster, while that great Master lived, and, after his death, he bore aloft the same standard and maintained the same cause. Mr. Everett spoke nothing more than the truth, when he said in Faneuil Hall, while all the bells were tolling, at the moment when the vessel bringing home the dead body of his lifelong friend cast anchor in Boston Harbor: 'If ever there was a truly disinterested patriot, Rufus Choate was that man. In his political career there was no shade of selfishness. Had he been willing to purchase advancement at the price often paid for it, there was never a moment, from the time he first made himself felt and known, that he could not have commanded anything that any party had to bestow. But he desired none of the rewards or honors of success.'

"He foresaw clearly that the division of the country into geographical parties must end in civil war. What he could not see was, that there was no other way—that only by cutting out slavery by the sword, could America secure Liberty and Union too—but to the last drop of his blood, and the last fibre of his being, he prayed and pleaded for the life of the nation, according to his light. Neither of these great patriots lived to see the fearful spectacle which they had so eloquently deprecated. But when at last the dread day came, and our young heroes marched forth to bleed and die for their country—their own sons among the foremost—they carried in their hearts the lessons which both had taught, and all Massachusetts, all New England, from the beginning, marched behind them, 'carrying the flag and keeping step to the music of the Union,' as he had bade them, and so I say, let us award to them both their due share of the glory.

"Thus to-day we consign this noble statue to the keeping of posterity, to remind them of 'the patriot, jurist, orator, scholar, citizen and friend,' whom we are proud to have known and loved."

The first part of 1898, besides going to Chicago to make an address, he seems to have spent mainly in professional labors. He talked at the dinner that the Alpha Delta Phi Society gave to him as their president on April 17, and he was a speaker at the National Conference of Charities and Correction at Carnegie Hall on May 18; but his main occupation is no doubt discovered when he writes to his wife on June 22:

" * * * This case has a cad of matter to be read and I find that I cannot possibly work to advantage in the country, when only home for a day or two. The distractions are altogether too great. * * * "

Again he says five days later:

" * * * I have been comfortable. In fact I have stayed up town for three days filling my head with the contents of twelve big volumes in preparation for my last case. This completes a year of thorough work which I shall probably not repeat. * * * "

He never did repeat it, as will be seen. He was half-way through his sixty-seventh year. He practised law after his return from England, but never again so strenuously as in this year.

Besides everything else in this busy year, with four hard cases and with three considerable addresses, there was an infusion of politics. He writes his wife on November 2, having got back to town:

" * * * I have got everything else out of the way now, so as to have 24 hours to get ready for my speech at the mass meeting tomorrow night, so as to have *something* to say, but I don't know what. I shall be heartily glad when this campaign is over, and think I may come up Saturday to get out of the way."

The mass-meeting that he speaks of was part of the campaign to make Theodore Roosevelt governor and to re-elect Judge Daly, to whom Croker had denied renomination. Mr. Choate's heart was in both of these efforts, and he spoke repeatedly in October and November. On October 5 he began his speech at Carnegie Hall by saying:

"I could not stay away from this meeting because I have known Colonel Roosevelt and loved Colonel Roosevelt from his cradle, and I know that there is not one drop of blood in his body or one fibre in his being that is not brave, honest and patriotic. He is just the man that in this emergency the State of New York wants for Governor, and it would be a great disgrace even to the Empire State, if the people should fail to put him in the Governor's chair."

The extreme activity of mind that characterized these multitudinous labors called for bodily support, and this letter to his daughter helps to an understanding of how this was maintained:

"Nov. 7, 1898.

"DEAR MABEL.

" * * * Yesterday after the rain stopped I took an entirely new walk and enjoyed it very much—Up the new Speedway following the bank of the Harlem River (a magnificent drive by the way) with the river on the right, and the bluff of the Washington Heights on the left, with all the fall foliage still on the trees, away up under High Bridge and Washington Bridge, to Dykeman St. which leads across from 206 St. to Kingsbridge Road—there striking the Lafayette Boulevard—getting a very poor lunch at the Abbey—down the Bank of the Hudson to the real Fort Washington, which I had never explored before, then along the bank of the River full of fishermen—with a three-masted schooner at 168th St. discharging lumber for a new school—away to Grant's Tomb, and there instead of climbing up, coasting along the Bank until I reached 104th St. where I took the cars for home—a good ten mile walk and just what I wanted after such a week. * * *

"Tonight everything promises well for the election of Roosevelt. In Wall St. today the bets are 2 to 1, on him. But I shall not be satisfied unless we elect Judge Daly and so give a grand coup to Crokerism, which is sadly needed. * * *   PAPA."

Early in November there began to be echoes in the papers of the possibility that the President would offer him the appointment of Ambassador to England. There was a Senator from New York to be elected, and this Ambassadorship to be filled. Mr. Choate and Mr. Root were talked of for both places. Another possible candidate for the Senatorship was Mr. Whitelaw Reid. It was understood that Mr. Platt, the manager of the Republican dispensary, was not favorable to the translation of Mr. Choate to the Senate. Mr. Platt was probably not favorable to the preferment of Mr. Choate in any direction, but as between having him sent to Washington and having him sent to London, he seems to have preferred that he should go to London. He was credited also with even greater reluctance to agree to the preferment of Mr. Reid than of Mr. Choate. That was the situation. Meanwhile Mr. Choate went right along with his customary activities, both frivolous and professional. He writes his wife on November 21:

"Everybody is preparing for the trip to Springfield on Saturday—that is to say all Harvard is doing so, and if Harvard doesn't win there will be weeping and wailing and gnashing of teeth, with me especially because I resolved last year to keep on going until Harvard should win, and I should not like the prospect of indefinite attendance at Springfield. * * * "

Again he writes to her a week later:

"Washington, D. C. Nov. 28, 1898.
Hotel Gordon.
" * * * Tomorrow morning the Attorney General is to take me to see the President but I don't think he will

say anything about the matter you are so much stirred up about. * * *

"The Supreme Court has violated the traditions of 110 years by taking a half hour's recess for lunch at two o'clock and then sitting a half hour longer until half past four. What are we coming to? It looks as if 'the floodgates' were opening and the 'foundation of things' breaking up. * * *

"I find this house very pleasant and comfortable. No interviewers, button holers or reporters, with their probes ready to jab you."

(November 29.) "You will think I am becoming very diplomatic when I tell you that before breakfast I wrote a note to Secretary Hay asking him to name a time when I could call to pay my respects and he replied 'right away.' So I went in and had a talk with him at a little after nine. Then the Attorney General took me to the White House at half past ten to see the President who was very cordial, but as a lot of Senators, all of whom I knew, were surrounding him and the Cabinet was about to assemble I didn't stop long. He inquired for you and especially for Jo, whose height seems to have made a great impression on him. I inquired for Mrs. McKinley and whether she was receiving today, which resulted in a telegram from Secy. Porter to me at Court, saying that she would like to see me at half past four. So as soon as Court adjourned I went again to the White House and saw them both, the poor President having taken his first rest for the day to receive me with her. Then I wound up with five o'clock tea with Mrs. Hay at her husband's request, and all this without a word on either side about anything in particular. So you see there is nothing in all the talk of the newspapers. For tomorrow evening I have two invitations to dinner—one from Sec'y Hay to meet Prest. Iglesias of Costa Rica, and one from Judge Brown to meet Lord Herschell,* but as I am bound to go to Albany Thursday morning to argue Laidlaw vs. Sage I was obliged to decline them both. * * *

J. H. C."

* Lord Herschell was the leading lawyer for Great Britain and Canada on the Commission that was trying to settle the Alaska Boundary controversy. In Thayer's "Life of John Hay" it says:

"On December 3, 1898, Hay wrote confidentially to Mr. Henry White in London: 'I hear from no less than three members of our Canadian Commission that by far the worst member of the Commission to deal with is Lord Herschell, who is more cantankerous than any of the Canadians, raises more petty points, and is harder than any of the Canadians to get along with. In fact he is the principal obstacle to a favorable arrangement. If you could in any discreet way, in conversation with Balfour or Villiers, or even Lord Salisbury, should occasion offer, intimate this state of things, so that they might speak a word which would moderate his excessive lawyer-like zeal to make a case, it would be a good thing.'

"On January 3, 1899, the Secretary complains again to Mr. White: 'Lord Herschell, with great dexterity and ability, represents his own side as granting everything and getting nothing, and yet I think the letter of Fairbanks [leading commissioner for the United States, and later Vice-President] shows with perfect clearness and candor that we are making great concessions and getting no credit for them.

"'In the case of Alaska, it is hard to treat with patience the claim set up by Lord Herschell that virtually the whole coast belongs to England, leaving us only a few jutting promontories without communication with each other. Without going into the historical or legal argument, as a mere matter of common sense it is impossible that any nation should ever have conceded, or any other nation have accepted, the cession of such a ridiculous and preposterous boundary line. We are absolutely driven to the conclusion that Lord Herschell put forward a claim that he had no belief or confidence in, for the mere purpose of trading it off for something substantial. And yet, the slightest suggestion that his claim is unfounded throws him into a fury.'

"Nevertheless, the Lord Chancellor stuck uncompromisingly to his demands and the Commission adjourned on February 20, 1899."

One of Mr. Choate's important diplomatic duties as ambassador was to co-operate with Mr. Hay, Lord Salisbury, and Lord Lansdowne in bringing the boundary dispute to settlement by a new tribunal, headed for England by Lord Chief Justice Alverstone, with two Canadians, Sir L. A. Jetté and A. B. Aylesworth, and with Senator Lodge, Secretary of War Root, and Ex-Senator George Turner to represent the United States. That tribunal reached a settlement.

A Washington despatch of this same date to *The Sun* says:

"Joseph H. Choate, of New York, whose name has been connected by rumor with the post of Ambassador to the Court of St. James, was among the callers who saw the President before the Cabinet met today. Mr. Choate said he merely called to pay his respects to the President. He is in Washington to argue the Dunlap alcohol case before the Supreme Court tomorrow. He expects to leave immediately after he speaks.

"'I must be in Albany the next morning,' he said to a reporter for *The Sun*, 'to argue before the Court of Appeals the celebrated case of Laidlaw vs. Sage.'

"'How many times has that been done?'

"'I think,' Mr. Choate answered, 'that I have presented the merits of that case to judges and juries six times; Thursday's effort will be the seventh.'

"Mr. Choate was asked regarding the report that he was to be appointed Ambassador to Great Britain.

"'I know nothing about it,' was his answer.

"'It is said today that the appointment has been determined on.'

"'So I see,' he responded, 'but I have heard nothing about it.'

"Mr. Choate's manner left the impression that he would not be greatly surprised if he should hear something about it. He expressed the opinion that Mr. Depew would be chosen Senator from New York."

Two weeks later the Philadelphia *Enquirer* observed:

"The New York correspondents of the London newspapers have been sending paragraphs by cable as to the outlook for Mr. Choate, of New York, being the next United States Ambassador to England, but they appear to have very vague ideas as to his position.* They unite in saying that he is the leader of the New York bar, which is correct, and that he is a man of no fortune nor any experience, fitting him for the position, save, perhaps, the gift of eloquence.

"Could anything be more pleasingly innocent than this? Do not these gentlemen know that Mr. Choate has the altogether delightful position of being able to pocket lots of retaining fees which represent a year's salary as Ambassador to England, while when it comes to sending in his bill for services rendered, the figures are apt to run to the salary of the President and all his Cabinet combined. Surely Mr. Choate has saved some of his income and not spent it every afternoon on his way up town after leaving his office."

On January 11, 1899, the President sent in his nomination to the Senate. There was a vast amount of comment on it in the newspapers, and it was commended with what amounted to a chorus of approval. *The Irish World* did not like it, but its objection to Mr. Choate as "a New England Englishman who hates Irishmen, their country and their faith," was one of very few that are recorded.

Life spoke of Mr. Choate's appointment as coming "like a large red apple to the boy who has been good." He had been good and he had been exceedingly diligent. For over forty years he had practised as a lawyer in New York and had done it for all there was in it, and he had

* So Mr. Root said nineteen years later that Mr. Choate's brilliant success as ambassador "had made his great reputation known to the public men of Europe, who at that time ordinarily knew little and cared less about American lawyers."

done an immense deal besides. Now that he was coming to the end of this extraordinary period of application to professional work, and was passing on to other things, it is interesting to look into his mind and discover some of the convictions that had come to lodge there. That was done in a way by Mr. Theodore Dreiser, since a novelist of reputation, who got a glimpse of Mr. Choate's mind late in 1897 and printed some of the results in the magazine called *Success* in January, 1898. He went to see Mr. Choate at his house; he said to him:

" 'You have had long years of distinction and comfort; do you find that success brings content and happiness?'

" 'Well,' he answered, contracting his brows with legal severity, 'constant labor is happiness, and success simply means ability to do more labor,—more deeds far-reaching in their power and effect. Such success brings about as much happiness as the world provides.'

" 'I mean,' I explained, 'the fruits of that which is conventionally accepted as success: few hours of toil, a luxuriously furnished home, hosts of friends, the applause of the people, sumptuous repasts, and content in idleness, knowing that enough has been done.'

" 'We never know that enough has been done,' said the lawyer. 'All this sounds pleasant, but the truth is that the men whose great efforts have made such things possible for themselves are the very last to desire them. You have described what appeals to the idler, the energy-less dreamer, the fashionable dawdler, and the listless voluptuary. Enjoyment of such things would sap the strength and deaden the ambition of a Lincoln. The man who has attained to the position where these things are possible is the one whose life has been a constant refutation of the need of these things. He is the one who has abstained, who has conserved his mental and physical strength by living a simple and frugal life. He has not taken more than he needed and never, if possible, less. His enjoyment has been in working, and I guarantee that you will find successful men ever to be plain-mannered persons of simple tastes, to whom sumptuous repasts are a bore, and luxury a thing apart. They may live surrounded by these things, but personally take little interest in them, knowing them to be mere trappings, which neither add to nor detract from character.'

" 'Is there no pleasure, then, in luxury and ease without toil?' I questioned.

" 'None,' said the speaker, emphatically. 'There is pleasure in rest after labor. It is gratifying to relax when you really need relaxation, to be weary and to be able to rest. But to enjoy anything you must feel the need of it. But no more,' he said, putting up his hand conclusively. 'Surely you have enough to make clear what you wish to know.'

"Mr. Choate had talked for ten minutes. His ease of manner, quickness of reply, smoothness of expression, and incisive diction, were fascinating beyond description."*

* In *Case and Comment* (the lawyers' magazine) for September, 1917, is an article—"Joseph H. Choate and Right Training for the Bar," by Mr. William V. Rowe, who was long and closely associated with Mr. Choate in practice. In the course of this article Mr. Rowe reviews the succession of Mr. Choate's chief cases in the forty years of his most active practice, and up to the time he went to England as Ambassador, as follows:

"As soon as Mr. Choate had finished a several months' trial of an action for libel, involving and vindicating the integrity and value of the Cesnola collection of Cypriote antiquities in the Metropolitan Museum of Art, he was at once called into legislative hearings on bills for the benefit of the Museum of Natural History, and was obliged to represent the interests of the West Shore, the North River Construction Company, and the New York Central Railroad, in suits to foreclose the mortgage of the West Shore Railway and to restrain, on complaint of a stockholder, the lease of the West Shore by the Central.

"The New York Central cases would hardly be closed before he might find it necessary to plunge into the hearings in the long controversy between Lord Dunraven and the New York Yacht Club over the famous international yacht race between '*Defender*' and '*Valkyrie III*,' in which the action of the yacht club had been criticised by the English challenger, and these hearings would perhaps be followed by the trial of the extraordinary case of Laidlaw *v.* Russell Sage, arising out of the dynamiting of Russell Sage and his alleged attempt to use the plaintiff as a shield, and presenting novel questions in the law of assault and trespass. Incidentally, it may be noted that this was the only case in which Mr. Choate was ever known to over-cross-examine—a common professional fault. His indignation had been so excited by the circumstances of the case that his cross-examination actually turned inside out the 'vest' and other personal garments of the defendant, the original history and condition of which the cross-examination fully exposed to the public gaze. In the years between 1880 and 1895 he was frequently employed in successful pioneer work in so-called Elevated Railroad cases, which were actions at law, condemnation proceedings, and suits in equity, brought to recover heavy damages arising out of the construction of the New York system of elevated railroads through and over the public streets, and which involved wholly novel questions in the law of easements relating to the rights of abutting owners to light, air, and access—cases in which Mr. Evarts and Mr. Choate were at times both engaged, and in which frequently arose the most difficult conceivable questions of title, including the title to old Dutch streets as affected by the civil law. At the same time, he was occupied for years with the defense of the Standard Oil Companies and the so-called Standard Oil Trust, in the famous 'Anti-trust Law' suits, including the cases attacking the Texas and Ohio Anti-trust Laws, and other cases covering the usual difficult, but at that time quite novel, Anti-trust Law questions, and in cases involving the valuation of oil properties, alleged breaches of warranty, building contracts, and many other matters, with constant legislative and congressional investigations. All this work was varied by great will contests, long drawn out, and great will construction suits, in the surrogates' or probate courts and through the medium of equity and partition suits, involving the Cruger, Vanderbilt, A. T. Stewart, Samuel J. Tilden, Hoyt, Drake, Hopkins-Searles, Vassar, Vanderpoel, and almost innumerable other wills which came before him year by year, presenting extremely important and embarrassing questions in the law relating to testamentary instruments and trusts and their construction, and covering all phases of insanity issues and the law of undue influence and testamentary capacity. This class of litigation included jury trials and the most carefully prepared cases on appeal in the higher courts. Landlord and tenant cases, arising, perhaps, in the form of ejectment suits for one of the Astor estates, would be followed by the important case against the Canada Southern Railway, testing before the Supreme Court of the United States the rights of domestic purchasers and holders of foreign-railway-company bonds, or the Brooklyn Bridge case, before the same court, involving the right to build and maintain the great and necessary structures connecting New York and Brooklyn, or the Stanford University case, from California, also before the Supreme Court, in which the United States sought to recover many millions from the Leland Stanford estate, the success of which suit would have deprived the University of a large part of its endowment, and in which case Mr. Choate's successful appeal for the University resembled Webster's appeal for Dartmouth College; and this, in turn, might be succeeded by the Bell Telephone Case, involving the entire Bell telephone patent. His work before the Supreme Court of the United States in all these years was continuous. The Behring Sea Case before that court, in which he appeared for the Canadian government, and which involved the right of the United States to seize and condemn Canadian and other vessels in Behring Sea, was matched in importance by the New York Indians Case, which had to do with the Indians' right to lands on their summary removal to limited reservations in other parts of the country; and these cases would no sooner be finished than he would be called into the case of the Pullman Palace Car Company against the Central Transportation Company, involving a great contract of lease, or the Southern Pacific Land Grant Case, the Chinese Exclusion Cases, the Alcohol-in-the-Arts Case, involving rebates of millions of dollars under the tariff laws, or the Massachusetts Fisheries Case (Manchester v. Massachusetts), relating to the state's right to protect fisheries in arms of the sea within or beyond the 3-mile limit. He would hardly have finished such a long series of cases before the Supreme Court before he would be called into an admiralty collision suit for the White Star Line, developing novel and abstruse problems in hydraulics and suction-action, in the case of overtaking ships of varying tonnage and draught, or suits presenting equally novel and complicated bill of lading problems arising out of the fire on the Inman Line pier and the destruction of the cargo of the steamship *Egypt* of the old National Line. While these cases were under way, he would, perhaps, be consulting with Mr. Evarts over the trial and argument of cases involving the whole common law of covenants and conditions subsequent as applied to deeds of property abutting on portions of the old Bloomingdale Road, as affected, in turn, by New York's great Riverside Park Improvement, or would be preparing to argue before the Supreme Court of the United States or elsewhere the great constitutional questions in the Income Tax Cases, the Reciprocal and Retaliatory Taxation Cases against insurance companies, the Kansas Prohibition Law Cases, the California Irrigation Law Cases, and the Neagle Case, this last involving the assault by Judge Terry, of California, on Mr. Justice Field, which raised the whole question of the power of the Supreme Court to protect itself and its officers within the jurisdiction of a state; or, after arguing in Washington the constitutionality of the Federal and state inheritance taxes, we might find him called in to his triumphant and spirited vindication of the rights of the bar, as against aggressions of the bench, in the contempt proceedings instituted by Recorder Smythe of New York, against Mr. Goff (afterwards recorder, and now Mr. Justice Goff, of the New York Supreme Court)—a peculiarly satisfactory and successful experience for Mr. Choate, in which he made one of his most forceful, eloquent, and convincing appeals to judicial as well as to human nature. While advising with Mr. Evarts as to the replevin action by the Turkish government, for which they were acting, to recover a consignment of rifles, he might find himself in the midst of the preparation for the trial of the greatest action for deceit (in the form of a suit in equity for an accounting) ever brought in New York—the controversy between the Banque-Franco-Egyptienne, of Paris, and various leading New York bankers over the sale of the old New York, Boston & Montreal bonds—or might be considering with his other partner, Mr. Southmayd, the firm's opinion as to a railroad reorganization plan. One week would find him occupied in the New York court of appeals with the so-called Maynard Election Fraud Cases and the cases involving the inheritance taxes under the Vassar will, with other questions affecting Vassar College, and the next week would see him before the Interstate Commerce Commission, representing the Orange County Farmers of New York, in a long and successful controversy with all the railroads centring in New York and Jersey City over the freight rates on New York city's milk supply. The very next week, in turn, he would himself represent the same railroads, or some of them, before that Commission or before a congressional or legislative committee, on a question of rates, of regulation, or of taxation. While he was settling the membership law for clubs and exchanges in what was practically the pioneer American litigation on that subject, in the famous cases of Loubat *v.* Union Club and Hutchinson *v.* New York Stock Exchange, he was also settling important features of the law of arbitration in a great building contract case. After a prodigious winter's work in will contests, and various important arguments before the court of appeals in New York and the Supreme Court at Washington, he devoted the entire summer and fall of the year 1894 to the work of the New York Constitutional Convention, of which he was President, and whose proposed constitution, due chiefly to his personal advocacy, was fully and triumphantly adopted by the people of the state, and is still in existence and serviceable. From that work his normal activities would drive him, perhaps, into an intricate partnership accounting with the estate of Paran Stevens, over a complicated hotel business, or into a long trial of a jury case, in which he appeared on behalf of the Western Union Telegraph Company and Jay Gould, involving questions of contract and tort in its relations with the old Bankers & Merchants Company and other telegraph companies—one of the trials in these cases furnishing us with the only instance (due in part to extraordinary heat in the month of June) in which Mr. Choate's voice was ever known to weaken through huskiness. Following these, he was liable at any time to be drawn into the accountings of the executors and trustees under the Astor and various other wills, or to be called upon to advise in relation to the last professional service of Mr. Evarts, rendered to the High Court of Chancery of England in its capacity as guardian of infants. For many years he found himself employed before the court of claims or special commissions, or before the Supreme Court of the United States, in the Berdan Arms Case and other difficult cases, and in the claims arising out of the Alabama Awards, and, later, in the Spanish Treaty Claims, followed by many extraordinary drawback and other revenue cases, some of which went to the Supreme Court. And, to cap the climax, he was occasionally, as we have heretofore pointed out, called into great patent cases; for example, that involving the whole Bell telephone patent. As evidence of his complete mastery of the problems of intensively specialized modern business law, reference may be made to his successful handling, following his return from the English ambassadorship, of the various controversies arising out of the receivership and proposed readjustment and reorganization of the affairs of the Third Avenue Railway Company of New York."

CHAPTER VIII

IN ENGLAND AS AMBASSADOR

Mr. Choate, his wife, and daughter sailed on the *St. Paul* for Southampton on February 22, 1899. The night before he sailed he went to a great dinner of the Harvard Club at the Waldorf-Astoria, where he was the leading guest of the evening and was cheered and drunk to and sung to to the full extent of Harvard energies. "Last night," he said, "I talked to a great company of lawyers, whose first feeling was how glad they were that I was going. (Laughter.) I speak to-night to a great company of Harvard men, whose last thought, I hope, is how sorry we are." (Prolonged cheering.)

Mr. Choate's good-bys were a serious matter, or would have been to anybody but him. Besides the lawyers he spoke of, the Union League Club gave him a farewell dinner. He went early to the pier and went aboard to receive his friends. Fifty lawyers came to see him off, *The Evening Telegram* said. At all events he got away very cheerfully.

He got to Southampton on the 1st of March, was met by the Mayor and a deputation partly British and partly American from the Embassy, received an illuminated address from the Southampton Chamber of Commerce and made his first speech as Ambassador. In London he put up at Claridge's. The next matter was a house. He could not get the house that his predecessor, Mr. Hay, had had, but with Mrs. Choate's complicity and assistance he presently acquired Lord Curzon's house, No. 1 Carlton House Terrace, which Levi Leiter, of Chicago, had given to his daughter Mary when she became Lady Curzon. It was a first-rate house for an Ambassador, in the same row with the house, No. 5, that Ambassador Hay had had. On the 6th of March he went to Windsor with Mrs. Choate and was presented to the Queen, for that year was still the nineteenth century and belonged to the Victorian age. His first considerable speech was at the dinner of the Associated Chambers of Commerce of the United Kingdom. Of this discourse a London commentator said:

"Since Lord Dufferin left the diplomatic service, it would be hard to find a single member of the diplomatic corps who could be relied on to make such an impression on a mixed and critical audience as Mr. Choate produced apparently without an effort on his first public appearance in London. He was speaking to the nation as well as to the Chambers of Commerce. There is a rational frankness and lucid unconventionality about the American Ambassador's style which is found to be extremely attractive, especially by those who are sorely wearied by the rounded periods and studied impromptus of average British eloquence. Mr. Choate was boldly and successfully outspoken about the very things on which educated Englishmen think much but say little in public and he expressed average opinion here quite as much as that of his own country. To refer in a maiden speech to the War of 1812, to the international disputes on the Oregon and north-eastern boundary questions, the Confederate cruisers, the *Trent* seizure, and the Venezuelan message required no less magnetism than diplomacy—if these topics were to be successfully employed by Mr. Choate as stepping stones to the goal of international understanding. There was thus more to be found in the speech than the racy adroitness of a trained advocate. It was the utterance of a clear and sagacious mind speaking for two great nations; a mind more intent on the reality of things than the glitter and graces of words, and yet with finished mastery of style that hid the art concealed."

So in England at least that speech was highly successful. When cabled home it gave a chance for criticism. One passage of it that concerned the Venezuela disturbance ran:

"You know that on our side of the water we love occasionally to twist the lion's tail for the mere sport of hearing him roar. Well, that time he disappointed us. He would not roar at all. He sat silent as the Sphinx, and, by dint of mutual forbearance—our sober second thought aiding your sober first thought—we averted everything but a mere war of words."

The Sun complained of that. "What are the facts?" it said. "They are that from first to last the United States, as represented by President Cleveland, had but one thought, always sober, namely, that the dispute between England and Venezuela should be submitted to arbitration; and that England's first thought of refusing arbitration was followed by a second thought, of admirable sobriety also, that arbitration should be submitted to."

In April Mrs. Choate was away in Paris, getting clothes, and there are letters:

To His Wife

"American Embassy, London,
15 April, 1899.

"To begin at the point where you left me. I went 'round to St. Michael's Church in Chester Square and heard my old friend Bishop Whipple preach a most animated discourse on Indians and such to a very crowded audience. His pretty young wife was with him, and 34 and 74 seem to get along well together. After tomorrow they are to be at Lady Ashburton's Kent House until May 13th, when they sail.

"Mr. Morgan came to lunch and seemed to enjoy it and approved the house very much.

"Lady Reay, seeing how bereaved I was by your departure and Mabel's has invited me to a family dinner on Friday. Today comes a letter to you from Mrs. Butler, of Cambridge, wife of the Master of Trinity, asking us to come and spend a Sunday there this Term, suggesting May 13th. What do you say to that?

"I hope that you have already given all your orders, been measured for all your dresses and have nothing to do but sit 'with your feet up.' You must not forget the heavy labors that await you in London."

(April 18.) "Yesterday I devoted the afternoon to personal calls and succeeded in making thirteen—only getting in at Sir Henry Irving's lodgings and the girl soon found that he was out after all. Today Jo is to take the carriage and do the like. I object to going out in so much style and greatly prefer a hansom, but I suppose must submit to being an Ambassador. * * *

"You say '*Don't eat things*' but would you have us starve? At tea I tried the *loaf cake* yesterday and found it quite good."

(April 20.) "In answer to the enclosed note from Lady Burdett-Coutts, I called on her this afternoon to see what she wanted.

"It was that you should attend at the Crystal Palace on the 13th of May, Saturday, at the annual meeting of the Royal Society for the Prevention of Cruelty to Animals and distribute the prizes to the children of the schools who compete for the best essay on the subject.

"The Queen and all the ladies of the Royal Family have from time to time rendered this service, and this time they wanted you. I told her that you felt highly honored and would like to serve them if disengaged, but was not sure of that; that there was a pending trip to Cambridge to visit the Master of Trinity on that same day and I did not know what you had decided about that—so on receipt of this I wish you would telegraph me what answer I shall make."

(April 21.) "The dinner of the Literary Fund came off last night and was very interesting. I sat on the Chairman's right and next to me was Lord Leven, through whose grounds we drove at Bournemouth, and Lord Edmund Fitzmaurice. The Chairman, Sir George Trevelyan, made a fine speech and so did the Master of Trinity. I send you the best account which was in the *Post*, though quite curtailed to make room for the Crewe-Primrose wedding which absorbed all London yesterday. The Bridal party drove through serried ranks of on lookers that would have done credit to Royalty. I told the Master of Trinity, who was very cordial about it, that we would I was quite sure come to them on the 13th and so I telegraphed you this morning that I would decline for you Baroness Burdett-Coutts affair which I dare say will relieve you. I also asked in the same telegram whether I should accept the Campbell-Bannermans' invitation for you and me and Mabel to dinner on the 10th of May which is your first drawing room day. I suppose you'll be very tired and Mabel too, but you can wind up the day with a reception at Lady Durning Lawrence 13 C. H. Terrace, which is so near. * * *

J. H. C."

The chairman of the Literary Fund dinner that he speaks of mentioned that the chairman of the first dinner (one hundred and nine years before) was Benjamin Franklin. Mr. Choate responded to the toast of "Literature." "The political ties by which Great Britain and America were once united are now," he said, "severed forever, but the literary ties which unite them have never been and never can be severed." He went on in that vein, observing finally that if he were asked for the names of two men who had done the most to strengthen the bonds of unity between the two great nations, he would name Sir George Trevelyan and Captain Alfred T. Mahan.

To His Wife

"London, 22 April, 1899.
"Last night Lady Reay's 'round table' proved to be quite a dinner-party. Mrs. Bernard Mallett sat next to me and said we must come down to Windsor again, and see the library and the many antiquities it contains in which she seems to take great interest. She is one of the Queen's secretaries, and will be on duty in July, and says if we will come she will give us tea in her room.

"Then there were Lady Munro-Ferguson—daughter of Lord Dufferin—a beautiful woman, and one of the Duke of Argyle's sons with a very handsome wife,—the Danish Minister with his wife and daughter, and a Lieut. General.

"The Prince of Wales receives me next Saturday."

(April 25.) "Last night I dined with Mr. Blyth to meet the Duke of Cambridge and all the swells of the Royal Academy, which has its opening and annual public dinner next Saturday. There must have been at least 60 present. I sat between Prince Edward of Saxe Weimar, an old English General and the host's brother, and opposite the Duke who is a fine old fellow of 80, cousin of the Queen and evidently a great favorite. I was surprised when I asked at what hour to order my carriage to be told 11½, but I managed to get away soon after 11. * * * "

(April 26.) "I didn't know that any report had got out of anything said by me at P. Bigelow's dinner and think Kitty must be mistaken. * * * "

(April 27.) "Last night I took Judge Andrews to the Eastern Dinner at Gray's Inn and we both enjoyed it immensely. They have a grand old hall which dates back over 500 years, one of the few real pieces of antiquity spared by the great fire, and ornamented with old portraits, among them Queen Elizabeth and Francis Bacon, both of whom are said to have danced there. Then they had a lot of quaint old customs which have come down through the same half century, and are continued just for that reason, and no other. Before we sat down little pellets of bread were passed round and a loving cup of punch to wash them down with through the whole company, for all the world like an old fashioned Presbyterian communion. There were a lot of young Indians at the students' table some of whom had white turbans and some black. Four of the students including one Indian were 'called to the bar' in the midst of the feast, and their healths drunk. For dessert we moved into another room to a new table and there was a new shuffle of the company. * * * "

(April 28.) "Sure enough some one sent me a report of my remarks at the Bigelow dinner but they were not very accurate and not at all mischievous. * * *

J. H. C."

A newspaper item, dated London, May 8, says:

"The United States Ambassador, Mr. Joseph H.
Choate, was the central figure at the annual meeting
today of the British and Foreign Sailors' Society at the
Mansion House.

"The Duke of Fife, in introducing Mr. Choate, said:
'I ask you to give a warm and vigorous welcome to one
of America's most brilliant sons.'

"Mr. Choate made a happy hit by saying, with reference to the name of the society, that he was neither British
nor foreign, but simply an American. 'But every American is entitled to feel sympathy with such a society as
this, in view of its historic interest, inasmuch as its
founder, Admiral Gambier, signed the treaty of peace
of 1814, a treaty which has never since been broken by
the two nations and, I trust, never will be.

"'Another reason why my sympathy is as I have stated,
is that in some measure I represent my large-hearted
President, whose letter, full of feeling, has just been read.
When we look across the page of history we see Nelson,
the great, typical sailor of all ages and races. But in
the past year two new heroes have come to stand by his
side in our own Dewey and Sampson.'"

President McKinley said in his letter: "This is a great
year for the Anglo-Saxon race, and the sailors of both
nations are coming in for a full share of praise for their
splendid achievements."

On May 27 he went to the dinner for the Actors' Fund
and gave the toast "The Drama." He had been studying, he said, that great national institution of England,
the dinner for charitable purposes, and he made some
amusing observations about that. He had never himself

been connected, he said, with the drama except in one capacity, and that was as one of the audience. That, in one respect, was perhaps the most important part of the drama; for what became of playwrights, actors, scene-shifters, ballet-dancers, and all the rest if there was no audience? For many years past American actors and actresses had done much to ennoble their calling, and when they had come to England they had been received with enthusiasm. It was Charlotte Cushman who said: "To me it seems that when God conceived the world, that was poetry. He formed it, and that was sculpture. He colored it—that was painting. He peopled it with living beings—that was the Grand Divine Eternal Drama." He went on to talk of English actors from David Garrick to Henry Irving. Lord Dartmouth was the chairman of the dinner, and he told about his ancestor who was secretary in the Colonies before the Revolution, "a true friend," he said, "of liberty and justice," so that he had the confidence of the American people and Dartmouth College was named after him.

It is noted in the *Pall Mall Gazette* of June 6, that at a hospital bazaar in Marylebone, "one of the most interesting of the stalls is the American and Kensington stall, presided over by Mrs. Choate, the wife of the American Ambassador, and largely occupied with articles sent by American manufacturers in London."

Among the visits that Mr. and Mrs. Choate made after the 12th of August was one to Mr. Carnegie, as to which he says:

"Skibo Castle, Ardgay, N. B.
Tuesday, 22 Augt. '99.
"Dear Jo:
" * * * We are having a very good time at Skibo— out of doors all the time in the most delightful country—

and I begin to understand the charm of the Highlands. But *you* must learn to *shoot*. No young man here amounts to much without that, and I am ready to present you with a good gun, as soon as you will undertake to try your hand at it. Yesterday we had a 'deer drive' and brought home six, and I very much regretted that I had never learned the art. * * *

FATHER."

To His Wife

"American Embassy, London
21 Septr., 1899

"The talk is still of war, but the delay confirms my belief that there will be no war. Cruger will yield enough to enable the English to avoid such a catastrophe.

"The tide of home-going Americans still continues, and many of them come to the office. Today Admiral Walker and Colonel Hines called to see me; they are on the Commission to examine and report on the whole subject of an interoceanic canal and have been in Paris to see what remains of the Panama Canal, of which as the result, they seem to think very well.

"Whether I shall be able to come before Saturday night is not yet certain. My interview with Lord Salisbury tomorrow is at so late an hour that I may not be able to complete my report to Washington in time to take the train that evening, but I shall do my best in that direction.

"London is perfectly delightful—cool and bracing and absolutely clear, so that the sunshine and moonlight are as good as you have.

"We don't like dining out of the house, but as it is best for a day or two, can stand it.

"Tell Mabel that Major is fine, but as they are still repairing both on the Mall and Bird Cage Walk she could not ride if she were here. To go all the way to Hyde Park corner on the pavement would be too dangerous. The other horses are all in first rate shape."

From the time he could afford it until late in life Mr. Choate concerned himself to have horses fit to ride and rode them habitually. It was one means he used to keep in working condition. There is much about horses in his letters.

He made a speech at the opening of the Sutherland Institute at Longton, in Staffordshire, on October 27— an amusing, informing, ingratiating discourse about as usual.

"And now a word or two about the Anglo-Saxons. Now the pure and simple Anglo-Saxon race is a matter of history, somewhat remote, possibly. Features of it survive. Its grand, impelling power survives. Its devotion to justice and freedom and civilization survives. But the Anglo-Saxon race has been a little diluted; it has been a little mixed. Didn't the Danes come and leave their mark in these Islands? And did not the Normans come, and for a little while, a few centuries, appear to get the better of the Anglo-Saxons? Now here is his Grace, the Duke of Sutherland, posing as an Anglo-Saxon. I don't know, but if we had a skilful analysis of his blood, if Pasteur or some equally skilful scientist could draw some of that rich liquid from his veins and examine it, they would find little of the Anglo-Saxon, a good deal of Scotch, some Norman, and what part of it would be finally eliminated and set aside as pure Anglo-

Saxon liquid, I for one cannot guess, and I do not believe he can. Why, I saw at Trentham today a huge volume of the Sutherland pedigree. It would require a careful reading of all its pages in the light of history, geography, and family life. Well now, when you come upon our side of the water there is a still more modern blend. We get the Anglo-Saxon once or twice removed, all mingling with the Danes and Normans. Then what took place? Why, there flowed into our national veins copious streams of rich blood from other nations of Europe. First came the Huguenots, refugees for liberty, and their strain was mingled with ours. Then came the Irish, bringing in a rich vein in addition to our blood, rendering great service on many fields, and many successive services on many fields, and in many successive generations. The Scotch came away back with William Penn, and afterwards. They occupied whole counties and their generous blood entered in to make our composition. And then the German came, a most copious tide of kindred blood, and that has mingled in our veins. And since then all the Scandinavian regions, and Italy finally have sent rich contributions. Now then what is the result? Why a new man has been created. He fills with seething masses of population all the region that lies between the Alleghanies and the Rocky Mountains. He rules America. He is not an Englishman, nor a Scotchman, nor an Irishman, nor an imitation of any of these nations of Europe; but he combines them all. And in the composition is a new and perfect blend. What will come of it time will only show. I can speak for his indomitable will to maintain liberty and his high resolve that that liberty shall always be protected by law. Now then, we are under divers obligations by this kinship which we bear not only to England, not only to Scotland and Ireland, and to Germany, but to all these nations of which we are in part made up. And if I understand rightly the will and purpose of the American people, it is to maintain peace and friendship with all so long as it can possibly be done with honor. Of you we feel sure. Of the others we feel sure. For eighty-five years we have settled all our controversies with you, with peace and honor; and, if I rightly recollect, we have not had a quarrel that required a resort to force with any of the others. Well, what do you see? It is not exactly an Anglo-Saxon race. I prefer the other form, in which his Grace has expressed it—the English-speaking peoples. I think the English-speaking people, scattered on all the continents, and all the islands of the sea, has achieved, and is daily achieving wonders for civilization. It seems to me to have borne in mind more thoroughly and directly than any other people the injunction that was first laid upon mankind: 'Be fruitful and multiply and replenish the earth, and subdue it; and have dominion over the fish of the sea, and over the fowl of the air, and all the cattle, and over all the earth, and over every creeping thing that creepeth upon the earth.' And so I say, as a concluding sentiment on behalf of these English-speaking peoples throughout the world, wherever they have dominion, under whichever flag, may they be true to their responsibilities and maintain always honor, justice, civilization, and liberty."

On November 4 he and Mrs. Choate gave a dinner to ex-President Harrison and had the Marquis of Salisbury, the Archbishop of Canterbury, the Lord Chancellor, the Marquis of Lansdowne, Lord Wolseley, the Bishop of London, Mr. Balfour, Mr. James Bryce, and other very distinguished people to meet him. On the 10th of November he responded to the toast on "Literature" at the sixth annual dinner of the Sir Walter Scott Club in Edinburgh. He could talk from his heart about Walter Scott, and he did. A passage out of this address may be quoted for what it tells about the speaker; he said:

"Carlyle has said, after nobly describing Scott as the pride of all Scotsmen, giving him credit for an open soul, a wide, far-reaching soul that carried him out in absolute sympathy with all human things and people, after giving him credit for that wonderful and innate love of the beauty of nature and the power of describing it, and his infinite sympathy with men as well as with nature—he has in one of his most accurate utterances said that if literature has no other task than pleasantly to amuse indolent, languid men, why, here in Scott was the perfection of literature. Well, now, for one I must confess that every now and then I am one of those indolent, languid men—and as I look along these tables, if I rightly study your character and moods, I suspect that this is a great group of those indolent, languid men who believe that it is not only the task, but it is one of the greatest tasks, of literature to amuse and to entertain mankind. Why, I have often thought that I would rather have been the author of one such book as 'Waverley,' or 'Kenilworth,' or 'Henry Esmond,' or 'Romola,' than to achieve any other kind of personal, professional, or public fame. The good that these books do us, the rest they give us, the enjoyment they yield us among the hundreds of millions that read the language in which they are written is absolutely infinite, and the fame that the author of such a book wins rivals, if it does not outshine, all other kinds of fame. Look at it now. 'Waverley' was written in 1814—a memorable event in the history of British literature. The battle of Waterloo was fought in the next year—one of the great critical battles of all human history. Eighty-five years have gone by since then, and which name is now the dearer to mankind; which one now enjoys the wider and the better fame—Wellington or Walter Scott? I shall not answer that question. I leave every man to answer it for himself."

He and Mrs. Choate went to Windsor on November 21 to dine and to meet the Kaiser, who was a guest there. On the 30th he went to the Thanksgiving Day dinner of the Americans in London. He spoke, of course; very interesting words, containing what his Edinburgh speech contained and what in all his speeches he managed to include—the message of British-American friendship. "Truly," he said in Edinburgh in starting his discourse, "your country, Mr. President, and mine are connected by bonds of sympathy, which were never stronger and closer than at this very hour. When Dandie Dinmont had listened to the reading of Mrs. Margaret Bertram's will, he threw himself back and gave utterance to that great saying: 'Blood is thicker than water.' Little did he dream that he was giving to two great nations a watchword for the exchange of their love and greetings eighty years afterwards."

To His Wife

"Dunraven Castle, Bridgend, Glamorgan.
27 November, 1899.

"If I had thought there was any possibility of your being well enough I should have telegraphed you this morning to be sure and come tomorrow morning, for the air here would cure anything. The castle looks right out upon the sea, and this morning we looked out upon bright sunshine and blue water, very near the house, and in a few minutes a great herd of deer came running over the downs and stopped under the windows as if to be admired, as you may be sure they were. We look out west upon the ocean with nothing between us and New York, but to the south through a mist the coast of North Devon is dimly seen. The air is very bracing and I have been walking all day—in the forenoon with a pretty woman, Mrs. Skeffington-Smith, whose husband is a captain in the Cold Stream Guards and was in the battle of Belmont only last week. In the afternoon I went alone while the rest were on the golf grounds where Mabel did not play, but went around with her kodak. The party is very small—six that were invited having failed like you. Lord and Lady Dunraven and Lady Aileen, their unmarried daughter, are most cordial and hospitable and make everything go well."

Mr. Choate had been counsel for the New York Yacht Club in a case where Lord Dunraven was concerned, but apparently no hard feelings had survived the hearing.

To the Same

"London,
20 December, 1899.

"Tonight Mr. Hay will arrive and I have invited him to lunch tomorrow and to dinner on Friday. He will be set upon apparently by all the people in town who have relatives prisoners in Pretoria, and who are all anxious to send out by him letters, money, clothes, chocolates, and other good things to their imprisoned friends.

Just now seems to be the darkest hour that England has known for many years, and I see that even such pro-Boer sheets as the New York *Sun* and *World* are beginning to relent of their hostility.

"It will be a most dull Christmas in London. All who are not gone to the country are overwhelmed with anxiety and distress about their friends at the front.

"There is no news today from the war, but everybody seems much encouraged by the appointment of Generals Roberts and Kitchener to go to the Cape."

To the Same

"Coombe Abbey, Coventry.
26 Dec. 1899.

"You certainly have lost a visit to one of the loveliest old houses in England—a veritable old Abbey, with the cloisters turned into galleries and but for the 'new wing' it would be most unique. * * * The house is full of interesting pictures—Vandykes & Lelys, and a Charles I. or II. by Vandyke would pass for a portrait of the present Earl. I have a big room which was intended for you, covered with tapestries of fine quality. The company consists of the Bradley Martins & Mrs. Sherman, Lady Strafford & her daughter, Mrs. Keppel, Lady Violet Finch, Hon. Mr. St. Aubyn, and Mr. Fredk. Martin, a brother of Bradley, & Mr. Bishop.

"By some strange blunder the baggage of Mrs. Keppel and Mr. Bishop 'went on,' and so for 24 hours they have had to appear in borrowed plumage, and as I am the only man in the house with a big enough neck for him I had to lend him shirt, collar & cravat, and Mrs. K. came down to dinner in a dressing gown of Lady Craven's. * * *   J. H. C."

Mrs. Choate lost the visit to Coombe Abbey because she had succumbed to the winter climate of London and come down with influenza or bronchitis, as did also Joseph Choate, Jr. They got out of London and went to Cannes as soon as they could. Miss Mabel Choate succumbed a little later and followed them to Cannes about the end of January. The Ambassador, who was proof against many things, including climate, stayed on in London until the end of March, when he joined his family at Cannes. He and Mrs. Choate had had a plan to go to Greece for his two months' leave in the spring, and he was very desirous to carry it out. They started, but as will be gathered from the later letters, Miss Choate's recruited strength was still unequal to the journey and they had to come back to Cannes. There Mrs. Choate and her daughter stayed on, and the Ambassador, after a few weeks with them at Cannes and a fortnight at Grasse, a little village on the heights back from the sea, finally went back to London about the middle of May. Through the rest of the season Mrs. Choate was in London with her husband, and Miss Choate lived, invalided, in a cottage at Wimbledon. In August she and her mother went to St. Moritz. There Mr. Choate joined them towards the end of September and went across the Maloja Pass down as far as Menaggio, but there Mrs. Choate fell ill. The Ambassador went back to London; his wife and daughter brought up at Lucerne and did not get back to London until Christmas. Of course so much illness made it a hard year for the Ambassador's family, but after that they had better luck and Mrs. Choate was able to stay pretty constantly in London with her husband except for short trips, and in the winter of 1902–1903 they all had "a wonderful three months' journey

to Constantinople, Greece, and Egypt," of which there
is no available record because Mr. and Mrs. Choate and
their daughter were together.

While in England Mr. Choate and his family spent
their summers in various ways: in 1899, visiting; in
1900, on the Continent; in 1901 and 1902 he took a
house in North Berwick, Scotland; in 1903 they came
home for J. H. Choate, Jr.'s, wedding, and then went to
the Continent; in 1904 he took a house in Hertfordshire
to be near their friends the Mount-Stephens, and liked
that best of all.

The letters that follow are to Mrs. Choate, at Cannes,
or wherever they found her, with her daughter. There
is a record of Mr. Choate's speaking at the opening of a
new public library at Acton on January 4. On January
19 he writes to his wife:

" * * * My dinner at the Antiquary's was very enjoyable, and that last night at Mrs. Ritchie's a great
success. Of course I had the honor of taking the Princess
out to dinner and found her very lovely. She spoke of
Lady Waterlow and is evidently very fond of her. The
women were all American, Mrs. Ronalds, Adair, New-
house, Blow, Miss Astrop. * * * "

To the Same

"1, Carlton House Terrace, S. W.
22 Jany. 1900.

" * * * The war news today showing very heavy
fighting without definite results makes people very rest-
less and anxious. I met your friend Sidney Colvin 'round
at the Club just now, and he seemed to think it was not
good—and as he sees everybody and hears everything

that probably indicates the general feeling in London tonight. I have had quite a busy afternoon in spite of the rain—lunched at the Carters' with Lady Grey Egerton, Mr. & Mrs. Prescott Lawrence and Mrs. Padelford & one English gentleman whom I did not know but he looked like a Bentinck. I drove out to Sir Gorell Barnes's to make our visit call and in honor of Henry's birthday. Lady Barnes I thought seemed much better than in the country but said she was about the same. Called at Lady Tweeddale's and there were Lord Egerton and the Duchess of Buckingham, both of whom expressed great regret that Jo missed his visit to them at New Year's, and still more that he was prevented by influenza. The Duchess said she had it two years ago, *and had never been well since.* I told her she kept up appearances wonderfully for nobody looked better. Lady Jeune was not at home, but Mrs. Bradley Martin at Claridge's was. She said that Mrs. Sherman was quite poorly and showed me a letter from her in which she said she had sent for Sir William Broadbent, who had put her to bed, and surrounded her with the entire contents of a drug store. They had a funny adventure last night. Went to the great concert at Albert Hall and got out at half past eleven and got into their carriage to drive home but didn't reach their hotel till ten minutes of one. They got into an absolutely dense fog, through which nothing could be seen and nothing could move. The police said that if they went straight on, they would be safe. Pretty soon they found the carriage on the side walk, whereupon Mrs. M. got out, and holding that tiny footman by the hand, she in evening shoes and he in his tiny boots, they walked the rest of the way to Claridge's, feeling their way mostly along the fronts of the houses.

"Your description of the glorious sunshine, air and scenery at Cannes almost lights London up, but there are no changes here yet. Fog yesterday and rain to-day. * * * "

(January 23.) "*Horrid ink!* I don't find it easy to write 1900 yet, having for 68 years tomorrow written 18—. It seems to take twice as long to get used to the change as at the turn of an ordinary year. * * *

"Mr. White returned yesterday and reported seeing you at the Station and in good shape. So I have no doubt the air of Cannes is doing you much good. Mabel I am happy to say is progressing and seems really to enjoy the rest cure. * * * When she and you are both away I don't see who is to attend to the wandering Americans, who are already beginning to arrive. Two daughters of Chief Justice Fuller are at the Carlton and what can I do for them? I think I must have a female attaché of the Embassy whose business shall be to take care of these visitors. One of them lives in Tacoma and her husband, Mr. Wallace, is a Democratic politician who says they are going to reorganize the Democratic party, get rid of Bryan, nominate Dewey, and get rid of all of us at one swoop. So you see we may get home next year after all.

"I attended the Memorial Service for Lord Lothian at the Chapel Royal today, a very fine service and well attended, Lord Salisbury being present, the actual burial taking place at New Battle Abbey at the same hour. * * *

J. H. C."

(January 25.) " * * * The war news doesn't come and everybody is very much on the strain. It still looks as if

Buller hadn't force enough to do what he has undertaken, but if he does it, it will be a famous victory. Did you read Lord Rosebery's speech at Chatham? Much the best speech yet delivered on the Liberal side or perhaps on any side since the war began. Unless some good news comes before Parliament meets there will be a great to-do there. Some scapegoat must be found, but it seems to me that the ministry are all equally responsible for the situation and they will stand by each other like men. * * *

"I enclose a good letter from George and one from a woman whose crochet lace you seem to have misappropriated. Poor thing! I suppose it ought to have been returned at once, but it can't be found. Where is it?

"Jo's letter to Mabel gives a glowing description of all your doings & surroundings. I am glad he declined to play poker with the Grand Duke."

(January 25.) "Mabel did not show me till I had sealed up my letter last night your very handsome birthday present—which was most welcome and handsome. My desk will now be admirably equipped, and I shall have you ever in my thoughts. I also had a cable from Beaman expressing the good wishes of all hands there. Only think of Mr. Evarts reaching his 82nd birthday two weeks from yesterday. I must write to Eliot to send him some flowers from us as usual. I have purchased a pair of silver candle sticks for Miss Lilian Pauncefote which will go forward by the 'bag' in season for her wedding. Today I had the Fullers (daughters of the Chief Justice), Mrs. Wallace and Mrs. Francis, at lunch and we got along admirably with the aid of Mrs. Carter (who was good enough to come and preside) her husband and Bayard (Cutting).

"All London is in a ferment today over the capture

of Spion Kop by General Warren.   I hope it means a speedier end to this terrible war. * * *

"The Bishop of London & Mrs. Creighton have asked us to dinner at London House on Feb. 7th, but I have declined for you and Mabel telling her that that was the day you had fixed for coming home, but that I didn't dare to say that you would be home in time.   Colonel Hozier was so touched by the 'Ambassador's graciousness' in returning his call in person, that he wrote inviting you and me and Mabel to dine with him at the Cavalry Club on the 30th, which of course had to be declined.   Today has been almost as fine as a winter day in New York only warmer, and the grass in the Parks in sheltered places is quite green.   Really the winter here seems to be only a rainy season."

(January 26.)   "London is down again today upon the report of the loss of Spion Kop.   I fear it will greatly prolong the war, and entail a vast amount of suffering on both sides. * * *

"Today I had Sir Chicken Lo-fen-luh, the Chinese Minister to lunch, as he wanted to talk over some business with me.   He is very good company indeed and was splendidly dressed.   He had heard nothing of the deposition of the Chinese Emperor of which the papers are full, and says the real power in China is the Dowager Empress. * * * "

"Terling Place, Witham, Essex.
28 Jan'y. 1900.

"You would have been delighted with this place and party.   Lady Rayleigh is delightful, very like her brother Arthur Balfour & I think infinitely proud of him.   She plays the organ very nicely and is very jolly though not very well just now.   And not only would she have taken

Jo's heart, but I wish he could have been with us when Lord Rayleigh took us 'round his laboratory and showed us all his apparatus for the most delicate chemical experiments. He had some 'liquid air' there, and though it was some hundred degrees below zero in temperature, when he poured it from one glass to another it was set violently boiling by contact with the warm air.

"The company consisted of Lord & Lady Salisbury and Lady Evelyn, Lady Sophia Palmer, Lord Selborne's sister, & Lady Mabel, his daughter, Mr. & Mrs. Mallett, Miss Baffie Balfour, and Lord & Lady Battersea, with a couple of young men, Mr. Noel Buxton & Mr. Ronald Malcolm.

"Lord Rayleigh has a great landed estate—several thousand acres—has more than 500 cows to be milked every day and sends the product to the London market. Hatfield Peverel is right in the heart of the County of Essex, and as Lady R. had a great quantity of books of history of the country I looked them over. I was interested to find my own name (Joseph Choate) on the poll lists in various parts of the country scattered along anywhere in the last hundred years.

"The news today is the worst since the war began— this second defeat of Buller and the retreat across the Ingela in spite of his promise that there should be 'no turning back' is a bitter pill for people here to swallow. The opening of the Parliament tomorrow promises to be most interesting. * * * "

"1, Carlton House Terrace, S. W.
31 Jany, 1900.
" * * * Yesterday I attended the opening of Parliament, which seems to have disappointed everybody.

The Government people had an uphill road, and to judge from what all the papers say have failed to satisfy public expectations by their explanations. But it seems to me that little good comes from that sort of talk. If the war must be fought to a finish, better to drop all criminations & agree upon the best mode of doing it. As long as the quarrel with the enemy lasts, quarreling among themselves should be postponed. But of course you won't quote me about this unhappy business. Sir Stafford Northcote was inducted with all the ancient ceremonies. Both houses were packed above & below—peeresses invaded the diplomatic gallery and I found myself seated between Lady Londonderry and Lady Gwendolen Cecil. Tonight I am to work out your dinner at Lady C. Beresford's—a send off for Lord Charles, who starts tomorrow for the Mediterranean Squadron. The Queen telegraphed me yesterday to know how Mr. Phelps was—of course through Sir Arthur Bigge. She seems much interested in his illness."

(February 7.) "Tonight I dine at the Bishop of London's; tomorrow I'm determined to go to the theatre; Friday at Mrs. Padelford's; Saturday at Lady Hilda Brodrick's, and Sunday lunch with Lady Dorothy Nevill. So you see I am seeking consolation where I can best find it."

(February 8.) "Americans are beginning to come in force, and this morning I have had quite a reception. Among them was a handsome girl, a Miss Weld from Dedham, daughter of my old friend General Weld. She said she went to dancing school with Jo—met him at the Van Dyck Gallery the other day but he didn't recog-

nize her—which was a pity—she was so very nice. Then
there was another very good looking girl, Miss Smith,
who said her mother was a Miss Palmer of Cleveland &
went to school with you there.

"The Bishop of London's (Creighton) dinner was very
ecclesiastical. Convocation is sitting and so they are
all in town. Lincoln, Chichester and Winchester, and an
ex-Bishop Barry, from Australia were all there & Scott
Holland, Canon of St. Paul's, the great radical, the
dowager Duchess of Bedford and Mr. & Mrs. Francis
Buxton were other guests. The oldest Creighton girl
is on the *Teutonic* returning from America where she
has been four months visiting the Chapmans, Nortons,
Eliots, etc., etc., and having a great time. Her mother
is afraid she has been thoroughly spoiled—thinks the
women of America are wholly given up to hen parties,
hen dinners, hen receptions, etc. I told her I guessed it
would all come down to 'ladies luncheons' which were
universal. She thought that was very bad, because no
ladies ought to have any leisure for social purposes, until
evening. * * *.

"None of my secretaries here can read enough Ger-
man to spell out the Flinsch, Frisching imbroglio, but
Mr. Carter thinks it is betrothal and not marriage and
Jo may confirm that. It is very cold here still."

(February 9.) "Last night after a walk with Bayard
around Kensington Palace I took an early dinner at the
Athenaeum Club, and went to see 'The Only Way,' a
capital dramatization of 'The Tale of Two Cities'—
Dickens's best novel—which I enjoyed very much. The
only person I knew there was Lady Charles Beresford,
who is, I believe, a great lover of the drama. She in-

troduced me to two gentlemen in her box; one was an American actor, named Kittredge, about to make his debut here, and another as I understood her, a distinguished scene painter, but it may have been a painter of scenery. Today began in London's darkest style, but by eleven o'clock the sun and skies were brilliant.

"It looks to me now as though they were going to strike some more effective blows in South Africa, and with all their great Generals out there and 194,000 men they can hardly do less. Anything that will bring this frightful war to an end will be welcome."

(February 10.) "Last night at Mrs. Padelford's I met a lot of new people, among them Lady Winnington, one of the Spencer Churchill tribe and cousin of the Duke of Marlborough, who was very agreeable, Lord & Lady Saltoun, Lord Onslow and Lord Rowton—all very pleasant people. The Carters also were there, the hostess being a Baltimorean. I find it quite embarrassing to have all the ladies wait for me to start. * * *

"Another retreat of Buller across the Ingela. I should think he and everybody else would be tired. I'm afraid the end of the war is not in sight. * * * "

(February 12.) "I enjoyed the Brodricks' dinner very much. The Lord George Hamiltons were there, Lord Monk Bretton and a lot of other nice people. Lady Dorothy Nevill's lunch was most agreeable. It seems she has the blood of all the Walpoles, being a lineal descendant of Sir Robert. She had her nephew Lord Orford, Lord Cork, Mr. Gould of the Westminster and Col. Saunderson, who kicks up such a row with his brother Irishmen.

"There is no good news from the War yet and every-body is gloomy. I enclose a cutting from the New York *Sun*, which Allie Evarts sent me and said it was, he thought, a fair view of the inclination of feeling in America."

(February 14.) " * * * I have asked Mr. White to occupy our house and run it while we are away, with Jo thrown in. It will be so much better for all concerned that I hope he will do it, although he seemed to think it was too generous a proposition.

"Mrs. Locker-Lampson, to whom on receipt of your telegram I had telegraphed that I should surely come, called in person yesterday morning at the Embassy to make it positively certain. She is going to have a very nice party, including Lord & Lady Battersea & Sir Henry Fowler."

The next letter is to a noted art connoisseur and collector who was knighted in 1909 for his public services and benefactions.

"DEAR MR. COTES: "14 February, 1900.

"I have your very interesting note of the 12th relating to the bust of Washington which you so generously propose to present to the President with a view to its being placed in the Senate House in commemoration of Washington's birthday. I am sure that the President would gratefully accept it, but he could not control a place for it in the Senate Chamber, which must depend on the vote of the Senate or of one of its committees. But he could place it in the White House, or very likely it could find a place in the Congressional

Library. Please let me know if this would modify your wish to present it. If not, by your leave, I will write to the Secretary of State of your generous purpose. Of course it could not in any way reach its destination before the 22nd, but that is not essential.

Yours very truly,

"Merwin Russell Cotes, Esq."   JOSEPH H. CHOATE.

"21 February, 1900.

"DEAR COL. HAY:

"I sent with today's despatches a black Wedgewood bust of Washington, which Mr. Merwin Russell Cotes, of Bournemouth, desires to present to the United States on the occasion of Washington's Birthday. It has been long in his possession and is very highly prized by him. He says that many applications have been made to him to sell it, but that he has never been willing to part with it until now that he presents it to the United States through the President.

"It struck me as being a good likeness and a unique bust, and while he would prefer that it should find a place in the Senate, it will be satisfactory to him if it goes to the White House, or to the State Department or the Congressional Library; but he imposes no conditions, sending it as a free gift and a goodwill offering.

"A direct acknowledgment to him (I enclose his card) would doubtless please him very much.

Yours very truly,

JOSEPH H. CHOATE.

"Col. John Hay,
Secretary of State."

The bust was accepted and is in the Congressional Library.

To His Wife

(February 16.) "I came up from the Locker-Lamp-sons' this morning to attend to some business, and go down again this afternoon to return again for good to-morrow morning. I find it a very delightful place and am sorry that you and Mabel could not be there to en-joy it. It stormed hard all day yesterday so that we didn't step foot out doors, but there was plenty in the house to enjoy. In the first place there was a very pleas-ant company, Sir Henry Fowler, the Batterseas, the Grant Duffs, Col. Durand who wrote 'The Making of a Frontier' and who is now on furlough, and quite a lot of young people. The house is a most attractive one with many large rooms opening into one another. It looks as though it might have been originally an Abbey— grand oak beams and oak arches dating back to Eliz-beth's time, splendid oak panelling all over the house, iron fire backs dated 1584, etc., etc. They have been great collectors—etchings by Michael Angelo, Titian, Raphael—pretty much all the old masters; books every-where and one brick vaulted and brick arched room con-taining rare old editions—first editions of Spencer, Shake-speare and almost all the great men of letters. The L.L.'s are specially sympathetic with America and Americans as her father, Sir Curtis Lampson, was a Vermont Boy. He had a great deal to do with the first Atlantic cable and was knighted I believe for that. One of the sons is in the Foreign office and the other at Cambridge. To-day is a most brilliant day—bright and warm and soft— quite equal I think to any of your days on the Riviera, which Jo describes in most glowing colors. * * *

"I am to go to the Foreign office at 3:30 to exchange ratifications of the Samoan Treaty, which has at last been agreed on. Do you remember the black Wedge-wood bust of Washington (life size) which we saw at Bournemouth? Mr. Cotes now presents it to the President. * * *

                                                    J. H. C."

                                "1, Carlton House Terrace.
                                    February 17, 1900.
"DEAR MABEL.

  " * * * Yesterday I went to the Foreign Office to exchange the final ratification of the Samoa Treaty. I expected to receive a slip of paper to that effect from Lord Salisbury—instead of which he handed me a large box containing the parchment Treaty signed by the Queen herself, bound in the richest Morocco covers, very handsomely tooled and decorated with gold & colors, and resting upon the great seal of England in wax of khaki color—as big as a dessert plate and this encased in a silver box with the arms of England upon it. The Lord Chancellor, by the way, has to carry the great seal from which this impression is made about with him wherever he goes. Even when he goes to a country house party this huge seal has to go with him—the traditional theory, I suppose, being that he wears it round his neck or somewhere on his person wherever he goes.

  "The last *Life* has a cartoon of Mark Hanna's Dream of Imperialism. It represents him with the Queen prostrate before him, Lord Salisbury and myself holding up her train, while he is putting her crown on his own head, with all the magnates of both realms looking on in admiration. Jo is so captivated with it that he won't let me send it to you '*yet awhile.*' He and Bayard* are going to have an early dinner here at six, and taking an evening train for Sandwich and golf till Monday afternoon.

---

*W. Bayard Cutting, Jr., his private secretary.

"The better news from the war has set everybody up, so that it was, I think, a great mistake for Lord Pauncefote to announce so long before his daughter's wedding, as I see he has done, that all the festivities which were to attend it have been abandoned because of the War, and the gloom prevailing in London and all over England. Mr. Ritchie at his daughter's wedding was showing a cable from South Africa that they had captured a camp full of Cronje's stores, including *champagne* for the General—which made everybody very happy.

"So many steamers have been taken off the lines between here and New York for War purposes that we only get mails once a week and some of them are very late. * * *

                                                    PAPA."

To His Wife

"1, Carlton House Terrace, S. W.
                    19 Feby. 1900.

"Jo and Bayard came back from Sandwich this morning and seem to have had a splendid Sunday on the golf links, though today again has been extremely wet here, and I suppose it was the prospect of that at S. that brought them home so early. R. W. Gilder appeared at my office today, having arrived with his wife on the *Germanic* on Saturday and is at Morley's hotel in Trafalgar Square. This time he has been ordered off for four months, not having been very well. He first tried going to Tyringham in winter, but no sooner got a little better there than he was called to town. He leaves the *Century* in the charge of Johnson, and his children in the care of Dorothy and the oldest boy.

"I judge from your account that Mabel will certainly

not be fit to travel much before April and I shall
probably not hurry away from here on the 1st of March
as I hardly think I should enjoy a long stay at Cannes.
I don't want to travel as Ambassador, or to be haunted
by a valet everywhere. If you take Ralph and Lydie
we certainly ought to be very comfortable. I am rather
inclined to ask Bayard to be with us for three or four
weeks at least, so as to get him into good shape before
his family appear, whose presence will no doubt make
a double demand upon his services. There is to be a
Levee held by the Prince of Wales, just announced for
March 7th, and of course Bayard will want to go to
that, and as it is to be a Diplomatic affair perhaps
it will be well for me to stay. Tomorrow I shall try to
go into Cook's and talk things over with them, but I
shall begin by telling them how shabbily they treated
me in Sicily in 1897, when they promised to take back
any tickets we did not use, and then made us pay over
again for a part of the route on which the Railroad refused their tickets. It was so small an affair that I did
not think it worth while to sue them, but I vowed then
that I would never have anything more to do with them.
* * *

"Mr. Ritchie came over to my table at the Athenaeum
and asked me to send his thanks to you for looking out
for his daughter and I read him what you wrote about
her in the letter which I received today. He said they
had quite recovered from the effects of the wedding,
which must have been tiring.

"Jo has just opened a letter from the 19th Century
and was much tickled when a check of £5 for his article
fell out of it.

"I enclose a letter for Mabel and a note from her shoe

maker, and am happy to say that my new shoes have
come from New York.

"I wish every day that you were here, for while 'no
household is complete without a baby,' it is no household at all without the wife & mother.

                                        J. H. C."

He was the guest of the Authors' Club at dinner on
February 20. He talked of the importance of readers
to authors and reminded his fellow diners that the people
of the United States constituted the vast majority of
the English-speaking peoples of the globe, and as cus-
tomers of English writers were entitled to very generous
consideration. He told also about the public library
system in the United States and how of three hundred
and fifty-one towns in Massachusetts, in all but seven
the public had the use of public libraries provided at
the public expense. He spoke of the teachableness of
the people who spoke the English tongue and of the work
of Captain Mahan in telling Great Britain about her
sea power, and of Mr. Bryce in telling the Americans
about their institutions. It was this teachableness, he
said, in all people who spoke the English tongue, that
constituted their great power in the present and their
great prospect for the future.

To His Wife

"American Embassy, London.
21 February 1900.
"At last we have got a brilliant day in London and a
bulletin is said to have just been put out at the war-office
that Ladysmith was relieved, which relieves London
too. Jo and I attended the debate in the Commons and

sat four hours listening to Chamberlain's assailants and to Chamberlain himself. He got quite the best of them and was supported in resisting any further inquiry by a vote of nearly 2 to 1, although if there is any truth not yet known, it will doubtless come out some time or other. There was also quite a debate in the Lords the same day on Lord Wemyss's motion about the Militia (his ancient hobby) and Lord Halsbury said that if Lord Kimberley had not come to their aid, Lord W. would have beaten the Government. The dinner at the Lord Chancellor's was an uncommonly pleasant one, as I knew every one there except young Mr. Ridley (the Home Secretary's son) and his wife. Lady Jeune was there with her husband and pretty daughter, the Duke and Duchess of Somerset, the Duchess of Buckingham and Lord Egerton, the Rayleighs, Lord James and his daughter and the cunning Lady Dorothy Nevill, and there were many inquiries about you & Mabel. The Somersets have taken for next summer that pretty place of Sir Kenneth Matheson's, Gledfield House, Ardgay, to which we went from Loch Carron, close upon their footsteps, and they would like very much to have us pay them a visit there. I haven't yet heard from Washington about my 'leave of absence' but hope to in a day or two. * * * "It is now 2 o'clock and the sun has been shining brightly since morning—a rare thing."

(February 23.) "Jo mailed you a tremendous mail of New York and other letters, and another to Mabel. So, I suppose you did not miss one from me, but yesterday being our national holiday, I closed the office and we all went away, Jo and Bayard to play golf at Mitcham and I went out to Slough and over the ground, or a part of the ground that we traversed together in 1879—Stoke Pogis, Burnham Beeches, Eton & Windsor. I had quite lost all recollection of the beeches and certainly it is a wonderful place. The trees must be many hundred years old, and are scattered over 300 acres and more which the City of London has now purchased and made a public park, which will preserve these relics of a remote past for a long time yet. The walk from Slough, where I lunched at the Crown Hotel was most interesting. The Road passes right through Eton and it happening to be the play hours I must have seen pretty much the whole of the school. One great group, the principal one, stood in the road across a field which soon opened and out came the dogs—the Eton beagles—and boys and dogs were all off together hare-hunting. Another lot were at foot ball and still another practising some other game. The country all the way from Slough to Windsor was under water on both sides of the road from the freshet in the Thames which was very remarkable, giving the whole the appearance of the Lake country, with Windsor Castle rising out of the water. * * *

"Jo is off to Baker Street arranging to send Mabel's bicycle. Tell her that I will inquire promptly all about the route to Athens via Marseilles, but I want your word for it that she will be fit to go.

"I met the Tweedmouths at Lady Strafford's last night and found them most agreeable.   J. H. C."

"American Embassy, London.
24 Feb. 1900.
"Dear Mabel:—
" * * * Yesterday I made some calls—on Mrs. Forbes-Leith among others. I did not get in—but this morning

I got a note from her which I enclose, from which it appears that her whole family are involved in the war, and that she is quite broken up. I don't wonder at it—the strain of it all must be tremendous.

"I am getting to be regarded as musical. Lady Rayleigh reported me as '*very musical*' because I insisted upon hearing her play on her organ. And now Lady Clanwilliam has asked me to come in this afternoon and hear Lady Beatrice play on the violin. This is no doubt my reward for sitting quietly at Lady Strafford's while Mrs. Cory played 'the Prelude.' By the way, I made a terrible break with her for after she got through I observed a young lady sitting on a sofa at some distance who looked just like her, and I asked her—'Is that handsome young lady on the sofa who looks so much like you your daughter?' But it proved to be her *sister*, Lady Carew, who is four years younger. She got back on me very well by saying, 'No, go and ask her if she isn't my mother?' * * *

"The Daveys' dinner was quiet—as their son is in Ladysmith and General Gatacre is their son-in-law. These fearful times are very trying to them. PAPA."

To the Same

"American Embassy, London.
26 Feb. 1900.

" * * * I am inquiring about those Messagonic Steamers. * * * As the time approaches I find I hate to go away. London is just now the one interesting place.

"I have just received notice from the University of Edinburgh that they have resolved to offer me the Honorary Degree of Doctor of Laws, and inviting me

to come to Edinburgh on the 14th of April to receive
it, or if that should not be possible, then at the end of
July. * * *

PAPA."

To His Wife

"American Embassy, London.
28 Feb. 1900.

"I don't think we have ever been separated so long
but once—and that was when you took dear Effie to
Europe in 1891—and you may imagine that I am long-
ing very much to see you, to say nothing of Mabel.

"Today ends February and, it is hoped, the rainy
season with it.   Lately it has rained every day.

"I enclose a letter from Mrs. Locker-Lampson which
she sent me with an acknowledgment of a copy of the
'Reminiscences of Bishop Whipple' who was a frequent
visitor at her house.

"Everybody in England is happy now over the vic-
tories and if they only lead to speedy Peace the rest of
the world will rejoice with them.   But I'm afraid that
these 3000 are only a small part of the Boers that must
be captured before the war ends. * * *

"Tonight I have to drive away out to Hammersmith
to dine at Lady Frances Balfour's—my last dinner before I leave.   Mrs. Abbey now finds she can't be presented in March and wants to be transferred to May
which I fear will not be possible as the places then are
all full and every one else wants to be transferred in the
same way.   Apparently the March Drawing Room will
be very leanly attended. * * * "

(March 1.)   "At Lady Frances Balfour's last night
there was quite a jolly party—Lady Betty who reported
her husband as decidedly better but not out of bed yet.

He wanted something amusing to read and I have today sent him Dooley's two volumes. As he has been Chief Secretary for Ireland these five years it ought to amuse him. Then there was the hostess herself who still goes to the Commons almost every day, leaving Miss Baffic in charge of the household. She is wonderfully well up on all the questions and people of the day—Lord Robert Cecil who looks like a terrible invalid, but is practising law very vigorously—the Solicitor General—and Miss Beatrice Chamberlain. Today I am to receive a new Minister from the Netherlands and tomorrow Mons. Boncart who has just been raised to full minister from Switzerland, having long been only Minister Resident.
* * *

"Lady Battersea has invited me to go to Aston Clinton for this Sunday but as I have an engagement here on Sunday I have had to decline—besides it is pretty cold yet for country visits.

"Mr. Peck, Director in Chief of the U. S. Section of the Paris Exhibition, has just been in and says I *must* come there. If I can't go on America's day, July 4th, then certainly on British day, which is yet to be designated.

"Hoping so soon to see you and judge for myself.

J. H. C."

In March he had begun to plan for a holiday with his wife and daughter.

To His Wife

"American Embassy, London.
2 March, 1900.
"Your letter of the 27th & 28th reached me at breakfast this morning, but you could not then have received

my letter which gave the result of my inquiries about the steamship lines, trains, etc., for it must have answered very many of your questions. Everything must depend on Mabel's condition whether we go at all, or where or how or how far we go. The more I think of it the more decidedly I am of opinion that the land route is the best; all things considered, wherever we go, the voyage from Brindisi will be enough. I don't want to take a man along, they are so frightfully in the way, and I have so much of them here. I dislike them the more every day. Mabel thought you would want to take only one maid between you, but there is no reason why you shouldn't take both, and as Mabel is pretty sure to need all she can get out of Lydie I think you had better take Ralph. * * *

"Last night Jo and I saw a fine performance of 'She Stoops to Conquer'—the best I have ever seen. * * *

"Much love to Mabel—as for yourself it seems ages that you have been gone. We seem to have abandoned all our social duties, but in your absence I don't see how that can be helped."

(March 5.) "I was very glad to get your letter this morning. Going by way of Trieste will suit me very well. On looking it up we found it was a very hard journey indeed from Genoa to Trieste unless broken up into several days. Bayard will go as far as Paris with me and then take a train to Rome where he has a lot of friends just now, and join us at Brindisi where the Trieste boats always touch. We are not going to take the train de luxe. We think it is too expensive for us; it is only good for the more delicate clay, but the cost is most exorbitant.* So we take the 11 o'clock train Friday, reach Paris at 7 P. M., cross to the P. M. & L. Station where I take the train for Cannes and he half an hour later the train for Rome. Mr. & Mrs. Albert Vickers invited us to dinner. Do you know them? Mrs. Forbes-Leith leaves on Wednesday (by the same train we take) with nurse, maid and two grandchildren, for Costebel. I'm afraid that going so loaded up she won't get much rest.

"I am going to give a lunch party on Thursday for Col. Sanger and his wife who arrived today from New York. She was a Stebbins and he a long time in my office.

"Mr. White arrives tomorrow."

(March 8.) "At last I see a clear prospect of getting off tomorrow morning which I believe will bring me to Cannes on Saturday about 1. * * * I have had to hustle today as there were no end of last things to do, and I gave a lunch party at 2 to the Sangers consisting of the Bryces, Trevelyans, Carters, Lady Dorothy Nevill and my 'new flame,' Mrs. Jack Gordon. It all went off exceptionally well, and everybody was so grieved that you and Mabel couldn't be there. Lady Dorothy was great fun. She and Mr. Bryce, utter antipodes in everything, sat together and harmonized at every point.

"Tonight I have Bishop Potter, Percy Grant and Mr. White for dinner. The Bishop and Grant, his chaplain, are on their way from a voyage 'round the world, and sail on Saturday morning.

"The Queen has arrived and the whole town is wide awake, great crowds everywhere, and much enthusiasm.

---

* He is still the same man for whom the one-dollar stateroom on the Newport boat was good enough.

Her announced trip to Ireland is thought to be a grand coup.

"Really, my dear, we have been so long apart that I have almost forgotten how you look, but I shall soon realize it.

J. H. C."

He got duly to Cannes, and wrote from there (Hotel Bellevue) on April 3 to his son:

"DEAR JO:—

" * * * I have written to 'Middleman' of Edinburgh to have my gown, hood and mortar board ready for the 14th, and to Rapkine to send him my measure. Those are prescribed requisites. Think of me in a *scarlet* gown.

FATHER."

On April 10, writing to his wife from the Embassy in London, he says:

"I had a very comfortable journey, and arrived at Charing Cross on the minute, to find Mr. White, Jo, Bayard, Creber & Horsman waiting for me at the station which was of course very pleasant. * * * It is finer here today than any one day at Cannes during my stay there. * * *

"I haven't been here long enough yet to hear any news. Jo was with Mrs. Craigie again at one of her theatre box parties last night and this afternoon he and Bayard have gone somewhere to play golf. White & Bayard took me last night to the Empire to see a variety show which was very good.

"I see by Smalley's letter this morning in *The Times*

that the Senate Foreign Relations Committee has concluded to drop the Hay-Pauncefote Treaty until after election, and so everything valuable has to yield to politics. Don't forget to write me every day, if it be only five lines, to say how Mabel progresses."

To the Same

"Howick, Lesbury, Northumberland.
16 April 1900.

"I was kept so constantly on the run in Edinburgh that I really didn't find time to write and was obliged to finish 'Red Pottage' which I had happened to take up on my first arrival. A strange book for a young girl to write. There was an immoral strain about it I thought, which seemed to leave a bad taste behind. As I found to my surprise that there was no day train to Scotland on Good Friday, I took the Thursday night train up, which gave me just three days in Edinburgh, and every hour was pleasantly spent. Only there is a disposition everywhere to see and exhibit an Ambassador and so I was kept going. Sir William Muir, the head of the College, entertained me most hospitably at Dean Park House, and his daughter, Mrs. Arbuthnot was most charming. She is the sister of Genl. Wauchope's widow, and of course the General's recent and tragic death has subdued the entire household very much. They seem to be as much in the dark as everybody else as to what passed between him and General Methuen just before his last fight. Sir William is a remarkable man, 81 years old this month, and yet he is out every morning on his bicycle at half past seven, then back to his bath and breakfast, and after that on horseback to the University where he is busy all day. He is an old Indian veteran of the Civil Service, was shut up for five months with his wife and four of his children in Fort Agra during the great Rebellion of 1857, and has survived to write many books about India, Mahomet, the Mamelukes, etc., etc., etc., one of which he has given with an inscription to 'H. E. the Right Honorable *Mrs*. Choate, in token of regret that she could not accompany' etc., etc., etc. He is Principal of the University, and Lord Dufferin the 'Lord Rector' came over from Ireland for the occasion; then we had Lord Leven who is again in Edinburgh getting ready for his brief reign again as Lord High Commissioner next month, and Prof. Masson, the author of the great 'Life of Milton,' came over from his home in the country to spend the Sunday with me. The function at the conferring of the degrees was very orderly and interesting, and I was specially pleased that there were no expectations or call for a 'speech' and no salutations from the boys. I was arrayed in a scarlet robe with blue facings—a black velvet square cap—and when I had been summoned to the platform, before a crowded house, a master of ceremonies related on the part of the Senators all the virtues I had and a great many more, and at the conclusion of the speech at his request the President laid another cap on my head, I kneeling, and pronounced me a Doctor of Laws; then another official in light uniform put the Doctor's Hood, black silk with blue lining, over my head —and having signed the roll of Honorary Graduates, I gave place to the next. This was very interesting, as the lady, Miss Ormerod (pronounced in two syllables *Orme-Rod*) was the first woman on whom the University had ever conferred this degree. She hadn't slept a wink the night before—poor thing—being so nervous in anticipation of the function, but she went through it very well and was received with great applause, as indeed I was myself, as Edinburgh seems to be very partial to me. Among the graduates of the year who received their first degree in course there were a great many young women, about a fifth part of all I should think, and as each degree was indicated by a different color the scene was quite spirited. In the evening Sir William gave a big dinner to the Honorary Graduates at his house, at which besides those I have already mentioned, there were many other dignitaries of the University. I see that the London papers of today give the substance of the day's doings, but as you will probably want all 'the particulars' I enclose cuttings from today's *Scotsman* which will probably interest you. Miss Ormerod is a very celebrated entomologist and does great services throughout England and Scotland in advising farmers and gardeners how to resist the ravages of the various insects against whom you are constantly waging war, just as the Department of Agriculture does for us in America.

"I quite fell in love with Mrs. Arbuthnot, Sir William's youngest daughter, who lives with him and takes care of him—the mother, Lady Muir, having died three years ago, having celebrated their golden wedding some years before. Mrs. A. married a barrister in London some 20 years older than herself and was left a widow ten years ago with three children. She has a house also at North Berwick which she regards as a summer paradise.

"Sunday is kept very strictly in Edinburgh and a vast deal of church going is done. I heard a young enthusiast, Mr. Black,* who is making a great sensation there. The son of a Rothsay baker he has worked his way by dint of brains at a very early age to the head of one of

* Rev. Hugh Black, well known as a preacher.

the principal churches. A long queue of expectant hearers forms before the church whenever he is to preach to get admission to the free seats, and yet he is not at all a revivalist, so far as I could judge at one hearing. As my departure from the house of the 'principal' on Sunday would have been regarded as Sabbath breaking of the worst kind, I did not leave until this morning, and reached here about noon. Jo has been here since Friday and returns tonight to take charge of the Embassy tomorrow. Bayard writes that he has a cantankerous liver, so I suppose he is not good for much and will be very glad to see Jo.

"This is a most interesting house, having been the home of Earl Grey of the Reform Bill, 1832—the grandfather of the present Earl, and is full of historical reminiscences. Lord and Lady Grey are most agreeable and hospitable. Lord Howick, 20, is at Cambridge, home for the holidays—a part of them only, for he is reading for honors. Lady Victoria, 22, a god-daughter of the Queen, Lady Sybil, 18, and Lady Evelyn, 14, make up the family, and Jo must have found them most delightful. Then there is a Miss Pease, of Alnmouth, not far from here, whose father and mother we met at Fulham last spring when we visited the Bishop.

"I have your two letters of Tuesday and Wednesday last which told good accounts of Mabel and promised still better, for which I was duly thankful. I think I shall go to London on Wednesday—certainly not later than Thursday. In the meantime I expect to receive here at least three or four of your delayed letters, and hope you will receive this long discourse as an equivalent for them all. Would that we might count upon being together in London again very soon.   J. H. C."

"It is too late and dark to reread this letter. So you must correct any errors."

The Scotsman, April 16, 1900, said:

"Howick Hall, where the American Ambassador is at present staying, is the beautiful seat of the Earl Greys, one of the notable Northumberland mansions. It occupies a site near the Turris de Howyke, which was one of the fourteenth century castles of Northumbria. In its situation, Howick Hall is matchless, buried in a dene of great natural beauty, and with a prospect seaward towards the blue North Sea. The mansion was built in 1792, from the designs of Mr. Newton of Newcastle. The internal decorations are of classic interest, and the pictures and statuary are of great historical import. Here is a canvas of Dr. Franklin, taken from his house in Philadelphia, during the War of Independence by Major Andre, the 'amiable spy' of Charles Lamb;* another of the Emperor Napoleon, painted during the Hundred Days, the bees on the frame of which were taken from the Emperor's throne. Family heirlooms are notable every-

---

* This picture of Franklin hangs now in the White House at Washington, bearing this inscription:

BENJAMIN FRANKLIN BY BENJAMIN WILSON
Painted in 1759
Taken from Franklin's house by Major Andre
Carried to England by General Sir Charles Grey and now
returned to the United States by Earl Grey

The letters following tell the story of its transfer.

GOVERNMENT HOUSE
OTTAWA

DEAR DR. WEIR MITCHELL,   17th April, 1906.
    I have received a letter from the President telling me that I am most welcome to send you the enclosed copies of the correspondence which has taken place

where. In the library is the gold timepiece given to Mr. Albert Grey by the Queen on the occasion of his marriage. Howick derives much of its present charm from the care and interest bestowed on it by the distinguished earl, who settled here in the early days of the century. Almost every tree he himself planted during his long lifetime, and the flower gardens today are things of beauty. In the family church near at hand a beautiful marble tomb

between him and me with regard to the Franklin portrait, with permission to you to make of them such use as you may see fit.

I remain,

Yours very truly,

GREY.

Dr. Weir Mitchell.

GOVERNMENT HOUSE
OTTAWA

7th Feb. 1906.

MY DEAR MR. PRESIDENT:

The fortune of war and the accident of inheritance have made me the owner of the portrait of Franklin, which Major Andre took out of his house in Philadelphia and gave to his Commanding Officer, my great Grandfather, General Sir Charles Grey.

This portrait which Franklin stated was "allowed by those who have seen it to have great merit as a picture in every respect" has for over a century occupied the chief place of honour on the walls of my Northumbrian home. Mr. Choate has suggested to me that the approaching Franklin Bi-Centenary Celebration at Philadelphia on the 20th of April, provides a fitting opportunity for restoring to the American people a picture which they will be glad to recover. I gladly fell in with his suggestion.

In a letter from Franklin written from Philadelphia October 23rd 1788 to Madame Lavoisier, he says: "Our English enemies, when they were in possession of this city and my house made a prisoner of my portrait and carried it off with them."

As your English friend I desire to give my prisoner after a lapse of 130 years, his liberty, and shall be obliged to you if you will name the officer into whose custody you wish me to deliver him. If agreeable to you I should be much pleased if he should find a final resting place in the White House, but I leave this to your judgment.

I remain, with great respect, and in all friendship

Yours truly

GREY.

To the President.

THE WHITE HOUSE
WASHINGTON

Personal

Feb. 12, 1906.

MY DEAR LORD GREY,

I shall send up an officer to receive that portrait; and I cannot sufficiently thank you for your thoughtful and generous gift. The announcement shall be made by Mr. Choate at the time and place that you suggest. I shall then formally thank you for your great and thoughtful courtesy. Meanwhile let me say is erected to his memory and that of the countess. A former chaplain of Charles I is said to have been at one time Rector of Howick. We might mention that in the hall of the mansion the fame of the second earl is recalled by the statue of him by Campbell, which was presented to the countess by the friends of the earl on the occasion of his retirement from office in 1834."

privately how much I appreciate not only what you have done, but the spirit in which you have done it and the way in which the manner of doing it adds to the generosity of the gift itself. I shall have placed on the portrait—which shall of course be kept at the White House, as you desire—the circumstances of its taking and return.

With heartiest regard, Sincerely yours, THEODORE ROOSEVELT.

8 East Sixty Third Street,
DEAR LORD GREY, 16th June 1906.

I am sending you direct from Philadelphia a faithful copy (by [William M.] Chase a well known artist approved by the American Philosophical Society) of your portrait of Franklin so generously presented by you to the American Nation, which I beg you to accept as a slight token of my regard and of my thorough appreciation of your most beneficent act. It should reach you by Express in a few days.

Yours most truly

JOSEPH H. CHOATE.

GOVERNMENT HOUSE
OTTAWA

MY DEAR MR. CHOATE, July 3, 06.

Your Franklin is looking at me from over the fireplace in my new room, at present the only picture on its walls, and I cannot tell you how greatly delighted I am with it, portrait, frame and all. I have pasted your letter on the back of the panel. I am not using the language of flattery when I say that I value the picture with which you have so generously presented me, and the circumstances under which I have come into its possession, even more than I valued the original which is to find an honoured place in the White House.

Your picture arrived during my absence and was unpacked by my comptroller. He called in the Howick housemaid to know whether in her opinion it was the original sent here by mistake or the copy, and she swore by all the experience of manifold dustings and sweepings in past years that it was the original on which she had exercised her elbow sufficiently often to know what she was saying.

It is admirably painted. I should like to write a line of thanks to Mr. Chase for having painted a copy which will be a treasured possession in the house of Grey so long as that family may continue. I hope my son's marriage on June 16th with Selborne's daughter may provide the fruitful security of its continuance.

I remain in the hope that you are in your usual vigorous health and youthful vigour and with my kindest regards to Mrs. Choate

Ever yours most truly and gratefully,

GREY.

To His Wife   "Howick.
                                18 April 1900.

"Yesterday we had a very lively day, driving to Bamburgh Castle—an old Saxon and afterwards Norman stronghold on the shore of the North Sea, some 15 miles away. The whole household went, including another visitor, Miss Willmott, a great enthusiast in gardening. In truth I think she was here to give the Countess lessons in that gentle art, and she is to be Vice-President of the International Congress to be held next July at the Crystal Palace to celebrate the Centennial of the *Sweet pea !*
* * *
                                J. H. C."

                        "American Embassy, London.
                        20 April 1900.

"Dear Mabel:—
    " * * * This has been an absolutely perfect day in London—soft, warm and balmy, and every moment out of doors was delightful. I have been three hours this afternoon on the top of an omnibus—various omnibuses in fact—watching the teeming life of this great city. There is nothing like it under the sun and I hope that by and by you will be well enough and strong enough to go about and enjoy such things with me. * * *
                                Papa."

                To His Wife

                        "American Embassy, London.
                        26 April 1900.

" * * * Last night I attended the Lord Mayor's Easter Banquet, and as I was the only Ambassador present, I had to speak for the Diplomatic Corps. They all seemed pleased, but as the papers do not make much of this spring occasion there is no very good report of what I said. Perhaps if you read this cutting from *The Standard* and the one I sent Mabel from *The Telegraph* you will have almost all that appeared. * * *

"Dr. T. DeWitt Talmage has just been in. He has been raising money in America for the sufferers, by the Indian famine—a very good thing. * * * "

(April 27.) "There are lots of picture exhibitions about now opening. The Guildhall, the New Gallery, the Royal Water Color already, and next week the Academy, where I see that Sydney Cooper, R. A. is to have *four* pictures hung—all the work of his 97th year, and his critics say that he still paints as well as ever. * * *

J. H. C."

"American Embassy, London.
27 April 1900.
"Dear Mabel.

" * * * I am afraid I should make your mouth water if I told you all we did yesterday afternoon, Suzette & I. We drove down first to the Guildhall and you know how interesting it is to drive through the crowded thoroughfares down town. The City is now having an exhibition of 120 pictures—free for the people—in a building adjoining the Guildhall—Sargent's Miss Astor, Whistler's Carlyle, a splendid group by Abbey, (King Lear and his daughters) and a lovely woman by Herkomer, we thought were the best and all very fine. In fact there was not much else to speak of in the Exhibition except five grossly realistic women clothed only in their hair. Then we went into the Guildhall itself. The room where the Aldermen sit is very fine—the walls are panelled in old oak, and the arms of each successive Lord Mayor for a hundred years on the panels and the glass. Then the attendants found out who I was and we were ushered into the Hall where the Lord Mayor was holding the Court of the Common Council, another very beautiful room with Gothic arched galleries all around above, which formed excellent frames for the spectators. We of course were taken right by the Lord Mayor's seat, and our entrance was quite an ovation. The Council happened at the moment to be discussing what rate of toll should be levied on American cattle coming into the City, which I suppose comes within their jurisdiction because they have charge of the markets. But they suspended business, rose up, clapping hands and cheering, and the Lord Mayor exclaimed 'Of course you all recognize the American Ambassador.' In truth I think they had almost all been at the Easter Banquet with their wives the night before which perhaps increased their enthusiasm. We sat a while to witness the proceedings and when we went out there was more clapping, so that I had to reappear in front of the curtain which draped the door and make another bow. Finally they lighted the great Hall with electricity for us to see the splendid oak roof which was put on after the great fire in 1666? to replace the roof then burned. The walls were not injured, and date back some centuries before that, I believe. In fact, the G. H. has been the 'City Hall' of the City and of the old guilds ever since it was a city.

"Then we drove down over Tower Bridge and back, which gave us the finest view of the exterior of the Tower, showing the various buildings which go to make it up distinctly, and on the way home inspected All Hallows Church, Barking, the oldest in town I think except the

Chapel St. Peter's ad Vincula in the Tower itself. It wholly escaped the fire and dates back to the 12th century, the Norman style very obvious. There are many wonderful old brasses there, inscriptions and figures on tombs & graves, some of which were mutilated in Cromwell's time & before. Then Suzette left me at Mr. Astor's Embankment house, where he was having a reception (by card) from 4 to 6—a wonderful house with carved wood in imitation or in the style of the old Guild houses— and with the portraits of his ancestors—the 2 John Jacobs and Wm. B. & his own—all very good. But I have come to the end of the paper & my time. They showed us the record of the baptism of William Penn in the register, which also had an entry of the marriage of John Quincy Adams.'

PAPA."

To His Wife

"American Embassy, London.
3 May 1900. Thursday.
"We have a real April day today, sunshine and showers alternating every hour.

"The Cuttings have come and the Butlers, but only an hour ago, so that I have not seen them yet. Tomorrow night I have quite a dinner party—Lord and Lady George Hamilton, Mr. and Mrs. Jack Morgan, Lord and Lady Arthur Wellesley, their daughter and her young man, Mr. Robbie James, Mrs. Padelford, and Justine and Bayard—fifteen.

"Tonight I am to dine at the Abbeys' to fulfil an engagement which I suppose she tried to make with you, and as Carl also expects to dine out I have invited Carter and his wife to dine with Suzette and Jo.

" * * * I have been negotiating today with Madame

de Staal and Madame Costaki Anthropoulos Pasha for
the discharge of your duties by them at the coming Drawing Rooms, when so many of our fair countrywomen are
to be presented. What a pity you can't be here. Now
I have got everybody on my back at once and must close
this scrawl."

(May 5.) " * * * Yesterday I had a terribly busy
day, and as we had a dinner party at night I fear I didn't
write you. Finding that we had only fifteen, eight of
whom were men, leaving us short of one 'gell' as they call
them here, I borrowed Susie Butler for the occasion and
that made 16. I took out Lady George Hamilton, Lord
Arthur Wellesley, Suzette, Lord George, Lady Arthur,
Mr. James, the fiancé of Miss Wellesley, Mrs. Padelford,
and the young people were easily disposed of. Jo & I
thought it a close question of precedence between Lord
George and Lord Arthur—one the son of a Duke by birth,
and the other the grandson of a Duke but authorized
on the accession of his brother, to take precedence as
a Duke's son. Well, how should you have settled that?
"The dinner was quite successful and everybody
seemed to think that my grief at your absence and Mabel's
might be described as 'mitigated' but we do indeed find
it very hard to get along without you. * * *
"Carl and Suzette are doing well, though Carl is too
busy and too headachey. Yesterday I got them tickets
for the private view at the Academy, and this afternoon
before going to the R. A. Dinner, I am going to take
them to a musicale at Lady Carew's.
"Americans are beginning to crowd in upon the Embassy. One wants a lunatic sent home—another has
lost his passport—another is dying and must have aid,
etc., etc., etc. * * *   J. H. C."

(May 6.) "Last night we had the greatest and most tedious function of the year—the Royal Academy Dinner. It took five hours and was duller than usual, but I sat opposite Sargent's great picture of Percy Wyndham's daughters, and it is certainly very fine.

"This afternoon I had a call from Mr. & Mrs. Chapin, and from Mrs. Kinnicutt, who is here for a day or two. She wants Mabel to go back with them in July and stay with them at Lenox. So she seems to have no lack of invitations. What do you and she say to Sadie's invitation to go to Bar Harbor?

"The Countess Hoyos says she ought to go at once to the Swedish quack who is curing everybody. Her daughter has been ill for months and months, and finds no help but from him. I believe he is the same man who recreated Poultney Bigelow. * * *

"I don't know how you will catch on to all this turmoil when you come. People are beginning to hustle very much and you can imagine how helpless I am without you and Mabel. * * *

"I took Suzette through Kensington Palace, but she now says I didn't show her the best thing there—a little house on the grounds built by 'Indigo' Jones."

To His Wife

"Howick, Lesbury, Northumberland.
9 May 1900.
" * * * I arrived here last night in time to inspect Lady Grey's beautiful garden before dinner. She takes an immense interest in it, and certainly is having great success. But the great change in the place since I was here three weeks ago is in the park as you approach the house—where the whole ground is carpeted with nar-

cissus and yellow and red primroses, a sight that I have never seen in America.

"There came up on the same train with me yesterday a very pretty girl, Alice Grenfell from Taplow. We were the first arrivals. Next came the Dartmouths from Patshull. They had left there at eight and took more than twelve hours to come. The morning brought the Pembrokes and Mr. & Mrs. W. Ridley, Jr., and the Duke and Duchess with Col. & Mrs. Egerton have just come at 4½ P. M. It looks now as if we should have a rainy day for the function in Newcastle tomorrow—the opening of a Young Men's Christian Association Building. Then there is to be a luncheon and an inspection of the Armstrong works in the afternoon.

"On Thursday pretty much the whole party returns to London to be in time for Friday's Drawing Room. I see that Countess Deym has returned to London, so I suppose that she instead of Madame Anthropoulos Pasha will present our Americans on Monday. * * *

"We have an invitation for the Derby (the 30th) from 'Ella Burns, Farm Court, Leatherhead' which I suppose is Mrs. Walter Burns.

J. H. C."

To the Same

"American Embassy, London.
11 May 1900.

"As this is Drawing Room day and we lunch at one, we are making everything very short. * * *

"I have a letter from the Vice Chancellor of Cambridge University that they have voted to give me the degree of Doctor of Laws, on the 14th of June. Perhaps you will be able to go there with me."

(May 14.) " * * * The drawing room of Friday was a great success. All our American ladies got through in time to see the Queen, and of course they were all greatly delighted. Suzette with Mabel's train looked very well. When her name was called, the Queen cried out 'Who's that? What name did you say?' Madame de Staal gave out at the last moment and so they were presented by Countess Deym who looked very fine. Mrs. Butler's dress, green velvet, and the Stewart jewels, great emeralds in a necklace, were among the finest there, and Susie was very stunning. Everything went well. The Cuttings—mother & daughter—were much approved, and wouldn't have missed it for anything. Everybody was well tired out as it was a very long function. Countess Deym had to retire half an hour before the close, but no harm seems to have come from it to anybody, though I got a bad cold in driving out to Poultney Bigelow's house-warming in Chelsea afterwards, and stayed at home on Saturday and Sunday, and am all right again. Have been to the Drawing Room today, which was quite another affair—dull and tame—no Queen, no crowd, no enthusiasm, but Mrs. ——, our Major General's wife, attracted great attention by wearing a breast full of decorations which Ponsonby Fane reported to me with great disgust as soon as she arrived, but I couldn't see what I could do about it. * * *

J. H. C."

A London despatch to the New York *Tribune*, dated May 16, says:

"Joseph H. Choate, the United States Ambassador, was the special guest at dinner this evening of the Ancient Company of Fishmongers. The assemblage, which was very distinguished, included the Chinese, Swiss and Servian Ministers, Sir Thomas Henry Sanderson, Permanent Under Secretary of State for Foreign Affairs, and other Foreign Office officials; the Australian Federation delegates, the Colonial Agents, the Earl of Cork, Lord Denbigh and many members of the House of Commons. Early in his speech Mr. Choate remarked:

"'Forget your war and internal commotions and look quietly in the faces of the diplomatic representatives of the world, who are bringing you only messages of peace.'

"The applause that greeted this apparent commonplace could only be appreciated by those who knew that the principal topic of conversation had been the cordial reception of the Boer delegates in New York.

"Mr. Choate facetiously referred to the endless disputes over the fisheries questions, remarking that such matters, although vehemently discussed, would not make them enemies. He rather took the audience by surprise when he declared that 'in Westminster Hall and other homes of oratory in England there have been as many noble blows struck and as many pregnant words uttered on behalf of the independence of America as there have been for the integrity of the British Empire.'

"All the members of the United States Embassy were present, and Mr. Choate's reception throughout the evening was enthusiastic.

"Major-General Alfred Edward Turner in a remarkable speech frankly admitted that Great Britain was not able to support an army adequate to her defence, and he said: 'There is a danger nearer home and more immediate than we think.'"

There was a fire at the Embassy on the 8th of June,

and the papers report the Ambassador fighting it in a dressing-gown, but it was soon put out.

On the 9th of June Mr. Choate went to a dinner given at the Savoy Hotel to Sir Henry Irving, celebrating his return to his country from the profitable wilds of the United States.   Mr. Choate was a speaker along with the Lord Chief Justice, Sir Henry Irving, Mark Twain, Mr. Pinero, and others.   Towards the end of his remarks he said:

"I would like to put Sir Henry 'on the stand' and hear his view as to the relative capacity of these two great peoples for enthusiasm.   When I first came to reside among the English people I had supposed from the account they gave of themselves that they were a cold and unimpassioned people, unwilling to give way to their feelings, and that when an occasional ebullition of enthusiasm broke out on one side of the water they said, 'That is quite American, you know,' but that was before certain recent events which have shown them in their true colors—before the relief of Ladysmith and of Mafeking; in other words, before the relief of London.   When these wonderful events happened they went as wild as human nature could let them go.   Never do I recollect, never have I heard in our history of such a wild outbreak of the human spirit as occurred on those two nights in London.   It recalled the enthusiasm on the other side of the water when events made our experiment in self-government a final, an absolute, and a perpetual success."

On the 14th of June he went to the Leys School speech day at Cambridge and distributed the prizes.   The discourse that he made there was addressed partly to the boys and partly to the five hundred guests who were present. About prizes, he expressed his conviction that the boys who got them were those who had determined to have them. It was so, he thought, with the prizes of life. The men who had the will to get them, got them. He said he had known all the leading lawyers in America and many in England for forty years. "No two of them were alike in mental, moral, physical, and natural endowments except in one, and that was an absolute tenacity of purpose, striving like grim death for the object they had before them, ignoring everything but attaining that object by all the honorable means in their power." What prizes were worth the effort to get them, he did not discuss.

At the Fourth of July celebration of the American Society in London, Sir Henry Campbell-Bannerman proposed the health of the American Ambassador, of whom he said that they had learned to appreciate his qualities and that "those who are acquainted with our characteristic self-complacency will understand how superlative a compliment we pay to Mr. Choate when we say we look upon him as one of ourselves."

The Embassy was closed on the Fourth of July, but in the afternoon there was a reception to Americans and others at the Ambassador's residence. The *Mail and Express Bureau,* on July 11, says:

"Of course there was the usual crush at the Fourth of July reception at the American embassy on Wednesday last, when Mr. and Mrs. Choate were 'at home' to the thousand and one loyal children of Columbia who happened to be in London.

"Carlton House Terrace had, in fact, a thoroughly well 'Starred and Striped' atmosphere about it. As one turned round the corner from Pall Mall, or crossed from the Crimean monument at the bottom of Regent Street into the shadow of the Athenæum Club, one could catch the dazzling flutter of a great Stars and Stripes, almost covering the big balcony over the doorway of Mrs. Mackay's mansion at No. 6 Carlton House Terrace. In fact, so very hospitable did this banner of liberty look to innocent tourists that the silver queen's front door was besieged during the afternoon by crowds, who, thinking it the home of their Ambassador, demanded admittance.

"The polite and magnificent flunkeys had all their time cut out in answering their demands for admittance by 'No, madam, further on, at No. 1, is the residence of his excellency the American Ambassador.' There also did the Stars and Stripes make a brave showing, both outside and inside the house, and Mr. and Mrs. Choate stood patiently and apparently contentedly at the top of the great stairway from three oclock until well past six, welcoming the advancing and ever-increasing army."

The Sun of this date (July 4) deprecated in an editorial the practice that had grown up since many years of sending diplomatic representatives to England to talk. *The Sun* thought that "an Ambassador should speak but seldom, and he is always safe if he confines himself to the commonplace." It went on to say: "The continual celebration by the American Ambassador of the good relations between England and the United States tends to give foreign nations an incorrect notion of the facts. There is no special friendliness between these countries. Interest is the only real tie between nations, and that is liable to vary."

But it does not appear that this opinion had much influence at the time, or has had much since.

At the dinner given in the Middle Temple Hall by members of the Bench and Bar of England to meet the representatives of the Bench and Bar of the United States, the Lord Chancellor presided, with the American Ambassador on his right, and there was much talk by lawyers, including Mr. Depew.

A livelier occasion was the Albrighton Puppy Show at the Kennels at Whiston Cross, on July 28, which might have come bodily out of one of Trollope's novels, where the talk was all of hunting. There was a big luncheon served in a marquee, and after that there came the exercises, including the presentation to the late Master of Hounds of a portrait of himself. Mr. Choate was one of the talkers and fell in very heartily with the spirit of the occasion.

Early in August Mrs. Choate and her daughter went to St. Moritz, Switzerland, and there are letters again to her, but first one to his brother William:

"Sunday 5 August 1900
Wilton Park, Beaconsfield.

"DEAR WILLIAM:

"I am very sorry that you and Mary did not conclude to cross the ocean this summer, as we had fondly hoped and rather expected you would. Even if you had only taken time for a short stay in London, you would have found it most agreeable, and I could have done something to advance your pleasure, now that I know so many of the sort of people whom you would be glad to meet.

"I find the judges and lawyers most satisfactory acquaintances, although they have far less to do with public questions and affairs than the profession is accustomed to in America. Of the nineteen members of the present

THREE BROTHERS: WILLIAM G., CHARLES F., AND JOSEPH H. CHOATE.
From a snap-shot taken in 1895.

government only two, the Lord Chancellor and Lord James of Hereford, were bred to the bar. In fact the study of the law instead of being, as with us, almost the only avenue to public office and affairs, seems here to be regarded as not only unnecessary for that purpose, but as a positive hindrance.

"Young men start fresh from the University into preparation for public life, and enter at once upon a lifelong career of that sort. There being an immense leisure class here, who have never to think of earning their livings, but have a great and well sustained ambition to serve the country in one way or another, the system works wonderfully well, and not only the military, but the civil service is of a very high order indeed. Nobody is admitted into the lowest branch of this service until he has proved himself qualified upon strict examination, and, once in, there is rarely any advancement except for merit and fitness. Corruption is practically unknown and patronage plays but a very small part,—so that the inducement to young men of merit to enter the public service is very constant and great. They have much to learn from us in many ways and we no less to learn from them.

"I wish you could have been at the Lawyers' Dinner in the Middle Temple Hall on the 27th of July. The cream of the English Bench and Bar were there, Lord Russell only excepted, who was kept at home by illness. It was intended by them as a recognition and return of the great hospitality which many of them have received in America. Although our side was very respectably represented indeed, we did not come quite up to their mark, as we had not a single Federal Judge, and the Bench was spoken for by your friend Simeon E. Baldwin of the Court of Errors of Conn., and the Bar by young Mr. Beck, who has just been appointed Assistant U. S. Attorney General, both of whom acquitted themselves very finely indeed.

"I find the post of Ambassador a very pleasant one, but there isn't work enough in it to satisfy the cravings of one who has practiced law for forty years in America. There are a great many functions and a plenty of social duties, and I often find myself yearning for a good old-fashioned contest in Court. Then an Ambassador is practically tongue-tied, and can never speak his mind. I must say, however, that the question now up about China, both in our relations to that great relic of barbarism and to all the nations of Europe, is most intensely interesting, and gives ample room for thought. I fear that we have only seen the beginning of a very fearful business.

"Everybody here is most cordial not only to me, but to all Americans, and I suppose that no former representative of the United States has been surrounded by so pleasant an atmosphere.

"Our family life here has been sadly marred by Mabel's illness,—so that for four months since this year began we have had to do without her (six months without Mabel) and her mother, and now, on Thursday last, they started off again for St. Moritz and will hardly return I fear until October. But Mabel, I am delighted to say, is already very much better, and I have every reason to hope and believe that in the Fall when she returns she will be as well as ever. She has never been alarmingly ill, but had a bad nervous breakdown, from which it takes a long time and very careful treatment of herself to recover. She takes it very bravely—was in capital spirits when she left for the Continent and is evidently gaining all the time. She has a fixed idea, however, that the climate of England doesn't suit her, but I hope that will pass away as soon as she finds herself perfectly well again. She hasn't begun to bulge yet, but I fancy she will very soon. At Wimbledon she had a very quiet but most enjoyable summer, and has infinite faith in the high air of Switzerland as a panacea.

"Jo has pretty much made up his mind to come home next February, gather up the threads of his interrupted 'second year' at the Law School, finish his course there to a degree, and then as quickly as possible get into the law in New York. He has had a grand opportunity here and had an experience that he will never forget, which in all probability will enrich his whole after life. He is still only 24 and I want him to get started in the profession and in life while I can perhaps be of some service to him. I hope too that he will have an ambition for public life in which I think there is soon to be a much better chance and opening for young men in America than there has been in the past.

"I note the approach of your 70th birthday and am glad to hear that you are turning that somewhat startling goal in fine health and condition. But don't keep your nose down at the grindstone too long! You're entitled to good, long holidays now, and plenty of them, and I can see no object to be gained by slaving away much longer. I am much delighted to have broken out of harness when I did. I seem to be in the best of health, have 'put on' a stone here in England, and feel the full benefit of our Hodges constitution which certainly was the saving of the Choates,—or at least of our branch of them.

"The death of Jo. Sprague was somewhat startling. I had hoped in the evening of life to see something of him again, but he has vanished. If I recollect right, he has exactly repeated his father's experience, lived just as long and died in just the same way. I thought that long-lived strain of the Bartletts would have extended his thread of life.

"The new Quinquennial of Harvard has just come to me. I see that we are now within 250 of the goal of my ambition, the post of oldest surviving graduate, and they will get out of our way very rapidly—but with 39 men starting now in their 70th year on the average, we shall ourselves make more rapid progress than we have hitherto.

"I am spending Sunday and Monday, the bank holiday, with Mr. White, 1st Secretary of the Embassy. You may remember him and his wife, who was a daughter of our old friend Lewis M. Rutherford, who in my young days in the Century, from '58 to '70 or thereabouts, was a regular habitué there.

"Give my best love to Mary and do write and tell me how things go with you.

Ever your loving brother,

J. H. C.

"P. S.

"Our Secretary of State is winning all sorts of laurels here now. He seems to have stood alone in the faith that the Legations were safe, and shows the immense power of a buoyant and hopeful temperament."

To His Wife

"Wilton Park, Beaconsfield.
Sunday, 5 Augt. 1900.

" * * * Yesterday we had the function of the funeral service at the Chapel Royal for Duke Alfred. The company was very distinguished, including the Princess of

Wales, the Duchess of Argyle and York, and many minor
Royalties, domestic and foreign, all the great men of
the Kingdom, and the heads of all foreign missions. * * *

"Everybody here except Muriel and myself played
bridge last night, in fact till 20 minutes of one this morning. It seems just now to exclude all other evening occupations, and whoever doesn't understand and play the
game, is 'not in it.' They all seem to be taking lessons
of my old friend Miss Clapp, of Pittsfield, who started
whist teaching in America and who is now the rage for
bridge in London. The Carters and Bayard are very
deep in it.

"Mr. White reports you and Mabel as 'both splendid' and 'not tired at all,' so I hope to hear the best reports of your progress to the end.

"The Shah is not coming and the lunch at Hatfield
has been countermanded.
                                                        J. H. C."

To the Same

"1, Carlton House Terrace, S. W.
                Monday, 7 August 1900.
"I returned from Mr. White's this morning, having
spent two solid days of rain at Wilton Park. But the
house party was very pleasant, and we talked and read,
and, will you believe it, played bridge! Having had no
experience of the game before, I did not cut any great
figure. * * *

"There is nothing authentic today from China, although a rumor by way of Washington that the allies
in a reconnaissance in force have had a hard fight about
8 miles from Tientsin, and lost 1200 killed and wounded,

but the Chinese retreated.   I fear they will find it a hard
journey to Pekin.

"Parliament adjourns tomorrow and Lord Salisbury
expects to go next week to some German bath to recruit.
Arthur Balfour seems to get angry in the House every
day, from which I infer that he is very tired. * * *

J. H. C."

(August 13.)   " * * * I was much interested in the
contents of Cordelia's letter which you wrote me. * * *
"I was not at all surprised by what her friend's friend
wrote about you.   Only I do not see why any one who
knew you should have doubted your success in London.
If we could only avoid these long breakups you would
certainly carry all before you.   There are no women like
American women to adapt themselves to new circumstances and you have done it admirably and nobly.

"Lord Russell's* death was a very great shock to us
all.   I suppose they felt certain that if let alone he would
certainly die and so they performed the fatal operation.
He was the most *live* man that I have met in England,
and I shall miss him very much. * * * "

(August 14.)   " * * * Yesterday afternoon I spent
at Kew Gardens with Mr. Francis Rawle, who was or
seemed to be very much pleased.   This morning he
and Mr. White breakfasted with me *at 8*, and we drove
together to the Brompton Oratory to attend the Requiem
Mass for the soul of the Lord Chief Justice.   I tried to
extract some meaning from some part of the service but
failed utterly.   No wonder the English people so long ago
made up their minds to have done with it.   The papers

* Charles Russell, C. J.

already begin to talk of his successor. The prize—and it is a very great one—seems to lie between the Master of the Rolls, Sir Robert Finlay (The Attorney General) and Sir Edward Clarke.

"Tomorrow we are to take a day off and visit Admiral Watson on the U. S. Cruiser *Baltimore* at Gravesend. * * *

"I have actually cleared up my table and not a loose paper left on it. Dr. Jacobi is here. I did not know before that Dr. J. was a Prussian Revolutionist of 1848, and escaped after several years in the State Prison. Did you?"

(August 16.) " * * * There is a *Journal* report from New York this afternoon that the Allies have entered Pekin but nobody seems to believe it, although for some days now it has looked as if it might come true any day, and certainly it is high time that this fearful suspense were ended.

"We had quite an excursion yesterday to visit the *Baltimore* at Gravesend, where Admiral Watson entertained us in fine fashion, and at our departure fired an Ambassador's salute of nineteen guns.

"You will find Major & Mrs. Cassatt a decided acquisition to the Embassy—most presentable in every way, and well disposed to make themselves useful and agreeable. * * *

"Last evening as I was driving through the Park with Mr. Carter and Major Cassatt we met with quite a tragic incident. We passed where a lady had just been thrown from her horse and frightfully injured. The police were just carrying her off to the Hospital, without the least idea who she was, but Mr. Cassatt searched her riding habit which they had taken off, and found her card—a Miss Page of 43 Trejunter Road, so we drove there, informed the family, took in her two sisters and left them at the Hospital just as the Doctors had examined the wounded one and moved her into the ward. It proved to be a terrible case—one eye destroyed, the cheekbone broken and a severe concussion of the brain. When her brother called this morning to thank me, she had not recovered consciousness, but for all that the Doctors thought she would recover. * * *

"You ask about Col. Hay. I don't think his sickness amounts to anything. He doesn't stand badgering and baiting quite as well as President McKinley does, and no doubt the vast amount of abuse he is getting from the Democrats worries him more than it ought. I think he's 'all right.' * * * "

"American Embassy, London.
18 August 1900.

"DEAR MABEL:—

"You have no idea how dead London is getting to be. At the house we are reduced to our lowest terms. Ralph has gone to her home, Creber to his, Charles is off with Jo who gives no sign except to send a box of game from Glen Urquhart, Henry has left, and not a sound is heard below stairs. I take my lunch and dinner at the Clubs and am only at home early in the morning and late at night. So it is at the office—an occasional Christian Endeavourer stranded, and now and then an American traveler to say 'How d'y do?' are all that we have in the place of the crowds of June & July. Do you know the ——s of 5th Avenue, New York? They called yesterday and were a queer couple. She seemed to be double his age, and did the talking—a good deal of idle talk it was—and when she got up to go she said 'I had a dream about you seven years ago, and have wanted to see you ever since, and now I am satisfied.' I tried to get her to tell me her dream but she could only do that sometime 'when we were alone.'

"My dinner at the Carlton Hotel went off very well. Mr. & Mrs. Smith though not quite fresh from 47th St. had more or less to tell about New York politics and business. * * *

"Mrs. Smith rather takes my view of that marriage of Miss —— as a failure—calls it a Platonic arrangement—a drawback too, because the nice people who used to invite her out to dinner now invite her with her husband and as he is always away she has to decline for both and so gets no dinner. * * *

"I have just heard from the Foreign Office that they have authentic news from Pekin that the Allies entered there on the 15th. * * *

PAPA."

To the Same

"American Embassy, London.
21 August 1900.
" * * * Yesterday I saw Prescott Butler and his entire family who sail tomorrow on the *Oceanic*. Mr. White and I called on them and they were all out but Prescott who had been ill in bed for a week with lumbago, while in Amsterdam, and looked quite pulled down. So I took him out for an airing, to High Gate and Hampstead Heath which seemed to interest him very much. Then in the evening I dined with them and today (if

it does not rain) I am going to drive them out to the Star & Garter at Richmond. Mrs. Butler was very funny, as usual. * * *

"Bainbridge Colby has just called. * * * He says that Ellery Sedgwick has moved to New York and taken editorial charge of Frank Leslie's weekly paper. There is a nominal Editor in Chief but Ellery does the work and gets a good salary. Ellery's mother has been quite ill, * * * but Mr. Sedgwick still defies all the laws and goes on eating lobster and washing it down with punch, and is very well and jolly. Mr. McKim who is 'shooting' with Schuyler, Cadwalader & Co. in Scotland writes to Mr. White that Mr. Carter at the age of 73 tramps all day over the moors after grouse without fatigue, while he himself was tired out—but two years ago Carter did the same thing and overdid it, having a bad winter afterwards.

"Now I have told you all the news I have, so goodbye.

PAPA."

To His Wife

"American Embassy, London.
22 August 1900.

"I enclose a letter from Lady Kay-Shuttleworth which explains itself. I am going there on my way home from Edinburgh, to a presentation of prizes, and I do hope that you will be able to go along as they are very nice people. I hope to get away from here so as to join you at St. Moritz about the end of the first week of September, and in the meantime expect to go to Col. Barnardiston's in Sudbury near Groton which he thinks is the cradle of the Choates, and also to Lincoln and for a short

visit to the Batterseas at Cromer, said to be a most delightful part of England.

"Be sure to write me what to wear for September in
the Engadine.   I shall count the days till I can be with
you again."

(August 27.) "I got back this morning from the Rye's,
Sudbury, where I went to visit Col. Barnardiston.   Lady
Florence, his wife, is a sister of the late Lord Dartmouth,
and of course an Aunt of the present Earl.   They have
eleven children, five sons and six daughters, of whom
the oldest son only is married, and by him they have
only one grandchild (a harder case even than mine).
The son married a Miss Floyd-Jones of South Oyster
Bay and I am sure that you would like her.   They live
in the midst of a lot of interesting old English Churches,
which we visited in long excursions, and one old English
House (Melford Hall) of which I sent you a photograph
direct from the store where I bought it.   The churches
we visited were at Levenham, Melford, Bury St. Edmunds and Groton and Boxford,—all very ancient and
fascinating.   At Groton I saw the Church Register with
the entry of the baptism of our supposed original progeni-
tor 'John Choate, June 24th, 1624' and there are many
circumstances that point to his being the man, but I
don't feel quite sure.

"Bury St. Edmunds is the seat of the famous Monas-
tery of St. Edmund, at whose altar the Barons assembled and registered their vow to extort from King John
the signing of Magna Charta. * * *

"I expect to go to Lincoln tomorrow afternoon, then
to Peterborough and Ely, a sort of Cathedral tour, and
to bring up at Lady Battersea's in Cromer on Friday.

"The news from China is still very muddy. There seems to be nobody at Peking for the Allies either to fight or negotiate with."

(August 28.) " * * * I am now getting quite in the notion of going to Oberammergau on my way to you. I find that there are performances of the Passion play on the 8th & 9th, & that it is 40 miles by rail from Munich. * * * If you were along I should have no hesitation about it, but it would be a 2 or 3 days journey from where you are to get there, which doubtless you would hardly think worth while. This play I believe is only performed once in ten years, and Lord & Lady Halifax whom I met on Sunday, gave me a very different idea of it from any I had before. They had just returned from there.

"This morning I gave the order to the Eagle Range Company to put into our house, or rather Lord Curzon's, one of their best Eagle ranges, 6 ft. 6, according to the estimates they gave you last Spring. Coal is still going up and even at the present rates we shall save a good part of the prime cost in a single winter, and stop a shocking waste. * * * "

To the Same

"Lamb Hotel, Ely.

31 August 1900.

"I'm very sorry not to have written you since I left London on Tuesday, but you know how it is yourself in travelling and sight-seeing. Every moment seems taken up until you have to go to bed.

"I have abandoned the idea of going to Oberammergau. As the play lasts till the end of September perhaps you and I, if you very much desire it, can go there then. * * *

"These cathedrals are very absorbing and delightful though none of them equal in grandeur York Minster which you have seen, although, as I think, with the restrictions of visiting, we didn't see half enough of it. * * *

"The cathedral bells are ringing for the morning service which is the best time to get the effect of the whole."

"The Pleasaunce, Overstrand, Cromer.
Sunday, 2 Sept. 1900.

"DEAR MABEL.

" * * * Here I am on the sea shore, on the northern coast of Norfolk, and the Batterseas have a most charming house, as you might suppose, full of beautiful things, each perfect in its kind. Paintings, water colors, engravings, photographs, a library of 5,000 books, many of them in the finest bindings, and a wonderful garden, where, although on the sea shore and exposed to the most bleak winds, yet the air is so soft that everything flourishes with the greatest luxuriance. I was mortified to think of our own poor orchard in Stockbridge— to see dwarf apple trees set out only last year, already bearing big apples. Climate is everything. * * *

"As I write, in a huge room beautifully equipped (occupied by the Princess Louise last week) I am looking out upon the North Sea, and see the ships go sailing by, and men, women and children wandering about the beach. Right before me overhanging the beach is the cliff which serves as a promenade for the whole neighborhood. I am quite sure you would like it.

"I enclose George's last letter. He was so much pleased with a postal you sent him. You must send him one every little while.

PAPA."

To His Wife

"The Pleasaunce, Overstrand, Cromer.
Monday, 3 Sept. 1900.

"My brief but somewhat frantic efforts for the Passion play on the 9th have ended in nothing. Cook reported today that no room whatever could be had at Oberammergau at that time, and that our only way would be to go by train Sunday morning from Munich to O., see the play and return the same day, 4 hours in the cars *each* way, to which I said no and immediately telegraphed you an hour ago 'could get no rooms and should start for St. Moritz on Friday morning.' * * * Then we have had that charming young Lady Dorothy Nevill, who started out with us for a walk yesterday afternoon and returned because the wind was disarranging her '*hair.*' [She was then 74.]

"To think that I shall actually be with you at the end of the week.

J. H. C."

To the Same

"American Embassy, London.
5 Septr. 1900.

" * * * I am in a terrible hurry to get to you & Mabel.

J. H. C."

"Hotel Victoria, Menaggio,
Lac de Como, 27 Sept. 1900.

"DEAR JO:—

" * * * As I expected when I left, nothing of importance seems to have happened in my absence. Anybody who expects any particular progress to be made in this China business in any particular time is bound to be mistaken. Too many cooks may not spoil this broth but they will give it plenty of time to cool. I have not seen or heard anything yet which commits our government to a wholly separate settlement on the points which concern all the powers alike. Has any such thing come from Washington? I am too far out of the world to know much that is going on. The papers when we get them are always two days old and sometimes three. * * *

FATHER."

To His Wife

"American Embassy, London.
5 Octr. 1900.

"Badly as I felt when I saw you and Mabel disappearing in the distance under your umbrellas, as soon as I struck the cooler atmosphere of Lake Lucerne, with its blue water and bluer sky, it operated like a powerful tonic and made a new man of me. Really there was something very lowering in the air of Lake Como, and if Mabel suffers from it in any way I should not hesitate to move right up to Switzerland, where you will be sure of a better state of things. And then London is simply *perfect*—cool, clear, bright and bracing. Nobody could help being well here just now.

"On the night train I got along very well, only the narrow and confined cabins are altogether too close. But in the morning the porter brought me a very nice breakfast—coffee, French bread and actually fresh eggs, laid by a French hen, not an Italian. Our passage across the Channel was a little rough. In fact it was a regular game of *bowls* all the way, and as every spot on deck was occupied I stayed in my cabin all the way across, reading the English newspapers. Creber, Horsman from the house, and White, Cutting and Hodson from the Embassy met me at the station and I was much delighted to find myself in London again—only they had a hot fire to welcome me in the library; but cheerful lights, welcoming books, running water and one's own comfortable bed, after those fearful narrow cribs on which we have been sleeping for the last four weeks were a great comfort and delight. On the boat at Lugano I was accosted by Mr. Haynes, who said he knew me by my pictures. It was he who married Miss Law, and on her death inherited the villa above Cadenabbia of which you spoke. He said it was full of the rarest curios which she had spent her life in collecting. He was most kind and assisted me very much, being familiar with the road over which he had passed many times, especially at Bâle, where there were many complicated things to be done. First, we had to put all our hand luggage together in the waiting room under the charge of his maid, while we went into a building across the street to the Wagon-Lit office and secured my sleeping berth; then back to the station to entrust our large baggage receipts to a porter who disappeared with them in the night. After a ¼ hour's waiting he came again but without the trunks and took us to a solitary room in a distant part of the building, where we found them in charge of a Customs officer (Swiss) who, on production of my card, chalked them and delivered them to the porter, who shouldered them off to the weighing room, where they had to be weighed. Then the tickets to London had to be taken to another office & stamped. I could hardly have done

it without Mr. Haynes who had been through it many
times before and was most patient.   I don't think you
could do it even with Lydie, but as you are going to stop
over at Bâle you will have no trouble.   You had better
let me arrange from here about your passage home when
the time comes.   You will be saved some trouble and
some extras.

"Lord & Lady Rayleigh came all the way from Lugano
to Bâle, a most gorgeous scenery all the way.   We dined
together and they were very pleasant.

"The elections seem to be going as we thought, very
strongly in support of the Government. * * * "

"American Embassy, London.
6 October 1900.

"DEAR MABEL.

" * * * Yesterday I took the carriage and made up
a lot of calls especially to enquire after our sick friends.
The Bishop of London seems to have had an experience
not unlike your own.   Mrs. Creighton who was as sound
as ever, said that he had been behaving very badly.
Right in the midst of their vacation—in the Tyrol I
believe—he broke right down.   She thought he hadn't
been well for some time, but there his digestion gave out
entirely and she had to bring him right home to Fulham.
He failed at his weakest point.   I told her I had thought
last winter that he couldn't keep on at that pace.   Well,
the Doctor got hold of him and put him on a strictly
meat diet, and prescribed 2 months rest from everything
but the actual business of the diocese, and he is doing
very well, though Mrs. Creighton confessed that she was
acting the part of a dragon over him and not letting
anybody see him, but letting him read novels, etc., etc.

The business of the diocese is considerable for he was holding an ordination, and the Hall of Fulham Palace was lined with anxious looking young men, who I suppose were waiting to hear their fate. The butler told me that they entertained 20 of them over night. * * *

FATHER."

"American Embassy, London.
Monday, 8 Oct. 1900.

"DEAR MABEL:—

"I enclose a letter for you from the Hotel Metropole, Folkestone—also, the only piece of Italian paper which I had left, 5 lire.

"By the way, will you go *the next time you go out* to that little store where we bought the stamps and pay the man that .75¾ of a lira which he overpaid me in making change. I meant to have done this before I left and it has been on my conscience ever since. It's a small thing to us, but no doubt of great importance to him. * * *

"Mama's friend, Mrs. —— of the —— is coming to see me to-morrow before sailing for America. Some people left their cards at the house on Saturday with a card from —— that they were her dearest friends. What shall I do with them? * * *

PAPA."

To His Wife

"American Embassy, London.
Tuesday, 9 Oct. 1900.

" * * * I have a note from Lord James of Hereford this morning inviting you and me to go to them in the country on the 21st which I shall probably accept. The Halsburys are to be there.

"I caught a glimpse of the Bishop of London yesterday driving in an open carriage, very much muffled up although the day was warm, and looking very serious.

"Bayard seems destined to adventure. Yesterday afternoon when he went home to his rooms, he found a great crowd surrounding the house, and blocking up the stair-way. A burglar had been sacking his rooms, turning everything inside out, and pocketing all his jewelry—had been overtaken by his valet and landlady, and had finally taken refuge in the attic, at which point the police, who had been loudly called, arrived and captured him after the landlady had driven him downstairs. This morning Bayard and Hodson are following him up at Court.

"Nothing new about China."

(October 10.) "There is nothing new about China. Today the Dowager Empress is reported seriously ill. If she would die it would help the situation amazingly.

"If I weren't so busy I should be quite lonesome.

J. H. C."

"American Embassy, London.
12 Octr. 1900.

"DEAR MABEL:—

"I enclose two or three things that have come, but I doubt if they are of much account. I spend most of the time these few days at the house, at work on my address for Edinburgh which I must finish by Sunday night, as it's very irksome to have such a thing hanging over one, and then the more I work upon it the more interested I get. But these days are quite too fine to spend in doors.
* * *

"Nothing new about China, except that the French note seems to suit everybody but our people, whose views upon it you will see in today's papers.   PAPA."

To His Wife

"1, Carlton House Terrace, S. W.
        Monday evening, October 1900.
"I hope you are all right by this time, but do not feel sure, as letters from Mabel and Mrs. Hardcastle written on Saturday indicate that you are still in the Doctor's hands. I am very sorry indeed about this and don't want you to come back to London until you have regained all the pounds you have lost. How came you to do so? I suppose it must have come from the strange fancy that all women have of taking meals out of doors.

"I have just returned from Lord James's. * * * My visit to Lord James was most pleasant. The Halsburys were there and full of kind inquiries about you. I didn't tell them anything about your having been unwell, but I boasted greatly on Mabel, and jeered at them for not having gone to Promontogno. Winston Churchill went up and returned with us—talked all the time and was most amusing. He is brimming over with the enthusiasm of youth, knows it all on every subject, and seemed to think his opinion entitled to weight as against us all. But he was great fun. The Cuttings and the Grews and the Holmeses all sail on Wednesday, and I went to bid them good bye this afternoon.

"Did I tell you that Bayard's burglar got six months at hard labor? I thought it a ridiculously light sentence. * * * "

To the Same

(October 15.) "Tomorrow is our wedding day and I wish we could then repair unto the Bell at Edmonton all in a chaise and pair, but as that cannot be I can only thank you for the 39th or 3900th time for the day, and hope we may have many returns of it and sometimes be together again. * * *

"I can't get on with that address. There is nothing so hard as to sit down in cold blood and get up such a thing before it is absolutely necessary, but I do want to get it out of the way. Perhaps as Mabel has been reading up about Lincoln she can give me some ideas, but the great difficulty is what *not* to say.

"You have all been invited to the American Society's Thanksgiving Dinner for Nov. 29th and are requested to make a note of it."

(October 16.) "Do you remember all about this day 39 years ago, and all the particulars? Certainly it took a great deal of courage on your part to embark on such an enterprise with an unknown man! Well, in spite of all our sorrows and trials, the balance has been in our favor. We have had a most happy life and have a vast deal to be thankful for, and now that Mabel is all right again we may look forward with hope to the end. I only wish you were here, and trust that all the returns of this, our great anniversary, we may spend together. * * *

"My little dinner last night was quite a success, although there were but four of us.—Mr. Coolidge, Mr. & Mrs. Newbold and myself, the young lady being confined to her bed with a bad cold. They seemed to like being invited and to enjoy their dinner, which was a very good one, and having been in the diplomatic line themselves, they were full of curiosity and interest. * * *

"Most of today I have given to Sir Henry Irving's matinee for the relief of the Galveston sufferers. Drury Lane Theatre was packed from floor to ceiling and the programme was four hours long, *three* of which I endured and enjoyed. I had taken four tickets, one for each member of my family, but as none of them appeared likely to go, I invited Mr. Coolidge and his two granddaughters. * * * The performances were very good, but I quite agree with Mrs. Delafield that 2 hours are enough for any entertainment. * * *

                                                    J. H. C."

(October 18.) "I didn't write to you yesterday because I was bound to finish my Edinburgh address and devoted every minute to that. Fortunately it is finished and will trouble me no more.

"I sent my check yesterday for £50 to Sir Henry Irving to add to his Galveston Fund which I was glad to hear from him would reach about £1300, a very generous thing for those actors & actresses to do. * * *

"I wish you were here to go to the James's with me tomorrow. For the next Sunday I have another very nice invitation from Lady George Hamilton to go to them at Deal Castle which I am accepting. * * *

"The new range works very satisfactorily, and seems to do all sorts of cooking very well. Creber says it hardly burns 1/10 as much coal as the old plan.

"Mr. Bryan seems to be making a great noise and stir in New York, but there isn't the least symptom that he is making any impression on the voters, so I look upon the election as being practically settled already. * * * "

"American Embassy, London.
23 October 1900.
"DEAR MABEL:—

" * * * I have just been to the Grosvenor-Bell wedding at a queer church in Duke St., Grosvenor Square. There was quite a large company of Anglo Americans, and after the wedding we had to adjourn to Mr. Bell's quarters at the Alexander Palace Hotel, where there was a sumptuous breakfast followed by many dullest speeches of which one was made of course by the Ambassador. * * *

"You should have seen Major in the Park this morning. He was all 'in the air' and as we went by Wellington Barracks and the band discoursed eloquent music, he discoursed eloquently too.

"Thursday I am to dine with the Maudslays and on Friday go to the Lord George Hamiltons' at Deal Castle. The Anglo-British agreement about China seems to suit everybody, except that our people want to know what the third section means, but this is between ourselves."

To His Wife

"American Embassy, London.
24 October 1900.

" * * * Today I have had charge of Senator Manderson and his wife, of Nebraska. He did me a good turn by preparing and delivering an address in my place before the American Bar Association when I came away, and so I wanted to do what I could for them. I took him to the Lord Chancellor's lunch to the Judges and Queen's Counsel in the House of Lords, and then we picked up Mrs. M. at the Metropole and went to the

Law Courts to see the procession, same that we saw last year, and after that to hear the remarks on Lord Russell by the Lord Chancellor and the Attorney General, all of which pleased him exceedingly. The new Lord Chief Justice looked splendidly on his first appearance in his new robes, and he got a great deal of applause. We were in the same gallery as last year. There I saw Lady Barnes quite recovered, and that dear old soul Lady Matthew, the wife of Mr. Justice Matthew, with whom we dined last year. They all ask for you and I tell them you are *very well*, taking no note of your late set back.

"All London is looking forward to Saturday—the reception of the C. I. V's. Windows to see the procession are selling at fabulous prices. * * * "

(October 27.) " * * * I found Lady Halsbury with a very bad cold last night. She had been in bed two days and looked not quite at her best, but was in good spirits and planning today to see the procession. Of course I played bridge with the Ld. Ch. and won 1s. 6d."

(October 29.) " * * * I wish you could have seen the crowd today that welcomed the C. I. V's home from the war. I have seen no such masses of people since that April morning when we looked down on that crowd in Wall St. that was called out by the news of Lincoln's assassination. I stood on the upper balcony of the Athenaeum Club, and as far as you see the crowd was solid. It was with the greatest difficulty that mounted soldiers could open a way for the little band of heroes. —Fourteen hundred, marching four abreast, dressed in khaki, worming their way through the black crowd— they were cheered at every point, but the greatest enthusiasm was reserved for the wounded and invalids who brought up the rear in carriages. All other parts of London seemed to be deserted for the line of procession from Paddington to the Mansion House. * * * "

(October 30.) " * * * Lady George Hamilton was full of inquiries about you and hopes that when I next come to Deal, you will come too. Deal Castle is a delightful old place, the simplest in the world, but a veritable medieval affair with a moat all about it, portcullis gate & big guns, and Lord George is Captain for life, as Lord Salisbury is of Walmer Castle, 1½ miles away."

(October 31.) " * * * The announcement has just come out that Lord Salisbury retires from the Foreign Office to remain Premier only and that Lord Lansdowne takes his place as Secretary for Foreign Affairs. I am very sorry to lose Lord Salisbury for he is a most pleasant man to do business with, and was always just & fair and well disposed to us. Of course Lord Lansdowne will also be a good man to deal with.

"You ask who Lady Joan Verney is. She is the elder daughter of Lord & Lady Desart, and a most charming little body. Her husband is in the foreign office. I suppose this change will greatly relieve the pressure on Lord Salisbury and give him time to look after all the departments. * * * "

(November 1.) " * * * Our dinner party last night went off in good style—even Jo ejaculated to that effect. The Desarts are daisies all of them. The Halsburys you know all about. The Lord Chancellor was jolly, and after dinner he and Ld. Desart and Lady Evelyn and I played bridge down stairs—a drawn game, as we hadn't time for a rubber, and Jo entertained the rest up stairs at the piano. Jim Barnes was a pleasing feature of the occasion.

"Today I had to go to another funeral service—that of the Prince Christian Victor at the Chapel Royal. I am sure this is a terrible blow to his mother.

"Next Wednesday I have to give away an American bride, Miss Carr, to the Earl of Newborough and to go to the Lord Mayor's dinner on the 9th.

"No doubt we shall get the news of McKinley's election on Wednesday afternoon. They seem to be getting unpleasantly rowdy in New York, but happily it will soon be all over.

"The funeral I went to last week was that of Sir Roderick Cameron, at the request of Madame Waddington, who was in some way connected."

"American Embassy, London.
5 November 1900.

"DEAR MABEL:—

"I have sent you by mail today a proof of my Edinburgh address, which as you cannot hear it, no doubt you and Mama will be interested to read in advance. I marked it 'private and confidential' that it should not go any further—or out of your hands. It has cost me lots of trouble and I hope the Scotsmen will like it.

"Well, the campaign in America is over, and now comes the election, which I am sure is coming out all right. I see that Roosevelt made nearly 500 speeches and stood bareheaded in the rain on Saturday, 7 hours, reviewing the procession—against his doctor's protest and is now ill in bed. It would not be wonderful if with such a helter-skelter mode of life he should come to grief.

"I am going to take Mr. Carter home to lunch with me to take care of Esther Hunt, and of course he has had to rush off and 'get shaved' as Bayard always has to. Why these young men who have nothing to do don't shave in the morning when they get up I don't see. * * * "

To the Same

"American Embassy, London.
Tuesday noon, Nov. 6.

" * * * I have just had a call from Miss Grace Carr whom I have to give away tomorrow at the Hotel Savoy to Lord Newborough. Isn't it funny what queer functions I have to perform? * * *

"Tomorrow afternoon no doubt we shall hear from the Election and when the decisive news comes I will try to send you a telegram, but it doesn't seem possible that there can be any disaster. The papers keep repeating and I as constantly denying that in the event of Mr. McKinley's Election Mr. Hay and I are to change places. Who can get up such silly stories? PAPA."

To His Wife

"1, Carlton House Terrace, S. W.
7 Nov. 1900.

"The great sensation of the day has been the election returns from America, as to which I caused two telegrams to be sent you on receipt of the first news. Every new report only increases McKinley's majority, both electoral and popular, and he has a good strong Congress to back him. So I think we shall have a fine administration for four years. Bryan too has signified his purpose to take himself off. I think the result of the election creates as much interest and gives as much pleasure here as at home.

"My wedding today went off very well. The old Savoy Chapel is a charming place for such a ceremony, and the bride was really very pretty. A breakfast afterwards at the Savoy Hotel, but the only persons that I knew there were Col. & Mrs. Hunsiker. He is the Carnegie agent here and a great friend of Mr. Fleishman's. * * * "

(November 10.) " * * * I enclose cuttings from *The Times* of today about the Guildhall Banquet last night. It was an amazing affair in that grand old Hall, about 900 people dining, quite half ladies. I sat between Lady Gwendolyn Cecil and Lady George Hamilton. I, and my speech too, were enthusiastically received. In fact the interest of the English people in the result of our Election seems quite equal to our own. * * * "

The Lord Mayor's banquet is a great show and one of the great public occasions of the London year. The Lord Mayor, who gives the feast, comes to it announced by a fanfare of trumpets, accompanied by the Lady Mayoress and attended by sword and mace bearers, and his lady by maids of honor, to a raised platform at the end of a great reception-room. The company is large—Mr. Choate says nine hundred—and everybody who goes wears the most decorative raiment they have; so that, as the London *Times* says of this banquet, "there was the customary display of gorgeous uniforms, beautiful dresses, orders, diamonds, costly plate and flowers, to which the Guildhall, brilliantly lighted so as to exhibit its fine architectural proportions to the best advantage, afforded an appropriate and admirable setting." The main speakers were Mr. Goschen for the navy, Colonel McKinnon for the army, Lord Salisbury for the ministers, and the American Ambassador for the foreign ministers. It was in this speech that Mr. Choate told his celebrated historical narrative of Downing Street and how it got its name:

"I hardly know," he said, "to what I am to attribute the honor of being selected to speak for all the foreign representatives. There are many of them that have been here much longer than I, whose faces are much more familiar to you. Probably I owe it to the fact that I am the only Ambassador present, possibly to the more significant fact that perhaps I know more about Downing Street, whose pavement we tread every week in our visits to her Majesty's Minister for Foreign Affairs, than any one of them. The truth is that Downing Street, if it may be called a street at all—which I somewhat doubt —is altogether an American street, and, however the representatives of other nations may feel, we are entirely at home there. I will show you how it is an American street, and how it derives its origin and its history from the earliest periods of the English colonies in America. I doubt whether many within sound of my voice know why it is called Downing Street. Now, at the school which I had the good fortune to attend, I am afraid to say how many years ago, in Massachusetts—the best colony that was ever planted under the English flag, and planted in the best way, because you drove them out to shift for themselves—at that school over the archway of entrance there were inscribed the words *Schola publica prima*—the first school organized in Massachusetts—and underneath was inscribed the name of George Downing, the first pupil of that school. Then in Harvard College we find him a graduate of that institution in the first year that it sent any youths into the world, the year 1642. He soon found his way to England. He became the chaplain of Colonel Oakey's army under Cromwell, and he soon began to display the most extraordinary faculties in the art of diplomacy of any man of his day. It was the old diplomacy. It was not anything like the new diplomacy that Lord Salisbury and the Foreign Ministers here present practise. It was the old kind. Downing developed a wonderful mastery of the art of hoodwinking, in which that kind of diplomacy chiefly consisted. In the first place he hoodwinked Cromwell himself, which showed he was a very astute young man, and persuaded him to send him as Ambassador to The Hague. Well, after the Protector died, he tried his arts upon the Rump, and he hoodwinked the Rump, and they reappointed him Ambassador to The Hague. And when the Restoration came, he practised his wily arts upon the Merry Monarch, and induced him to send him again as Ambassador to The Hague. Three great triumphs in diplomacy—all by one man. In those days, when the King shuffled his cards—and I believe he shuffled them very often—changes of office took place as if by magic, and he who had been in the Foreign Office was transferred to the War Office, and he who had been in the Board of Works was transferred to the Home Office, with the same happy facility with which those changes now take place, by the mere nod of the Prime Minister. Downing seems to have had

opportunities which none of her Majesty's present ministers enjoy—he made lots of money, and finally he induced the Merry Monarch to grant him a great tract of
land at Westminster provided—or so the grant ran—
that the houses to be built upon the premises so near
to the Royal Palace shall be handsome and graceful.
If you will stand at the mouth—shall I call it the mouth?
—of Downing Street and gaze across the way to Whitehall where Charles in his merry moods was always ban-
quetting and looking out of the window, you will appreciate the reason of this proviso. So he built him a
house possibly in Whitehall, and he built more mansions
between there and Westminster Abbey, and the old annals of the time describe those houses as 'pleasant mansions,' having a back fronting upon St. James's Park—
the exact description of the Foreign Office to-day. For
it also has a back fronting on St. James's Park, and really
it is the most important side, because that is where her
Majesty's Minister for Foreign Affairs always finds his
way in and out, with a private key by the back front
door. In the natural course of things Downing would
have been haled to Tyburn and hanged by the neck
until dead, but he won his way into the favor of King
Charles by claiming that the King must forgive his past
backslidings because of the vicious principles that he
had sucked in in his early New England education.
Finally he died, and by his will he devised his mansion
and estates and farm at Westminster to his children,
and now they are long since gone, leaving no wrack behind except a little bit of ground a hundred yards long
and twenty yards wide, sometimes narrowing to ten,
which bears still his illustrious name. It is the smallest
and at the same time the greatest street in the world,

because it lies at the hub of the gigantic wheel which encircles the globe under the name of the British Empire. It is all American. I have shown you why it is called Downing Street. But why, Lord Salisbury, is it called a street? I have always thought that a street was a way through from one place to some other place. This does not come within that definition. I have heard it called a *cul-de-sac*—that has no outlet except at one end—a place where you can get in but cannot get out. How, however, other nations may find it, we Americans, by reason of our prescriptive rights in the premises, find it to be a thoroughfare. We feel entirely at home in it. Our feet are on our native heath. We can go in and go out, and give and take on equal terms. And now I will conclude with one word; perhaps it is the only proper word I ought to have said. On behalf of the entire Diplomatic Corps, whom I am happy here to represent, words would fail me to express the delight which we have found up to this hour in our intercourse with Lord Salisbury, and the very great regret we feel that we shall see his face in the Foreign Office no more. I hope in his higher and grander station he will not wholly ignore us. I hope he will rather imitate the example of the retired tallow-chandler who, parting with a great business which he had followed with eminent success and with great personal delight, wiped his eyes as he was leaving the premises and promised that on melting days he would in spirit always be ready to be with them. I believe—I know—that a good deal of the friendly relations which exist between all the great nations of the earth that are represented at this Court of Great Britain, and the preservation of the peace of the world, have in large measure depended upon the just and fair spirit, the patience and the forbearance, the hearty good-will and the fairness which he has manifested towards us, and his considerate regard for the rights of all other nations, while maintaining with the utmost tenacity and stoutness the rights of his own."

> "Hatfield House, Hatfield, Herts.
> Sunday 11 Nov. 1900.

"DEAR MABEL:—

"Not half the glories of Hatfield House have been told. I wish that you and Mama could have been here with me today. The house itself is one of the most beautifully preserved of the old houses of England, and close by is the old palace of Henry VII. where Elizabeth lived during bloody Mary's reign—a prisoner part of the time —and this house is full of most interesting pictures, tapestries, armor, etc., etc. Lord Salisbury under his own roof is even more delightful than at the Foreign Office and that is saying a good deal. The party included Eustace Balfour & his daughter Baffie, Lord Rowton, Lord Percy—'Harry Percy' as they call him, recalling Shakespeare's 'Harry to Harry shall hot horse to horse,' etc., etc., Lady Ampthill, Eric Barrington & Mrs. B.— great friends of the Dunhams, several Cecils besides Lord Robert and Lord Hugh—about 20 at table.

"My speech at the Lord Mayor's banquet seems to have been the talk of the town for 24 hours. It seems that nobody knew the origin and history of the name Downing St. till I told it, and my demonstration that it was an American Street took everybody by surprise, it being the sacred centre of the British Empire. * * *

PAPA."

Mr. Choate's address on Abraham Lincoln, delivered in the Music Hall at Edinburgh on the 13th of November, is one of his most ambitious and notable speeches. Lincoln was a fresher subject to average English minds in 1900 than he would be now since Lord Charnwood has written his life and Drinkwater's play about him has had so remarkable a success. Lord Rosebery, in introducing Mr. Choate, spoke of his selecting for his discourse "the most interesting subject, I think, that was within the range of possibility—the great man whom he personally knew and saw in the flesh." The address is the leading one in the volume that contains the more finished discourses that Mr. Choate made while Ambassador. It was printed at full length in the New York *Times* on the day of its delivery, and other New York papers had more or less of it. *The Sun* went through it carefully for defects and snarled about as usual.

"Dalmeny House, Edinburgh.
14 Nov. 1900.
"Dear Mabel:—
"I am much obliged for your letter of Sunday—and as you give us no idea of your future movements I continue to write to you at Luzerne, although I have more than half an idea that I shall find you at home when I get there on Friday night. The 'address' came off very satisfactorily last night. Lord Rosebery and I went in 'à la postilion,' and Jo drove in with the other young men—the secretary, the agricultural agent, and Mr. C. P. Trevelyan, M.P., who came up along with us. The audience was closely packed and was most responsive and enthusiastic, seeming to take every point as quickly and sympathetically as a New York audience would have done. I think the Scotch are a little closer to the Americans than any other people. Lord Rose-

bery lives like a prince, and Dalmeny looking out upon
the Firth of Forth, and within a stone's throw of it, is
most charmingly situated.   Then close by, right at the
edge of the water is his old 13th Century Castle where
he sleeps and I guess spends most of his time here.   There
he keeps many most interesting treasures.   The entire
family consists of himself and Lady Sybil who since the
marriage of her sister must have many lonely hours.
They are most cordial and hospitable.

"Tonight I am going to the Archers' dinner in Edinburgh and tomorrow go to Burnley but as Sir Ughtred
Kay-Shuttleworth is laid up with influenza in London,
and Lady S. is kept there with him, I shall go from there
on Friday to London.   Ever lovingly yours, PAPA."

His errand at Burnley was to distribute awards to
the students at the Mechanics Institute of that town.
He talked to them about education, which he said was
the chief industry of the United States.   He reminded
them too that they were Lancashire people and that
Lancashire, in spite of the cotton famine, had supported
Lincoln in the Civil War.

"Gawthorpe Hall, Burnley,
Lancashire, Friday Nov. 16.
'DEAREST MABEL:—
" * * * My visit to Edinburgh was most enjoyable
throughout.   Lord Rosebery is a perfect host, and Lady
Sybil does her part exceedingly well.   Wednesday night
I went with Lord R. to the annual dinner of the Scots
Archers in Holyrood Palace, in that long gallery that
has the portraits of the Scottish Kings for 600 years,

all just alike and painted to order by the yard by one artist. The Duke of Buccleuch presided, and of course we all had to talk a little. I chaffed the company to their apparently great satisfaction, and Lord Rosebery did the like.

"Gawthorpe Hall is a charming spot and house,—an oasis in this great manufacturing region, an old Jacobean mansion in fact commenced in the time of Elizabeth and finished just about the date of her death. Wonderfully well preserved—with many rich memorials of the past—portraits, carvings, etc., etc. Miss Nina Kay-Shuttleworth, a charming girl, does the honors in the absence of her father and mother most admirably for me and Sir Spencer Walpole, the only other guest. At the meeting last night I was made much of—presented with an address in a highly illuminated book, with a speech by his worship the Mayor, and talked for an half hour in a somewhat lively strain about education to an audience of 1500 mostly operatives. I will send you the first report I can get.

PAPA."

To His Wife

"American Embassy, London.
17 Nov. 1900.

" * * * Everybody seems pleased with my Edinburgh address and also with the speech at the Guild hall, and I am expecting to hear, as Mr. Smalley cables to *The Times*, that on the other side of the water they have been equally well received. I send you today's *Anglo-American* which seems to have a lot to say about me. * * *

J. H. C."

In a letter to his daughter (November 26) he says:

"I suppose you have seen the accounts of Sir Arthur Sullivan's death. I am very sorry for it. He was one of the most agreeable men I have met here."

He went to the Thanksgiving dinner of the American Society in London at the Hotel Cecil and told the diners why he thought of the United States as "a sort of Cinderella in the family of nations."

He writes to his wife (November 29):

" * * * I am expected to lead another bride to the altar next week—a Miss Langham of San Francisco (Do you know her?) who is to be married to Baron von Sternburg who used to be Secretary in the German Embassy at Washington. * * * "

"American Embassy, London.
1 December 1900.

"DEAR MABEL:—

"Writing 'December' reminds me that it is now almost a year since we had you and Mama both together —so we are both looking forward with great eagerness and delight to your speedy return. I had a lovely time last night at the Royal Society Dinner of which I send you a full verbatim account cut from the London *Times* of the proceedings. It was most delightful to be in close contact with such great men as Lord Lister and Lord Kelvin—who after wringing secrets from nature which have conferred lasting blessings on mankind, are as simple in bearing and modest in speech as children. The room was full of celebrated men whom it was most interesting to see, of a wholly different type from those who generally grace civic banquets. Tomorrow we are to have a quiet day at home, which you know I always enjoy very much. I am, however, to lunch at the deBilles, who have invited me to meet Sir Henry Howard who is beginning to be talked of as Lord Pauncefote's possible successor at Washington.

"I also send you a cutting from the New York *Sun* in which some sensible writer corrects *The Sun's* absurd criticism on my Lincoln Address. * * *

PAPA."

To His Wife

"American Embassy, London.
Dec. 2, 1900.

" * * * I am looking seriously into the subject of a stove for our hall, and think I have found one very like a New York Stewart's stove to burn anthracite coal. Of course it will not be ornamental, but it will I hope keep you and Mabel warm. After your recent experiences you will hardly be able to bear a cold house. * * * "

(December 5.) " * * * I had not heard of Mr. Pratt's death, hardly a surprise as he had been an invalid so long, but it takes another name from the list of the class of 1852.

"I gave a bride away today at St. George's Church, Hanover Square. The groom, Baron von Sternburg, was for many years Secretary of the German Embassy at Washington. The only people in the Church were the parson, the clerk, two charwomen & the sexton, the bride & groom, her mother and two sisters and myself,

and they drove straight from the Church to the station
en route for Paris, quite the quietest wedding I have
ever attended. * * *
J. H. C."

(Saturday.) "I was so very busy yesterday that I
got Jo to write you.

"In the evening I went down to Grub St. to the City
of London College, to distribute prizes, etc. I had to
travel largely on my muscle, so far as the address went,
but so far as I could judge it seemed to suit the occasion. * * *

"I see that Lord Wemyss at the age of 82 has just got
married. The English are a great people!
J. H. C."

(December 9.) " * * * Our stoves are up and are
working beautifully, and being of porcelain—or rather
terra cotta—they are not hideous, and are much less
in the way than you might suppose. I feel quite sure
that they will keep the house very comfortable through
the winter, and after that they can be put down stairs.
They have to be charged with fine anthracite coal once
a day, and the fire will never go out. * * * "

(December 10.) " * * * Lady Agnew is a near friend
of the new Lady Wemyss, and says she is a very attractive woman about 40 years old. Gossip says that the
marriage took place five months ago, and that his family
have only just now succeeded in overcoming his shyness
to announce it. * * *
J. H. C."

"American Embassy, London.
13 Dec'r. 1900.

"Dear Mabel.—

" * * * I spent two very pleasant hours yesterday at the British Museum (Natural History) at South Kensington with Prof. Ray Lankester who is the Director there, and wanted to show me about. It is quite the finest collection of its kind in the world. I saw the Great Auk—the remains of the Dodo, and the cast of the skull recently discovered in Java, and supposed to be the newly discovered 'missing link' between man & the monkey, but which Prof. Lankester thinks is only a very low type of man. The brain cavity is extremely flat & small. * * *

Papa."

"American Embassy, London.
16 Dec'r. 1900.

"Dearest Mabel:—

"What a shock it was this morning to get a cable from New York announcing that our dear Beaman had just died. I had heard of him constantly this winter as being in remarkably good health and spirits, and so this sudden news was all the more appalling. I really don't know what we shall do without him. I must have time to think. I immediately telegraphed Mama and already have her answer. To think of his being taken, and Mr. Evarts left, who has been trying to die now for four years. * * *

"I enclose a letter from George Von L. Meyer, our new Ambassador to Italy enclosing Julian Ralph's account and description of me at the Guildhall dinner which will probably just suit you. * * *

Papa."

Queen Victoria died January 22, 1901. One looks for Mr. Choate's reaction on that event, but there are

CHARLES C. BEAMAN, JOSEPH H. CHOATE, AND HENRY E. HOWLAND.

no available letters about it. Such as he wrote—and he must have written them—were doubtless to friends in England, and the great disturbance of the war, and all that has followed it, have made English letters very difficult of access. On January 30 he wrote to Secretary Hay:

"*Private and confidential.*

"DEAR COLONEL HAY:

"I· have acknowledged in my despatch of today the President's special authorization which you cabled me to represent him at the Queen's funeral—that I had immediately communicated it to the Foreign Office and was awaiting Lord Lansdowne's answer. I shall of course go to Windsor to the funeral, and shall probably go in the London procession in a state carriage as Mr. Reid did at the Jubilee. This procession is as I understand to be a strictly military one, and although many of the special envoys, most of whom are Royalties and great military officers, are to ride in it in full uniform, I have hinted to Lord Lansdowne that I thought I should hardly be paying proper respect to the occasion, to the King, and to the President, by appearing among them on horseback in a dress suit, or even a frock suit and a top hat, and that if there were to be state carriages in the procession as at the Jubilee, it would be more suitable for me to go in one of those. He appreciated the situation and as the arrangements are still in a formative state he said he would arrange it for me and I left it to him.

"I duly received your cipher cable 'order funeral wreath to be sent in the President's name at her Majesty's funeral,' and I immediately ordered from Green's what Mr. White and I after studying the matter carefully thought the proper thing. It is an exact counterpart of the wreath sent by the King and Queen of Italy to the funeral of the Duke of Clarence. The continental sovereigns and governments were sending most extravagant things, the King of Portugal's took 5 men to carry. We thought that without imitating this, the President's should be very handsome, chaste, and dignified, and that our choice was adequate for his great position.

"The wreath will be sent to Windsor on Friday morning, and I shall try to send you a photograph of it in due season. I have also filled an order from Mrs. Garfield for a wreath from her in grateful remembrance of the Queen's kindness at the time of her husband's death.

"I do not send you more details because the press gives them to you faster than we can, and quite in advance of the facts.

Most truly yours,

Joseph H. Choate.

"Col. John Hay."

"1 Feb'y, 1901.

"To Colonel Hay:

"Everything is in readiness for the Queen's funeral tomorrow. I am fortunately relieved of all my apprehensions about our personal part in the funeral procession in London by the final decision to confine it strictly to the Royal Family and their Royal guests and the grand military escort. With the other 'special representatives,' I am invited to join the procession at Windsor 'to assist in the interment' and afterwards to lunch with the King at the Castle.

"Everything just now is intensely interesting here.

"The President's wreath went down to Windsor this morning and was in all respects worthy of him and of the occasion.
                    Yours very truly,
                            JOSEPH H. CHOATE."

Professor Pickering, the Harvard astronomer, had requested the Ambassador to receive for him a gold medal awarded by the Royal Astronomical Society. Mr. Choate undertook this service, and writes:

                                "9 February, 1901.
"MY DEAR PROF. PICKERING:
    "I duly attended yesterday the meeting of the Royal Astronomical Society, and received on your behalf the beautiful gold medal, which I now have the pleasure of transmitting to you.
    "I wish you could have witnessed the enthusiasm with which the references to you and to Harvard were received by the interested audience. Your own letter also, which I had the pleasure and honor of reading was much applauded.
    "I congratulate you and Harvard very much on this most honorable achievement of yours. I cut from *The Times* of today a brief account of the meeting.
                    Yours very truly,
                            JOSEPH H. CHOATE.
"Prof. Edward C. Pickering."

"*Personal and confidential.*

                                "9 February, 1901.
"MY DEAR COLONEL HAY:
    "I hope the President will show to you my letter to him of this date, explaining the reasons which constrained

me to decline his very kind and cordial invitation to me to accept the place of Attorney-General. I have stated the matter exactly as I viewed it and trust that my conclusion and the reasons I assign for it will meet with your approval as well as his.

"We are looking for your son's arrival before this reaches you. If he can give any time to London he will have a warm reception here.

"The new King is making a decidedly favorable impression and is to open Parliament in person on Thursday next with great splendor.

Yours very truly
Jos. H. Choate."

Mr. Choate was in constant communication with Secretary Hay. In the season when diplomatic business was being transacted he wrote to him, usually with his own hand and often at considerable length, about concerns of government and especially about diplomatic negotiations, first with Lord Salisbury and afterwards with Lord Lansdowne. The letters copied here are on subjects of relatively less diplomatic importance than the main part of this correspondence. It should not be inferred from them that the ambassador's time and thought were chiefly taken up with social matters, addresses, and lighter duties. An important mass of correspondence running over six years attests the contrary and shows him as a diligent official, skilled and practised in the law and in all researches that are connected with it; devoting his talents, his energies, and his acquired knowledge to promoting the causes and the interests of the United States. In the Alaska boundary case, there is a series of his letters to General Foster, who was concerned in it for our government, giving him all possible help by suggestion, with information and by maps and other documents which he searched London, including the British Museum, to obtain.

On March 18 he was chairman at a lecture by Mr. Augustine Birrell at the Chelsea Town Hall in aid of the Cheyne Hospital. On March 21 he had something to say at the meeting for the London School of Economics, where Lord Rosebery made the chief address.

"American Embassy, London.
3 April 1901.

"DEAR MABEL:—

" * * * Tomorrow I go to Dorking to lunch with Mr. George Meredith. I wish I were as well up in 'The Egoist' as Jo is.

"Our little dinner last night for Professor Agassiz was very successful. It was fun to hear Sir Martin Conway describing to Lord Kelvin & Professor Agassiz his ascent of the 23000 feet peak in the Himalayas, most of the time cutting steps up the face of glaciers almost perpendicular like cataracts. The two others drinking it in as school boys would a new Arabian Nights story.

PAPA."

"American Embassy, London.
3 April 1901.

"DEAR JO:—

" * * * Tomorrow I go to Dorking to lunch with George Meredith. I am sure you would like to go with me, and discuss 'The Egoist'—to which I hardly feel equal—although fairly up in 'Richard Feverel' and 'Diana of the Crossways.' * * *

PAPA."

To the Same

(April 6.) " * * * I had a most interesting day with George Meredith. He lives in a cunning little cottage with a fine garden, an ideal place for a poet and a purely literary man, he is deaf and disabled in the legs, but as clear in the head as ever. He talks just like his books, is immensely devoted to French poetry and novels, speaks French, German, Greek and English apparently with equal facility, thinks 'Beauchamp's Career' his best book, says that when he wrote 'Diana' it was currently believed, and he was told positively, that Sidney Herbert (Dacier) gave Mrs. Norton (Diana) the secret from the minister (Sir Robert Peel) which was sold to *The Times*, but that subsequently it was all disproved.

"I asked him whether if he had to write 'Richard Feverel' again he would not rewrite the last chapter, and save the life of that dear young wife. He said 'no,' that 'the decrees of fate fall alike on the innocent and the guilty,' that Leslie Stephen had often asked him the same question and had stamped up and down his room declaring her death to be wilful murder on his part. He had a deal to say about Napoleon, of whom he was a great admirer, had studied his campaigns and could have pointed out to him many mistakes. * * *
FATHER."

To the Same

(May 4.) " * * * I am glad your interest in Law and the Law School revives so quickly and so emphatically. I am sure you will decide to 'stick' there for the 3rd year. I am decidedly in favor of that. Columbia Law School may hold out the same courses and have the same appearance on paper, but Harvard is in my judgment infinitely superior, and if you will take the trouble to read what Prof. Dicey and Sir F. Pollock say about it you will see they think so too. (The Pollocks by the way invited you to a supper party next week) I feel very certain of the superiority of the Harvard Professors, and of the superior tone of the school. The spirit of hard work that prevails there cannot be reproduced in New York, and the prestige of Harvard adds value to its degree. I know that your contemporaries will mostly have left, but you would not find them in the Columbia Law School either; they will all be in offices, etc., and I have seen enough of trying to do both office and Law School at the same time to be certain that there is no good in that. * * *   FATHER."

On the 4th of June the Ambassador gave a reception at No. 1 Carlton House Terrace, where five or six hundred guests came "to meet the delegates of the Chamber of Commerce of the State of New York." He took the chair in place of the Italian Ambassador, who could not come, at the annual meeting of the Dante Society on June 5, and in moving a vote of thanks to the lecturer, Mrs. Craigie, told about the Dante Club in Cambridge, Massachusetts, and Professor Fiske's gift of a remarkable collection of Dante books to the library of Cornell University. He spoke at the annual meeting of the Children's Country Holidays Fund on June 11. The next night he made a real speech at the public banquet in the Hotel Metropole to Sir John Tenniel of *Punch*. It was a remarkable dinner, to commemorate Sir John's fifty years of service for *Punch*, for more than forty of

which he had contributed week by week the chief cartoon. Mr. Arthur Balfour was chairman. Other speakers
besides him and Mr. Choate were the Duke of Devonshire and Mr. Birrell.

The Ambassador kept open house on the 4th of July,
and the *Daily Telegraph* says that "Mr. and Miss Choate
received visitors at the top of the staircase leading to
the drawing-room, to the number of about two thousand." That night he went to the 4th of July dinner
of the American Society in London, and there of course
addressed the company.

On July 13 he presided at Mr. Frederick Harrison's
lecture on the life and reign of Alfred the Great in connection with the Anglo-Saxon exhibition at the British
Museum. He was a speaker on July 15 at the dinner
of the Royal Free Hospital at the Hotel Cecil. He distributed prizes on Prize Day (July 22) at University
College School in London.

As has been noted, he took a house that summer at
North Berwick, near Edinburgh.

To His Wife

"Blythswood, Renfrew, N. B.
Sunday, 4 Augt. 1901.
"I was delighted to hear by your letter which reached
me before I left London, that you and Mabel and Mimsy
had all borne the very fatiguing journey so well.

"I reached here at half past seven, an hour late, and
as Lady Blythswood had written that they would send
for me to Paisley, and I had written her that I would
come Saturday by that train, I was a little surprised to

find no carriage, but I took a fly to the house—about three miles—and when I reached here it was quite evident that I was not expected. Lord Blythswood soon appeared, much surprised, and said they did not expect me till Tuesday the sixth. But I told him they certainly invited us from the 3rd to the 6th and I had written on Thursday that I would come Saturday. 'No' said he, 'your letter too said you would come Tuesday.' But my letter being fished up confirmed me—on that point at least. They are sure they invited us from the 6th to the 10th and had really on hearing I would come, invited a lot of people to meet me, most of whom fortunately are sick and couldn't come. I would have given anything to have had that letter inviting us which you so strangely destroyed. I hope you will never destroy another until the visit is made. You see it is necessary to have your credentials ready to produce. And hereafter I shall insist on keeping all in which I am concerned in my own custody. It is so easy to make such mistakes. And oddly enough, by a strange coincidence, when I asked Lady B. to produce your letter to her in which you said you had written that I would come from the 3rd to the 6th, she too had destroyed that before my arrival, but she said you wrote that I would come on the 6th. Did ever you hear of such a chapter of contradictions? However, they were most cordial and jolly and gave me as warm a welcome as if I had been expected and waited for, though they were much chagrined that I shouldn't have been sent for. There are here over Sunday only Genl. Trotter who is in command of this District at Stirling Castle, Lord Dundas, a son of the Zetlands, Mrs. Rowley & her daughter from Dublin and another lady whose name I have not yet acquired. But next week was to have been and is to be the great week. Lord Clanwilliam and his daughter Katharine come tomorrow and on Tuesday the brother of Lord Blythswood is expected to arrive from South Africa with his regiment—a regiment of this district.

"To add to the perplexity of the situation on my arrival, *my trunk had been left behind.* The train was so large that they had to run in three sections, and somehow in the confusion of rearranging the train at Glasgow, or just outside of Glasgow, my trunk and several others were left, but the Station Master said it would come by the next train *in five minutes.* However, I distrusted that very much, and came on here, leaving Laurence to wait for the trunk. I had to go to dinner as I was, and when we were nearly through with dinner the butler came to me and said that my servant had come but *without the trunk.* Lord B. was kind enough to send one of his own men back to Paisley with Laurence, with instructions to telegraph in all directions, but at half past 11, nothing had been heard of it, and I was constrained to borrow one of Lord B's nightgowns to go to bed in. The fit would have been as if Codling had tried one of Short's (now that probably touches an abyss all round, but read 'The Old Curiosity Shop'—little Nell). Not giving up all hopes, although things looked pretty desperate, I concluded to sit up till midnight in the hope that something would turn up, and sure enough, just as the clock struck 12, in came the trunk which had been found in the Station at Glasgow and sent back. So at last the fiat went forth 'requiescat in pace' and to bed I went.

"This is a very fine place. The Queen stayed here for three days in 1888, but it has some drawbacks—especially the River Clyde which runs through the Park, and is very foul. It does really smell terribly, and its bed is black as ink.

"There came up on the train with me a very pretty Mrs. Littleton, a cousin of Lady Jersey and a sister of Lady Alice Shaw-Stewart's husband. She was going beyond here to visit her parents, having just got the news of the death of her youngest brother—Shaw-Stewart, on his way home from South Africa on the same ship that brings B's brother's regiment to which he belonged.

"Preparations are already on foot to give me enough to do tomorrow. In the morning to visit the Cathedral which Macaulay describes as almost the only fine building of middle ages surviving in Scotland, and he gives a very striking account of the Presbyterians snow-balling the prelatists there as they came out—before the Government of Scotland got settled on the accession of William & Mary. Then we are to visit the Municipal buildings—thought by the people here to be the finest in the world—to lunch at a hotel in Glasgow, and in the afternoon to do the Exhibition or be done by it. As long as I stay—and in view of the horrid mistakes which I have related I can't quite tell how long that will be—there is likely to be quite a circus.

"Don't forget to write to George.

"I hear the motor coming for the mail, so goodbye.

J. H. C."

To the Same

"1, Carlton House Terrace, S. W.
19 August 1901.
" * * * On Saturday I went out to Wimbledon and lunched with Mrs. Ritchie—Thackeray's daughter—to

meet the Schuylers who have taken the house next door. Her house is full of most interesting memorials and reminiscences of her father—books, sketches, paintings, manuscripts—all delightful to see and she was most agreeable. Her husband is private Secretary to Lord George Hamilton at the India office, and as he is much confined there, and then is going into the Law, they have just concluded to give up their house and are to take one in town.

"On my return I drove to Paddington and spent Sunday at Wilton Park very pleasantly. The party was small—Mr. & Mrs. Winty Chanler—she is a sister or half sister of Marion Crawford—Mr. & Mrs. Edward Wharton—she the author of 'The Greater Inclination' and decidedly interesting—one of Governor Morton's daughters, George Pell & Mr. de Haviland, a tutor at Eton. * * *

"Lady Curzon has sent your letter to 'the Viceroy to answer.' They decline to renew the sunblinds over the skylight on the ground that they were 'put in order 2½ years ago, and that it is not their business to renew them. They have always closed all town houses they hired (5 in all) 8 mos. in the year, and so are not surprised at the wear & tear here, etc.' * * * "

To the Same

"American Embassy, London.
14 September 1901.
"I came down just at the right time. The sad news of the President's death reached London a few minutes after my arrival and I heard of it while at breakfast. The reaction from such buoyant hopes has completely overwhelmed every one, and there can hardly be more

genuine and widespread grief in New York than in London. My first act was to telegraph the news to Jo at Clonmel and to direct him to return immediately to North Berwick, and having an impression that he had left there to go to some place which you knew and I did not, I telegraphed to you asking you to do the same. I have his answer dated 1:25 stating that he will leave this afternoon at 3:25 if connections are possible. So, you will have him with you almost as soon as this letter.

"Of course we have been inundated with calls and with telegrams in showers from all parts. It is hard to keep up with them.

"Mrs. White and Mrs. Eustis were in this morning, and we talked over the question of mourning—and concluded that the ladies of the Embassy must wear dull black, as you did for the Queen, and crape about the hat or bonnet.

"There will doubtless be a memorial service, probably at Westminster, at which we should all go that can, and I hope you and Mabel & Jo will come down for it. It will be on the same day as the final interment of the President. I think it will be in the Abbey because Sub-dean Buckworth has been in this morning and is consulting Dean Bradly about it who is out of town.

"The flags on the public buildings are at half mast, and everybody is very, very sorry. * * * "

(September 16.) "As I telegraphed you this morning, there is to be a Memorial Service for the President at Westminster Abbey on Thursday at 12 noon, and as we are chief mourners, it is highly important that we should all attend if possible. * * * Of course we are all over head and ears in work. Mr. Woodward came back this

morning. The details of the preparation for this ceremony are immense, and by the aid of the Lord Chamberlain and the other Ambassadors who have had similar
functions, we hope to do it all right. A constant stream
of callers—such as Sir William & Lady Harcourt, Sir Wm.
MacCormac, half a dozen Filippinos with an interpreter,
Henry Higginson and scores of others all in rapid succession, and constant messages from all sorts of people
from Royal Dukes, down, for instance, to the Association
of Cab Drivers plying at Charing Cross.

"I shall rely on Jo to get you safely down here and
back & on Thursday he will have to help the Embassy
receive people at the Abbey. There will be only 950
seats but the whole of the rear and North Transept will
be open to the public. * * *

J. H. C."

To the Same

"The Athenaeum, Pall Mall, S. W.
22 Sept. 1901.

" * * * I have been pretty busy today getting off
the bag, with a long letter to Col. Hay about Treaty
matters—also we sent an autograph letter from Queen
Alexandra to Mrs. McKinley. Addresses and resolutions
continue to pour in from everywhere, but we are getting
the matter well in hand with printed forms of reply in
which the name of the sender is inserted by machine,
and my signature is all that is necessary.

"This afternoon I took the brougham and made my
necessary calls after the Abbey service—the three Ambassadors and Dean Bradly.

"Mrs. White is doing well with her broken foot, but
the Drs. say that she must not walk for two weeks. * * *

"Do look at this week's *Black & White* which I just took up on the table here—a most rugged and furrowed picture of me at my desk in the morning room receiving the news of the death of the President, and Mr. Woodward standing beside me. * * *

J. H. C."

(September 23.) "As I telegraphed you this morning on receipt of your letter, I really could not accept an invitation even from Mr. Balfour for next Sunday, as I shall probably be detained here. I must wait upon Lord Pauncefote who is in communication with Lord Lansdowne. Must also meet and discuss matters with Mr. Lodge who is an important factor just now,—and have a lot of other things on hand.

"I am happy to say that the letters about President McKinley are diminishing in number and importance and can mostly be attended to by others, although I have had to sign my name not less than 50 or 60 times today, and spent all day in the house preparing a long report on the 'London clause' in the North Atlantic Lines bills of lading—not quite all day because I was interrupted by visits from Lady Curzon with whom I went over the house. I don't think she found anything out of the way, or is at all disturbed. In Mabel's bath-room she discovered the weighing machine and got me to weigh her —8 stone 2—a gain she said of 4 pounds. Lord Pauncefote thought, and so did I, that she was handsomer than ever. She goes to India on Thursday. * * * "

(September 24.) " * * * This is one of our fateful days—dear Ruluff's birthday. Think of it that he would have been thirty-seven years old today—quite middle aged—and what a difference it might have made in our lot. I miss him and Effie more and more the older I grow. * * *

"Roosevelt seems to be starting off wonderfully well, and though he is so very different from McKinley I believe he is going to make a splendid President—a popular one he is bound to be. * * *"

(September 25.) " * * * I got a wedding present this morning for Helen Morton, a pair of claret jugs mounted with silver gilt—very handsome—only one of them is not yet made, but they promise to have it ready in ten days, on the 4th, the day before the wedding. That is to take place at the little Catholic Church in Chelsea. I have seen the happy man—quite a good looking Frenchman—also called this P. M. on Mrs. Morton—at the Coburg Hotel—where Helen is acquiring a 15 days residence under the English Law. They are quite worn out by the red tape details, and the requirements of the French lawyers. I fell into the arms of the whole lot in the Hallway of the Coburg—Mrs. Morton, Helen, Lina, Eustis, the bridegroom and his mother, the Duchess de Sagan, all discussing some of these fine points.

"My old friend Simon Sterne is dead of apoplexy in New York. I have had pleasant relations with him for 40 years and always enjoyed his intellectual cleverness. * * *

J. H. C."

"1 Carlton House Terrace,
Sept. 26, 1901.
"DEAR MABEL:—
" * * * I am to have an audience with the King tomorrow at 11. I sent my note asking for it last night—or rather had Woodward do so, addressed to Sir Francis Knollys at Marlborough House, thinking he was in at-

tendance there, but he was in Scotland and the note was
forwarded to him unopened, but he telegraphed its contents back and the King immediately named an hour.

"How fast events push each other off the scene! Here
we are receiving telegrams every 15 minutes from the
Central News reporting the progress of the two yachts
in the race at New York and they are very thrilling, very
close and very varying. For instance, at the end of 1 hr.
5 min. the yachts had covered 7 knots, the *Columbia*
leading 200 yards, but 15 minutes later '*Shamrock* drawn
up—Grand race wind decreasing' and wind decreasing
is supposed to be favorable to *Shamrock*. If I get anything decisive before 8 I shall telegraph you in the hope
of your getting it before you go to bed.

"I have had a long session today with Lord Pauncefote
and fear I shall have to have a good many more. * * *
PAPA."

The long session with Lord Pauncefote was about
the Panama Canal, and was doubtless part of the negotiations which substituted the Hay-Pauncefote treaty
for the Clayton-Bulwer treaty. Before the canal was
dug at the isthmus it had to be dug through the minds
of men, and in that excavation Mr. Choate was now
doing his part.

To His Wife

"The Athenaeum, Pall Mall, S. W.
27 Septr. 1901.
"I must write you one line although I have been writing again nearly all day. Dr. Kinnicutt, or Dr. Con-
necticut as Creber persists in calling him, called this
morning. They are back at Buckland's until they sail
next Wednesday.

"At 11 I drove in great state to Marlborough House and had my audience with the King to thank him in person for all the kindness and sympathy that he and the Queen have shown. His Majesty was in fine form—looking perfectly well, and in excellent spirits. You can safely contradict any stories you hear to the discredit of his health. He received me most cordially, put me in an armchair opposite his own, and had a great many things to say, was very solicitous about Mrs. McKinley and sent her a kind message of regard; was very much interested in President Roosevelt, seemed to be quite familiar with his record and admired him; asked very kindly for you, and after 20 minutes' conversation accompanied me to the door of the Indian room where I was received and asked me to send him photographs of McKinley & Roosevelt.

"Those people of whom I ordered the claret jugs for Helen Morton sent me word tonight that after all their promises they couldn't have them done for two weeks. So I have got to do that over again—a great bore for one who loves shopping so little."

(September 28.) " * * * I am getting telegrams every quarter of an hour from the race—the last word being, 'Both boats rounded stake boat, *Shamrock* 30 seconds ahead.' She must be doing much better than on Thursday. * * *

"Bishop Whipple is dead in Minnesota—a great loss.
                                        J. H. C."

A little later they went home and stayed over Christmas and well into the New Year. A dinner was given to Mr. Choate at the Lotos Club, and there is a record

of his remarks there.   In December he went to visit Mr.
George Vanderbilt at Biltmore in North Carolina.   It
was as though he had acquired the habit of making visits
at country houses and could not break it off all at once.
About Biltmore and his visit there he writes to his wife:

To His Wife
"Biltmore House
28 December, 1901.

"I take advantage of the first moment I have here to
tell you of our safe arrival.   Mr. and Mrs. Vanderbilt
are full of regrets at your absence and its cause, as are all
the rest of the party which consists of Commander and
Mrs. Cowles, your friend Mrs. Keyes and a Prince whose
name I have not yet got hold of.   Mr. Fred Stimson of
Boston and his pretty daughter, young Mr. Robbins and
his wife from New York, Mrs. Mead, whom we used to
know and like so much in 11th Street, Mr. John B.
Trevor, a Harvard Senior, and Mr. Gregory. * * *

"I shall not attempt to describe the house, which is
obviously the finest in America, but the dogs are truly
magnificent, and the baby a very lovely one—now six
months old.   She shakes hands with everybody and is
very jolly and sociable.   Mrs. Sears will be glad to know
that I promptly delivered Helen's present, which Mrs.
Vanderbilt received with great pleasure.

"My room in which I now am to get ready for dinner
is a most spacious one, with a fine open fireplace and
no steam heat, which seems to be just now the curse of
America."

"29th December.

"Since our leaving New York there has been nothing
but rain, and the downpour ever since our arrival has

been tremendous, but all hands have been out this afternoon for a stroll in the gardens and greenhouses—the latter very spacious and splendid, but with not a flower to show now as everything is preparing for winter. Although it is more than 2200 feet above the sea, the season is much milder and the summer much longer than in New York or Massachusetts, so that the best of grapes ripen in the open, and figs also. The hills all about are covered with rhododendrons, and in June it must be a paradise. There is almost no snow here in winter, and Asheville is thronged with winter patients.

"Mr. Vanderbilt frequently repeats his regrets that you are not here, and hopes your coming is only a pleasure deferred. I hope you will come some time in early summer and see Biltmore in all its glory. The library appeals to me as the most charming part of the house, and its contents include the rarest of volumes, which he has been collecting since he was 19, and could only have been bought at great price."

"30 December, 1901.

"At last the weather has cleared sufficiently to show us the snow that has fallen on the neighboring mountains, one of which is over 5000 feet high.

"The house constantly grows upon one and is truly a great affair—a worthy monument to Richard Hunt as his last work. You are reminded of that by Sargent's portrait painted here—a ghastly thing, exhibiting in most glaring way the dreadful disease of which he was dying. You would revel in the winter garden in the centre of the house, 60 feet high and full of palms and ferns with the loveliest fountain always flowing in a gentle way, inducing rest and sleep. The vast swimming tank under the main hall is a great resort for the young men after exercising—ten feet deep so that they can take a good dive. This forenoon we are to drive about the farms and see the wonderful stock. Mr. Vanderbilt is teaching the farmers about here the first rudiments of farming. They were a pretty hopeless set before.

"I wish you could see these great St. Bernards—five of them, father, mother and three children, all big and splendid. They seem to fill the billiard-room and are most affectionate."

"1 January, 1902.

"Last night the whole party sat up to greet the New Year and were very merry indeed, though the departure of Mr. and Mrs. Cowles in the afternoon left a great gap. There were games and dancing, hot punch served at the stroke of 12 and quite a revel even after that. Mrs. Vanderbilt fills her great place with the utmost fitness.

"I wish you could see the Albert Dürer room opening out of the library, and the Rembrandt gallery which leads to the Vanderbilts' private apartments—the latter really royal. The very choice prints and etchings of both artists are wonderful. Many cases of Rembrandt's etchings—two or three of the same subject—show the changes he made in the same picture from time to time in groupings, dress, expression, etc."

Mr. Choate's diplomatic labors and correspondence up to 1902 had to do chiefly with the matters of the Alaskan boundary, the seizure of American goods bound for Delagoa Bay, the amendment of the Clayton-Bulwer treaty to permit a new arrangement satisfactory to the United States about the building of the Panama Canal, and the questions that arose out of the Boxer rebellion in China, including a long, faithful and successful contention for the open door in that country. Besides these important matters of state, there was a considerable correspondence about the case of Mrs. Maybrick, which ended in a reduction of her sentence.

"American Embassy, London.
24 January 1902.
"DEAR MABEL:—
The 'evening of life' for me begins today at 70, and you will soon have to determine whether we shall settle in Salem finally or not. * * *   PAPA."

Mr. Choate used to threaten to go back to Salem to spend "the evening of his days," a plan his family did not favor. Partly to wean him from this inclination, they named the place at Stockbridge "Naumkeag," which is the Indian name for Salem, and means "Haven of Rest."

"American Embassy, London.
25 Feby. 1902.
"DEAR JO:—
" * * * I was shocked beyond expression this morning by your announcement that Professor Thayer had suddenly died, of which we had no intimation whatever, or even that he was ill. I agree with you that his loss to the Law School is irreparable. His commanding position there and from there was very lofty, and he was generally regarded in all the law schools and by the Bar throughout America as a very high authority on questions of Constitutional Law and of Evidence.

NAUMKEAG—THE GARDENS AND HOUSE, STOCKBRIDGE, MASS.

He was one of my oldest and dearest friends, and one of those upon whose continued friendship to the end I had confidently counted. In college days we were particularly intimate, and his tender and loving heart endeared him to his fellows, especially to those who were thrown in close contact with him. * * * FATHER."

On the 11th of March he was chairman of the annual dinner of the Fly Fishers Club at the Hotel Cecil and discussed many things about fly-fishing, the Puritan Fathers, fish breeding and planting in the United States, and other like matters.

"American Embassy, London.
15 March 1902.

"DEAR MABEL:—

"I enclose an account of last night's 'Drawing Room Court' the first of the new reign. There was a great crowd, about 800 passing before the King & Queen. It was held in the great Hall where you have attended State concerts.

"The King & Queen stood in front of the dais where at concerts they formerly sat, and we all passed before them. The King shook hands only with the Ambassadors, and after the Ambassadresses had passed and made their courtesies they stood on the left of the Royal party, and the Ambassadors on the steps of the throne. You will be glad to know that Mama looked very well, that her dress was very pretty, and that she stood it as well as anybody—though of course it was most fatiguing—much better than some of her more embonpoint colleagues who almost dropped with fatigue. In fact one of them did sit down—hiding behind Countess ——'s ample zone, until Sir Wm. Colville came and insisted on her going out or standing up.

"The Italian Ambassadress, Madame Panza, made her first appearance and is most charming. I took her out to supper (There was supper, and the whole thing was a great improvement on the old day drawing rooms).

PAPA."

"1, Carlton House Terrace, S. W.
16 April 1902.

"DEAR JO:—

" * * * Mama and Mabel went to Paris last Saturday to be gone for two weeks, so that I have been absolutely alone, as Emily Tuckerman who had stayed with us till they left, went to Torquay to visit the Godkins to return Saturday. Meantime I am getting up a dinner of 36 for the 28th and am also planning for a 'squash' for the same night. But I find it a great job to make out a list from our 'visitors' book, especially in mama's absence, as she knows so many of the people that I do not, and I may have to take a later day for it. We can not invite less than 2000 people but experts like Carter and Creber say that that is not too many to ask for such an occasion. * * *

"The arrangements for Coronation are proceeding, but not much that is very definite is yet announced. One thing, however, we have, positively and officially, which pleases me, viz. that the 'Resident Ambassadors' are not to go in the Coronation procession, but are to go directly to the Abbey. This solves the difficulty about a State Carriage, as it would have been absurd for me to go in a dress suit and a plain carriage among my colleagues all in their 'voitures de gala' and bedizened in splendid uniforms, and still more absurd to try to get up anything for the occasion. * * *   FATHER."

The matter of what the American Ambassador should do for a state carriage for the coronation was discussed in the newspapers of the day. A state carriage, proper for a very splendid street procession, is quite a serious detail of provision. It was discussed in the United States whether it was the duty of the government to provide one of these chariots, which cost, it seems, $12,000 or $15,000 and are of no possible use to an Ambassador after he retires from office. It will be understood how welcome the announcement was to Mr. Choate that the resident Ambassadors need not be part of the street show.

To His Wife

"American Embassy, London.
17 April 1902.
"Mr. White arrived today and we have all been at work all day on that terrible list aided as far as R. by your comments, but it is a terrible job. You mustn't be too hard upon Lady Mt. Edgecombe and Lady Clarendon for 'not having called' as they have both been dead many years and have a good excuse, but your mistake mitigated the dullness of our work. * * * "

"1 Carlton House Terrace,
18 April 1902.
"DEAR MABEL:—
"You and Mama may thank your stars that you have been out of the way while all this work in preparing the

'At Home' has been going on. We finished the list late last night, and today converted the long table in the dining room into a work table at which you might have seen me & Mr. White, Mr. Carter, Mr. Eustis, Mr. Woodward, Frank and Miss Garretson from the Embassy, and two men from Webster's, and Creber besides, all directing envelopes, and studying Red Books and Blue Books, Dodd, Lodge and Who's Who for addresses. Mr. White's and Mr. Carter's special knowledge of the people prove to be invaluable, and Mr. Woodward's executive faculty. More than 700 envelopes have already been directed and verified, and before midnight we hope the rest will be done, leaving only the cards for tomorrow and the sealing, stamping & mailing for Sunday, so that we hope all will reach their destination Monday. It will take more than £4. worth of postage stamps for them all. * * *

"I am afraid that you and Mama will think that great dinners and great receptions can be given without any trouble, but next time I will go to Paris and you two can stay at home and take charge. * * *   PAPA."

To His Wife

"1, Carlton House Terrace, S. W.
Monday 21 April 1902.

"We are proceeding apace in our preparations—eleven hundred cards have been stamped and mailed and I suppose the additional ones that will be called for will bring it up to 1200.

"Creber & Hicks will get up the dinner, and Kingston Miller & Co., who usually do our 4th of July, will attend to the Soirée. Of course we miss you and Mabel terribly in all this, and if you are really through with your dress-making, as you hoped to have got last Saturday night, the sooner you get home the better. The whole embassy thinks that your escape at this time was a perfect stroke of genius.

"Today has been a very full day—a ride, two delegations on what were supposed to be international matters but which turned out not to be so—the King's levee— the Evelyn Gifford wedding at the Church & at the house, the service performed by the Archbishop of Canterbury, Lord Salisbury & I signing the Register, and I led Lady Halsbury to the vestry and out of the Church. Emily Tuckerman arrived at four and the rest of the day has been spent in revising the last cards, etc. Although we left R. S. V. P. off, as you saw by the invitation sent you, answers are beginning to come in rapidly. To make more room in the house K. M. & Co. are to have a sutler's tent on the terrace where the whole service of the Soirée is to be done through the middle window, which we all think a capital idea. I believe Mr. Woodward is sending you a long list which we have culled out for omission unless you insist on sending them—mostly people whom we can find out nothing about. Our dinner will be 40."

The Ambassador's reception on the 28th of April is described apparently in the Paris edition of the New York *Herald* as "the largest function that has been given by the diplomatic corps in London, and if perfect appointments and a tremendous throng of distinguished men and beautiful women constitute any sort of standard to judge by, the function was an unqualified success."

He spoke on the 9th of May at a dinner to the American and colonial journalists in London, given by some of their English brethren in connection with the impend-

ing coronation. The Boer War ended towards the end
of May, 1902, and the coronation was fixed for the 26th
of June, but on the 24th the King took sick with peri-
typhlitis and had to have an operation, and the coronation had to be put off; but the operation succeeded remarkably, and he got well so fast that he was able to be
crowned on August 9.   The show was somewhat less
gorgeous than it would have been in June, but it was
still a great show.

"American Embassy, London.

5 June 1902.

"Dear Jo:—

"I must admit that in the matter of letters you have
been rather badly treated lately, but we went off to Jersey
and Guernsey (a delightful trip by the way) for the Whitsuntide holidays, and since our return the rush has been
simply terrific. * * * Nothing but the Coronation seems
to be thought of or in the way of being done.   Yesterday we received our invitations to the Abbey, very large
and handsome cards, of course, about 8 inches by ten,
simply inviting us to the Abbey to attend the Coronation, and saying that cards of admission and detailed
instructions would be sent us later.   These are directed
to the Ambassador, Mrs. Choate and Miss, and I understand that all those of the Embassy whose names are
on the Foreign office list received the same.   I still am
not without hope of getting you in somehow, as Lord
Lansdowne has said that he would do what he could
for me in that direction.

"I arranged a big dinner for Mr. Reid the day after
his expected arrival—June 12th. He expected to come
by the steamer which would bring him here on the 11th
but having got notice from Cambridge that they wanted

to make him an honorary LL.D. on the 10th he has taken an earlier steamer which brings him here on the 7th. But our dinner remains unchanged, and quite a lot of your very nice friends will be there, including Lord & Lady Grey & Lady Sybil, Lord & Lady Leven and Melville, the Duchess of Marlborough, Duke & Duchess of Sutherland, etc., so that I think Mr. & Mrs. Reid will be well content.

"Strangely enough the King & Queen & Princess Victoria fixed upon the day before (June 11th) for coming to dine with us, as they had accepted our invitation as long ago as April, and 'hoped to fix a day in May for it' but that month was too full. This of course is to be a very stately affair, and there we expect Mr. & Miss Balfour, Lord & Lady Lansdowne, Lord Rosebery, Lord & Lady Derby, Lord & Lady Spencer, the Bishop of London, Sir Wm. & Lady Harcourt, Pierpont Morgan, Mr. & Mrs. Reid, and others of like distinction, and the Whites & Carters & W. W.—the other members of the Embassy, Mrs. Sears, etc."

"DEAR JO:—   "Saturday June 7th.
    "I must send this letter unfinished.
    "We never get a moment now. Sarah Sears was presented last night successfully. * * *
                                          FATHER."

At the Fourth of July dinner of the American Society Mr. Choate proposed the health of the King, and naturally enlarged upon that subject, telling about the shock and disappointment of his illness, recalling his lively sympathy when the news of the death of President McKinley came, and rejoicing in the prospect that he would soon be well again.

Bishop Simpson had died, as he notes in a letter. As the representative of six millions of Methodists in America, Mr. Choate spoke about him at a meeting of Methodists in Wesley's chapel. He had a great admiration and regard for Bishop Simpson and recognized how remarkable and important a man he was.

He spoke very cheerfully on September 30 at the Cutlers' Feast at Sheffield, winding up with discourse on American competition, which he said the Sheffield cutlers need never fear so long as they could furnish the best goods at the lowest prices.

To His Wife

"American Embassy, London.
24 Sept. 1902.

"This ought to have been one of our great days—the birthday of our dear Ruluff. I woke at quarter before six to recall his first cry at that hour, thirty-eight years ago. What a comfort and support he would have been to us, as we grow older, in full manhood, with a group of children about him—those much coveted grandchildren whom we have so far missed. Certainly we miss him and dearest Effie more and more every year. But we must make the most of those who are left to us. * * *

"President Roosevelt's illness is startling but I think not very serious."

To the Same

"The Athenæum, Pall Mall S. W.
Monday evening, 13 Oct. 1902.

" * * * Today I have devoted to the Generals, Corbin, Young & Wood. I took them to the Palace for lunch where the King received them very graciously, showed them about the palace, kept them to see him award the medals to Kitchener and all his staff, mixed them up at the table with the British Generals, and just before we rose from the table, proposed the health of the President in a very hearty way. * * * ”

To the Same

"American Embassy, London.
14 Octr. 1902.
" * * * Today we are having mingled showers & sunshine and it is almost like summer. Tomorrow, I am going to the lunch which 'The Pilgrims' give to our three American Generals. By the time they get through my dinner on Friday I think they will need a sea voyage to recruit. They are being dined and wined quite as vigorously as we were in America.

"The King and W. Woodward and Wadsworth have all gone to Newmarket. How anybody can stand such frequent races quite passes my conprehension."

(Wadsworth, above mentioned, was Mr. Craig Wadsworth, third secretary of legation.)

(October 15.) " * * * I have just come from 'the Pilgrims' luncheon at the Carlton for Generals Corbin, Young and Wood—which was quite a jolly affair— and of course I had to help jollify it. I enclose the card. * * *

"Tomorrow is our great day—our greatest day. I hoped we should never spend it apart again."

On the 25th of October King Edward went in procession through the main streets of London. Writing to his wife on that day Mr. Choate says:

"The great procession is over, and the whole day has been quite successful. When I got here I found a letter from de Staal saying that voitures de gala were not to be allowed in going to the Guildhall today, and a telegram which came at midnight saying that the last order was, voitures de gala necessary for today. As I had already ordered the best turnout that Withers could furnish, I made no change. Genl. Wood arrived at eleven and we drove down together. I sat between the Lady Mayoress and the Italian Ambassador. All the Royalties were on hand except the Princess of Wales and the Duchess of Fife, and made a great show. Everything was very handsomely done, and the display of gold and silver was especially fine. I had not long been home before the procession began to pass our terrace, where were Mrs. Wodehouse and Eleanor, Miss Rose Lamb, Mr. & Mrs. Townsend & their two children, Mr. & Mrs. Hardy who are going to Madrid, Rev. Dr. Nevin and quite a lot besides. Creber had some cake, sandwiches and wine for them and everything was done well. * * * "

"1 Carlton House Terrace,
Oct. 27, 1902.

"DEAR MABEL:—
"Today we have had the great Thanksgiving Service at St. Paul's for the King's recovery, which of course was most splendid. Half an hour before the arrival of the King at eleven the great Cathedral was packed and everyone was in his place—or at least, so far as the Di-

plomatists were concerned, as nearly so as Sir Wm. Colville, who arranged it, would let them be. He put Jannis, the ace of spades Haytian Minister, up in the stalls, alongside of Baron de Staal and his wife, in seats specially reserved for Ambassadors and Royalties. So pretty soon he and his white wife had to be called down and put in lower seats. Then he put the Duchess de Mandas in a seat alongside of me, which was reserved and marked for Princess Henry of Battenberg, and when she arrived the Duchess had to go down, which was quite mortifying. The music was very grand—especially the Te Deum, which was truly wonderful. I drove General Wood down, but Mrs. Wood was in bed with a quinzy sore throat, which was very disappointing. The General seemed much impressed with the fact that yesterday I was the only Ambassador who was greeted with applause—once at Temple Bar, and again as we entered Guildhall. * * *

PAPA."

(October 28.) " * * * The King held a very brilliant review of the Guards this morning but I did not take the trouble to go or even to ask for tickets.

"Mrs. Chapin and her husband are at the Hans Crescent Hotel for about two weeks on the way to South Africa, and she wants very much to see you and Mabel before she goes. And that by the way reminds me of Alfred Lyttleton with whose wife she became so thick. He finished his job in Newfoundland, pocketed his fee of £2400, went to Boston and Harvard and was perfectly fascinated with both, thinks Harvard the greatest educational establishment in the world. It's a great pity that more responsible Englishmen don't go over. * * *

J. H. C."

In his letters to his son, who was starting in the practice of law in New York, there are detachable portions that are applicable to all young men undergoing that experience. Thus he writes on November 26, 1902:

"DEAR JO:—

" * * * We are all much interested in your accounts of your labors at the office—especially your pursuit of witnesses, a fine discipline for you as well as for them. I remember doing a lot of that sort of work myself. You can't see just how it helps you, but it does all the same. Every lawyer ought to know how all the work should be done from the bottom up. * * *   FATHER."

On the 11th of November he wrote to Colonel Hay, mentioning an application for leave of absence in 1903, "my purpose being, always with your approval," he said, "to be absent on leave for sixty days, more or less, from the 8th or 10th of December." Parliament, he said, would take a recess from about the middle of December to the middle of February, and there would be no time at which there would be likely to be less to do at the Embassy.

Agreeable to this plan he started off early in December, and made with his wife and daughter and his secretary, Mr. Woodward, a journey to Greece and Egypt that was in all ways fortunate and happy.

President Roosevelt and Colonel Hay so much appreciated Mr. Choate's high competence and value as a lawyer that they wished him to be counsel for the United States before the tribunal to which the Alaska Boundary case had been referred. As to that he says, on the 28th of February, to Colonel Hay:

"I received night before last your letter of the 17th. It at once occurred to me that there might be an incompatibility between my position as Ambassador and my acceptance of a retainer as counsel to conduct and argue the case before the Tribunal against the British Government to which I am accredited, and twenty-four hours' reflection has made me only the more doubtful of the propriety of my so doing. An ambassador seems to be regarded as standing in the shoes of his sovereign, and the diplomatic world and the British Government might regard it as derogating from the sovereign's dignity and character for him to step into the forensic arena in this way and besides, and more important, as counsel I might, and probably should have to say things about Canada, and possibly about Great Britain which might not be acceptable coming from an Ambassador. Counsel conducting a cause ought not to be under the same restraints that rest upon an Ambassador.

"At any rate I think I ought not to accept the appointment as counsel without advising Lord Lansdowne in advance lest he might say hereafter that he would have treated with me differently concerning anything referring to the Alaska boundary matter if he had known that besides being Ambassador, I was also the retained counsel against Great Britain.

"Thinking that these points have probably not occurred to you or to the President, I have sent you today a cipher cable, of which I enclose a copy. There certainly can be no difficulty in finding an abundance of adequate counsel. In my cable I have suggested Mr. Spooner, who would be admirable, and as it would all be in the recess of the Senate, I should think it would be a great advantage to him; and Mr. Root who knows all the

leading lawyers in America can easily give you the names
of others.

"In any event I will give all the assistance in my power
to our side of the case, and it might be advantageous
to have others as counsel, with me in the background
to advise and aid, as I probably could, and as I should
of course be expected by the British Government to do.
                    Very truly yours,
                        JOSEPH H. CHOATE."

                                        "6 March, 1903
"DEAR COLONEL HAY:
"I have just received your White cipher cable in answer to my two, in which you say: 'Your two telegrams
received. The President and I do not agree with you,
but we shall of course not impose on you a distasteful
duty,' which I accept as an acquiescence in my opinion,
which you read between the lines of my telegram, that
I ought not as Ambassador to undertake the added office
of counsel to argue before the Commission the case of
the United States against Great Britain. It is only in
that sense—of doing two incompatible things—of doing
as Ambassador what I ought not to, and what in my
judgment the whole diplomatic world would condemn,
that there is anything distasteful to me about what you
propose. I am sure that both you and the President
know me well enough to accept my assurance that I
should otherwise have taken the greatest delight in such
a service. I should not only have enjoyed it very much,
but should have considered it the crowning honor of my
long professional life. So, I am sure that you will not
regard me, for you cannot justly regard me, as shirking
or shrinking from a duty. Ever since I came here in

March, 1899, I have been in more or less constant communication with the Foreign Office in the discussion of this Alaska case, in endeavors to settle it, and in the argument of all the questions essential and incidental involved in it. My first private letter to you of May 19, 1899, shows how fully I was immersed in it from the start, and it was only just before the receipt of your last letter proposing to me this service as counsel that I was trying to get from Lord Lansdowne the report of Col. Cameron in 1886, the inventor of the Canadian claim, and who by the way I found was a son-in-law of Sir Charles Tupper. All this communication and intercourse was in a way necessarily confidential. It was under the seal of my diplomatic relations of my office of Ambassador. It brought me into relations first with Lord Salisbury and afterwards with Lord Lansdowne of a very confidential character, which they would never have thought of holding with me if they had supposed that I should afterwards appear in the rôle of counsel for the United States against Great Britain in this very case, and I cannot but think that they would feel justly aggrieved on the part of their government if after all my dealings with them I should so appear. And how could I expect to receive their full confidence again after such —I will not say a betrayal, but a disregard of what they had formerly given me? It is quite clear to me too that such a position would not only impair my own subsequent usefulness, but would seriously impair that of any subsequent Ambassador here who was also a lawyer. Assuming that I am better qualified than any other lawyer to argue the case, a very considerable part of my qualification would come from these long continued, confidential diplomatic dealings with the representatives of the British Government about it, and, as it seems to me, the highest consideration of international duty forbids me to make the proposed use of qualifications so acquired to argue the case. Wholly apart from the special considerations growing out of my long diplomatic relations to the case, there is, I think, an obvious incompatibility between the office of Ambassador and that of counsel retained to argue a case before a judicial tribunal on behalf of his own country against that to which he is accredited. The two services are absolutely distinct, and for exercise at the same time, quite inconsistent. Counsel so employed ought to be absolutely free to say whatever his duty to the case requires him to say, so in this case against Canada or against Great Britain, and it might be quite possible that he would have to say things that would hurt or wound the susceptibilities of those constituting the Government of the adverse party, and make him altogether a *persona non grata* with them. There is also a technical inconsistency between the two offices. The ambassador represents his sovereign in a special sense, and his intercourse with the Foreign Office is with the representative of the other sovereign on an equal footing, but when he goes into the judicial arena as a combatant, he meets an adversary who has not the same representative character, and must expect to give and take a very different kind of blow. It is on this ground that I believe that no sovereign in Europe would permit his ambassador in Great Britain, being also a lawyer, to go before a judicial tribunal to argue his case against Great Britain, and our Republic should be just as jealous of the dignity and strict propriety of its diplomatic representatives' conduct, as the proudest monarch.

"I think that considerations such as I have now pre-

sented account for the fact that although many eminent
lawyers have been employed as ambassadors and ministers, there is no precedent for such a representative accepting or being vested with the additional office of retained counsel to argue before a judicial tribunal the
case of his own government or country against the country to which he is accredited, and that, whether the
same case has been in his hands as a subject of diplomatic
intercourse or not. I do not believe that under any circumstances Great Britain would have permitted Lord
Pauncefote, who was also a lawyer of repute, to go
professionally before any judicial tribunal to conduct
a case on her behalf against the United States while he
was accredited there as her Minister or Ambassador,
least of all to present there a case which he had been for
years conducting in his diplomatic capacity confidentially
with the Secretary of State, and I think that her Government would naturally and justly apply the same standard to us and to other nations, and would reasonably
take umbrage, although they might never express it,
if I after four years of diplomatic dealings in which they
had uniformly treated me with the utmost confidence,
took charge of the same case in court as counsel against
them, in which service I could not forget or strip myself
of what had come to me in the confidence of the Foreign Office.

"But there is a service in the case of large value which
I can properly render, and which the British Government would naturally expect me to render, and that is
to aid and advise and support the efforts of the counsel
who shall be retained to try the case before the Commission, to the full extent which the Foreign Office will
advise with and support the law offices of the govern-

ment who will conduct it against us—and this service I intend most conscientiously to give. With such adequate counsel for the United States as you will employ, I can render almost as effectual aid out of court as I could in, and this I intend to do. To this end I have begun a careful study of the case with such materials as are at my command here, and shall from time to time communicate with General Foster and give him all such aid as I possibly can, as you requested in your letter of February 17.

"I shall much regret it if after full consideration of what I have said, the President and yourself are still unable to agree with me, but you will at any rate give me the credit of conscientiously weighing the matter and deciding it according to the best of my lights.

Yours very truly,
JOSEPH H. CHOATE."

Mr. Choate was the guest of the Society of the Pilgrims on March 3, 1903, and was a speaker, a little later, at the dinner of the Institute of British Architects.

To His Wife

"American Embassy, London.
16 May 1903.

"I have been struggling hard but without much success to get along without you but have not succeeded very well.

"My lecture went off very well, and to my great surprise I had a very sympathetic and interested audience. The newspapers could not make much of it. It was a hard thing to condense for I had already struck out every superfluous word. Even *The Times*, which tried hard, failed on that. * * *

J. H. C."

The lecture he speaks of was an address delivered before the Political and Social Education League, May 13, on the Supreme Court of the United States. It is included in the volume of his "Addresses" selected from those he made in England.

Another address, not so long, but included in the same volume, was that on Ralph Waldo Emerson, which he made a month later (June 18) at the Passmore Edwards Institute at the unveiling of a bust of Emerson. Besides these two addresses he made two more that year: on Education in America, August 1, and on Franklin, October 23, which the same book contains.

To His Daughter, in New York

"American Embassy, London.
20 May 1903.

" * * * What have I been doing since Saturday? Well, Mr. Phillips and I spent Sunday at Battle Abbey, and had of course a delightful time inquiring into antiquities, which the Graces seem to care nothing about, but fortunately Sir Augustus Webster, the owner, came to lunch and was able to tell us a good deal, and to put his foot on the very spot where King Harold fell. Imagine my delight! * * *

"Last night Mrs. Adair had a nice party and 'varieties' to meet the Prince and Princess of Wales, and in the afternoon I went down to help them open the Sailors'

Palace. We drove eight miles through solid London to reach the place at Limehouse.

"Today at the Lord Mayor's lunch I met that tall Prince Andrew of Greece, who sat next to your mother at the Egertons' dinner. He is here to marry one of the Battenberg princesses."

He wrote Colonel Hay in April:

"I have your letter of April 3 and am deeply touched by the high appreciation which you are kind enough to put upon the service that I might have rendered, if I could have conscientiously undertaken to act as counsel for the United States against Great Britain in the Alaska boundary case, but you hardly seem to consider that I based my objections not on personal, but purely upon public grounds.

"I think that I must, with your approval, unless some public question intervenes or threatens to prevent, go to New York to attend my son's wedding, which takes place at Albany on June 6th, and I have accordingly secured my passage for the 27th of May and to return on June 9th; giving me a week on the other side.

"But I want very much to see you and the President to talk with you about the Alaska case, the situation of which on this side I am not sure that you fully understand. I mean of course if you desire to see me about it, and I might be of some service to General Foster in regard to the counter case which will then be in course of preparation.

"And if for these purposes it will be more convenient to the President and yourself that I should come a little earlier or return a little later, I shall be obliged if you will let me know. I do not wish to be absent at this time longer than may be necessary."

The plan thus arranged for was carried out, and Mr. Choate was present with his wife and daughter at his son's marriage to Miss Cora Oliver on June 6, at Albany.

Mr. Choate's letters to Secretary Hay begin again on June 17, which means he had got back to London by that time. He stayed there, more or less diverted by week-end visits, through the summer.

On August 1, he made the discourse on Education in America, that is described in the book which contains it as an "inaugural address, at the opening of the summer meeting at Oxford."

"1 Carlton House Terrace.
Sept. 1, 1903.

"DEAR MABEL:—

"Mama has been good enough to do the writing, while I have been so busy. The fact is that going out of town every Sunday makes the week too short for anything, and I should not consent to it many weeks in succession. How the regular London man accomplishes anything with such constant breaks—52 in the year—passes my comprehension. Perhaps it accounts for the inefficiency which we hear so much complaint of.

"But we did have a capital time at Maiden Bradley with the Somersets. They are splendid people both of them—far and away in advance of the Smart Set, and know how to make their friends welcome. It is a charming old house about as large as our own house at Stockbridge so that they can have but few at a time. But Count and Countess Hayos and their daughter Camilla, the 'baby' as they call her, were there and we found them delightful, especially the latter with whom both the Duke and I fell very much in love.   In fact when the Duke sat with her by his side on the box I thought we were in very great danger for he kept his face down under her hat so constantly that the horses might have run away with us without his knowing anything about it. She has sent me her book, which I am going to read.   I hear it shows a great deal of talent. * * *   PAPA."

To His Wife

"1, Carlton House Terrace, S. W.
Saturday Evening.   Sept. 19, 1903.
"I wrote Mabel yesterday about Mimsy's return.   Since he came back I have tried my best to make him tell where he had been or what he had been doing, but couldn't get a word out of him, though I put him many questions that required a categorical answer.   This morning he fairly glued himself to me so that I could hardly move a step—and when I got into my bath so that he couldn't 'yub' he really did 'yowl.'   I think he was glad to get back. * * *

"The only amusing one in the whole Alaska group is Dickinson who tells a good many droll stories, among them one new one about the Pilgrim Fathers.   An ante-bellum Southerner was asked by an Englishman, if anything could possibly have prevented the Civil War.   'Oh, yes' said he 'there was one thing.'   'Well! what was it?'   'Why,' said he, 'if Plymouth Rock had landed on the Pilgrim Fathers, instead of the Pilgrim Fathers landing on Plymouth Rock, we should have had no war.'   Very true, and a great tribute to the Pilgrim Fathers. * * *

J. H. C."

"American Embassy, London.
22 Septr. 1903.

"DEAR JO:—

" * * * I have always said that clerks in law offices
are divided into two classes, those who *do* what they are
given to do, and those who come back with a very plausible reason why they haven't done it, and I want you
to belong to the first class—but it will involve a good
deal of self denial, and postponement of pleasure.
* * * "

(September 23). " * * * Of course there is a good
deal of drudgery and what seems very small business in
getting your foot on the bottom round of the ladder, but
there is no other way up that I know of, and you will
find it to pay in the end. And it's really nothing compared with the privations to which the young officers
submit who want to get on in the Army. * * *

FATHER."

To His Wife

" 1, Carlton House Terrace, S. W.
24 Septr. 1903.

"I must write you a line today of all days—for our
Ruluff would have been 39 years old this morning—an
incredible age for a boy of ours. But he will always be
the dear boy of almost twenty that we lost. But what
a pillar to lean on he would have been by now. * * *

"By the way, Fred tells me that Theodore who is now
75 or 76 receives $500 & a house from the College as
Emeritus Professor, and is too blind to do anything.
It occurs to me that if you intend to give him the full
benefit in his lifetime of the little fund you still have

from his mother, you might make him an allowance out
of it, assuming that he will live five years, say—one
fifth of it each year; and if he and we outlive that, and
he needs more we can help him out. Fred says he is
patience itself. * * *

J. H. C."

To the Same

"American Embassy, London.
3 Octr. 1903.

"What makes you think I don't half read your letters?
I devour them and am always very hungry for more.

"I was just sitting down to write to you last evening
when Lady De Grey, who had just arrived from Davos
with Lady Herbert came to see me—of course, in great
distress—to get me to advise and help her about the
funeral arrangements of her brother Sir Michael. She
could only persuade Belle, that is, Lady Herbert, to go
down to Wilton and be quiet by promising her to come
to me. I think they must have had a hard time at Davos,
for his one absorbing idea was to get back to America
where his heart and his duties were, and you know how
frightfully exhausting death always is to all but the one
who goes happily to sleep—and after his last hemorrhage
his heart began to fail and he fell asleep without any
idea that he was dying, of which they were all very glad.
But to go through the sad scene and then rush off all the
way from Davos to London was very hard, and I was
so sorry for them that I was glad to do for them what
little I could. I saw Lodge and proposed that as the
funeral was to be on Tuesday, the Alaska Tribunal should
adjourn for that day, to enable all its members to attend
the funeral at Wilton, which the family wished very much,

and we got up a telegram to Lord Alverstone at Cranleigh who proved to be of the same mind and I was able to inform her of that this morning. Of course that dispenses with any memorial service in town, as London is now so empty that there would be nobody to attend it.†
* * *

"Tell Mabel that between fifty and seventy is a very dangerous period for spinsters and they are more than likely to marry themselves into trouble.

"I haven't written you about my dinner of Thursday for the Meyers. After their great hospitality to us in Rome, and all that, I couldn't think of letting them spend a week in London without taking suitable notice of it. The dinner went off very well indeed, and proved to be quite a sociable and jolly affair. I had a round table for twelve at the alcoved end of the big restaurant at the Carlton, where it fitted in very well and was out of the way of other people, and as they all knew each other it went off well. Mrs. Root, unfortunately, was ill with a cold and unable to come, but Edith almost made good her place, and the other five ladies were Mrs. Meyer and Mrs. Lodge who sat on my right and left—Mrs. Witherbee, who is most agreeable and handsome too, and Mrs. Herbert Harriman, sister-in-law of Mrs. W. K. Vanderbilt, whom Billy Phillips told me about, and I made bold to invite her. She had just had a tooth pulled, but she accepted with alacrity, and perhaps was all the more lively for that, and Mrs. Newbold whom you know made the sixth—all attractive women, and Mr. Carter made the sixth man, and he is everybody's favorite. We

† Sir Michael Herbert was British Ambassador to the United States, and had signed with Mr. Hay the convention under which the Alaska Boundary Tribunal, then sitting, was created.

sat at the table till half past ten, instead of going out into the front hall for cigars & coffee, which I think is rather a trying place. * * * "

(October 5.) " * * * I have heard nothing more from Mr. Balfour except that he told Mr. White that he had told me we could have the house. But his life lately has been so full of difficulties that he probably hasn't had time to think of it again. The new Cabinet is coming out tomorrow, but I don't think that will end his difficulties. However, he takes things very easily and probably looks forward without distress to a vacation before long. * * * "

(October 6.) " * * * I am off in a few minutes to Wilton to attend Sir Michael Herbert's funeral. There is to be a memorial service after all, by order of the King, but I thought under all the circumstances that I should go to Wilton as Lady Herbert so much desired it. * * * "

(October 10.) " * * * The political campaign is already getting hot here, as you may believe when Lord Spencer last night denounced Mr. Chamberlain as a reckless and unscrupulous opponent—and Mr. Ritchie addressing his own constituents at Croydon, was interrupted from beginning to end of his speech by an unruly audience. * * * "

(October 15.) " * * * We were all disgusted with Lord Rosebery's way of speaking of the President in his speech at Sheffield."

(He spoke of him as "Teddy.")

(October 16.) " * * * I must write you a line today of all days in the year. Do you remember everything or anything about the 16th of October 42 years
ago? Forty-two years would have seemed a long way
to look forward, but how swiftly it has flown! On the
whole we have been greatly blessed—and have a very
great balance of good to be thankful for. * * * "

"1 Carlton House Terrace.
19 October 1903.

"Dear Mabel:—
" * * * It looks as if the Alaska Boundary case was
to be decided today or tomorrow and largely in our favor.
At least the *Associated Press* has so reported to America,
and today's papers are full of it. But I know nothing
about it, and shall not be sure until it is officially announced. There is many a slip betwixt the cup and the
lip, and the sessions are absolutely secret. * * *

"Today I presented to His Majesty our three commissioners—Root, Lodge and Turner—a brief and formal
function. He received us very pleasantly and looks in
excellent health. * * *
                                                        Papa."

To His Wife

"1, Carlton House Terrace, S. W.
19 October 1903.
" * * * To answer your other questions, I don't think
Lord Rosebery meant to reflect upon the President.
What we objected to was his calling him 'Teddy' in a
public speech. * * *
"If the Alaska Boundary is settled the way the papers
say this morning, it will be, I should think, satisfactory
to all Americans, but the Canadians may grumble. How-

ever, I have always believed that they know they had no case. What they wanted was to get a port, on that coast, to which they had no right, and in that they have been successfully baffled, if the decision comes out as it has been foretold. * * *

"Yesterday I walked Mr. Hardinge to Jordan's to see Wm. Penn's grave and the little Quaker meeting-house close by, and then a long stroll through the country back to Beaconsfield. Mrs. Hardinge is one of the Queen's women-in-waiting and I found her very attractive. She has to serve two weeks at a time twice a year, and when at Sandringham they make a part of the family and enjoy it very much. But at Buckingham Palace the Royal Family dine, etc., apart up stairs, and the 'Household' below & she doesn't enjoy it so much, especially as she has to go home at night. * * *

J. H. C."

"American Embassy, London.
20 October 1903.

"DEAR MABEL:—

" * * * We are all a little excited today over the announcement of the decision of the Alaska Boundary Commissioners giving us our main contentions, and at the same time giving Canada more than she was entitled to. It is happily all over, and though the Canadians may grumble a little while, I think they will rejoice with the rest that it is all over. It has run along now for fifteen years in one shape or another and stood in the way of settling other matters.

"Now, all the Alaskans scatter. The Lodges and Turners sail tomorrow and the Roots on Friday of next week. * * *

PAPA."

"American Embassy, London.
21 Octr. 1903.
"DEAR JO:—
"I sent you by Mrs. Lodge who sailed today and was kind enough to take it, Morley's Life of Gladstone, which is a great book about a great man, and I hope you will enjoy it. We are all rejoicing over the end of the long-drawn Alaska Boundary case. What I always contended for was fully sustained, and the Canadians got all they were, as I thought, entitled to and more. * * *

FATHER."

To His Wife

"Randolph Hotel, Oxford.
Monday, 26 Oct. 1903.
" * * * My Birmingham experience was most successful—a great audience very sympathetic and responsive. I think the address well timed, as the English people generally—including the best informed—have but little appreciation of Franklin. He was far too democratic to suit the titled classes, but at Birmingham they seemed to take him in at once. * * * "

The occasion of the address on Franklin was the annual prize distribution to students of Midland Institute at the Town Hall, Birmingham, on October 23.

"American Embassy, London.
28 October 1903.
"DEAR JO:—
" * * * I beg you not to be discouraged about the work or want of work at the office. As soon as they realize

that you are always on hand and eager to be useful, they will put upon you all that you can do. And although at first the matters entrusted to you will appear trifling and worthless which any boy might do, they will soon come to be more important. I went through the same ordeal of trying to make myself indispensable to a big office, and I know how it tires one's patience, but as I said before, it will pay in the end. * * * "

(November 3.) " * * * I see that the Canadians are still fretting over the Alaska decision, but they were very fortunate in getting so much, and their irritation will soon I think give way to great satisfaction."

To the Same

"American Embassy, London.
27 Nov. 1903.
" * * * I send you cuttings from today's *Times* and *Telegraph* about our Thanksgiving Dinner last night. From the two together you can gather a fairly good sketch of my speech, although both are much condensed. Mr. Bryan's I am sorry to say is not well reported. He spoke for nearly half an hour, a very finished oration, delivered most artistically, and made a decided impression. He is also making a favorable impression here personally. I had him to lunch with Mr. Balfour and others and they liked him very much, and he was at Mr. White's next day with Lord Rosebery, Ld. Salisbury & others and they liked him & think much better of him from having seen and known him. * * *   FATHER."

To the Same

"American Embassy, London.
29 Decr. 1903.

"We were all delighted with your letter of the 15th giving an account of your experience in the case of the Broad Exchange Co. It was very jolly in Mr. Sprague to give you such an opportunity, and it is quite evident that you seized it in a becoming spirit. * * * I remember well the first time I was allowed by B. E. & S.* to argue a case in Court. It was a little case in the Superior Court General Term, and I very nearly funked. But they soon gave me another chance in a Jury case, to defend an ejectment suit (Smith vs. Bruen). I was there saved by the skin of my teeth. The plaintiff's counsel having opened, I moved on the pleading *and his opening* to dismiss the complaint, and the Judge (D. P. Ingraham) being pleased with the audacity of such a stripling, and being always desirous of getting rid of a case on the easiest terms possible, granted my motion. There was no great merit in the performance but it quite set me up with that particular client and with the office. But you seem to have been put forward for the last encounter in a case of some importance with a leader of the Bar—who must have recalled many contests with me. * * *

FATHER."

The incorrigible optimist breaks out in his letter of January 27, 1904, to his daughter:

"Every day," he says, "makes me more confident that this horrible War threatened between Russia and

* Butler, Evarts, and Southmayd.

Japan will be avoided. They must and will find some way out of it—some other way. * * * "

But it was a case of confidence misplaced, as he admits in writing to her on February 10:

" * * * This horrid war so long threatened has begun at last, and I'm afraid it will be a long and bloody one. Russia has great staying powers and the Japs are full of indomitable spirit. Let us hope that no other Nations will be drawn in."

His diplomatic correspondence in these early months of 1904 was much concerned with the war and things growing out of it, including matters relating to China. He speaks of being more than usually busy, for which it helps to account that he had two addresses of more than usual consequence to prepare and deliver. One of them he made at the centenary of the British and Foreign Bible Society in London early in March, the other on March 19 at Edinburgh. Along with Doctor Payson Ingersoll, Corresponding Secretary of the American Bible Society, Mr. Choate was delegate and representative of the American Bible Society at the centenary meeting. He appeared therefore in a double capacity, both as delegate and as Ambassador. When he came to speak he first read to the meeting a message of congratulation from President Roosevelt. He then read a letter from the President and Secretary of the American Bible Society, which was the credentials of Doctor Ingersoll and himself, and went on as follows:

"I was going to say that the American Bible Society is your own offspring, but, inasmuch as you yourselves were only twelve years old when it came into being, I must regard you as our elder sister, and our elder sister it was who showed us the way, who encouraged us in our small beginning, who sent us a grant of five hundred pounds from her treasury to start with, which was a tremendous help in those days, and who has ever since been leading the way which we have been glad to follow.

"Let me say one word more about the American Bible Society. Like yourselves, it has had its struggles and its triumphs. Like yourselves, it has an immense work on hand. Like yourselves, it finds the demand far greater than the supply that it is able to furnish. It is no small undertaking to keep eighty millions of people supplied with a Bible in every house, and that has been their ambition. And then they have to meet about eight hundred thousand immigrants from foreign lands every year as they land in New York and other parts of the country, and I am sorry to say that they are not always provided with Bibles, and the Society has to take care of them. But with all that, I think its records will show, as in the past, that now and in the future it can be relied on to do almost as much for foreign lands as it does for its own people at home.

"Now this great harvest which this centenary demonstrates, is only, after all, what has grown up from the little seed which, nearly three hundred years ago, your fathers and our fathers united in planting in the distant wilderness. When the Pilgrim Fathers embarked in the *Mayflower* in 1620, and when, eight years afterwards, the great Puritan immigration from old England to New England set in, they carried with them, our fathers and the brothers of your fathers, carried with them, as their best possession—in fact the only one which was to have a lasting value—King James's Bible, upon which their infant state was built. It was their only book—their only readable book. I have read catalogues of the books which some who were best off among them had, and the Bible was the only readable book, and that was readable by every man, woman and child. It was the ark of their covenant, and, really, they did find, within those sacred covers, their shelter from the stormy blast and their eternal home. Their faith was founded upon it, and having no other book, you can realize how there they stood to find, not their religion only, but their literature, their biographies, their voyages and travels, their poetry, such as no poets have ever since produced, and that magnificent march of history from the beginning, and they searched and found in it the golden rule of life.

"I do not know that I can more forcibly bring before you how completely the Bible was their one treasure than by describing one of the few family Bibles that have come down from those days to ours—the only legacy that has reached the remote posterity of the family to which it belonged. It was read twice a day in every family by the head of the household, with all the members gathered about him, going in at Genesis and coming out at Revelations, the whole journey being accomplished twice every year between January and December. Dog's-eared?—that is a mild term to express its condition, for its leaves were absolutely worn away by the pious thumbs that had turned them. It was really the fact that New England, in its first generation, was the most biblical community on the face of the earth. Their laws, their customs, their language, their habits, were founded upon it, and in it they found their sole guide of life.

"Let me read a word from one of the greatest of their descendants, Phillips Brooks, that most noble product of New England culture, himself a true descendant of their blood. He said worthily of them (I could not begin to find language equal to his in point of expression): 'It never frightened a Puritan when you bade him stand still and listen to the voice of God. His closet and his church were full of the reverberations of the awful, gracious, beautiful voice for which he listened. He made little, too little, of sacraments and priests, because God was so intensely real to him. What should he do with lenses who stood thus full in the torrent of the sunshine?'

"Our New England fathers, with the Bible as the basis of their lives, realized that prayer of Erasmus, uttered one hundred years before they found foothold upon Plymouth Rock,—a prayer which it was often dangerous to breathe in those early days: 'I wish the Gospels were translated into the languages of all people, that they might be read and known not only by the Scotch and the Irish and the English, of course, but even by the Turks and the Saracens. I wish that the husbandman may sing parts of them at his plow; that the weaver may warble them at his shuttle; that the traveler may, with their narration, beguile the weariness of the way.'

"Well, our Pilgrim Fathers were exactly the kind of men that you might expect them to have been. I wish you would just imagine, for one moment, what our lives would be if, like them, the Bible were our only book. No newspapers, no weeklies, no magazines, no novels, no libraries, no school reading of any kind. I only hope that we, like them, would find our refuge where they so safely found theirs.

"In the days of their greatest poverty and distress, they founded Harvard College, in order, as they said, that the supply of learned and godly ministers might never fail, and they gave it a motto which holds to this day: 'To Christ and the Church,' and, what means the same thing, 'Veritas' (truth), and then they founded the great State of Massachusetts, which I shall not ask you for one moment to hear about. I can only say what Mr. Webster says of her: 'Massachusetts, she needs no eulogy. There she stands, behold her and judge for yourselves.'

"If you ask me what more has come of it, what other good things they founded upon the Bible, besides Plymouth Rock and Boston, I should say that a very large share of the good which has been wrought out in America from the beginning is traceable to their pious efforts, that if the common schools have found their way from the Atlantic to the Pacific; if slavery has been abolished; if the whole land has been changed from a wilderness into a garden of plenty, from ocean to ocean; if education has been fostered according to the best light of each generation since then; if industry, frugality and sobriety are the watchwords of the nation, as I believe them to be, I say it is largely due to those first emigrants, who landing with the English Bible in their hands and in their hearts, and assisted by men like themselves here in London, established themselves on the shores of America.

"Without detracting at all from the great part which has been contributed from other countries, we say that that little leaven has leavened the whole lump, and if you ask me what the signs of the leavening of the lump are, I point again to the work of the American Bible Society and its relation to that community. It is liberally supported and encouraged by many ardent friends in every state and in every territory of the Union. I point to the fame and influence which it has acquired throughout the land. I point to the millions of dollars which it is gathering in for this pious use, and to the scores of millions of Bibles which it has distributed, on the principle always of the whole Bible for the whole world, to all but the poor at cost, to everyone of the poor without money and without price.

"And now, before I sit down, I should like to make a claim for my country which may be a little surprising to this audience, and that is that one of. the first translations from the English text of the whole Bible into a heathen language, was made in the earliest days of Massachusetts with the great aid that was sent over to us from London. There came over to us in 1639 a poor clergyman from Jesus College, Cambridge. There he had been distinguished for his studies in theology and for the study of languages, and when he came to America he made himself busy in connection with that peaceful, harmless tribe of Indians who made their home in Massachusetts, and tried to teach them the word of God. After he had learned their language, and it took him about twelve years to learn, he sent over a cry for help, and he got a response. The same cry and the same response has been going on to this day: 'Can we to souls benighted the lamp of life deny?' What was the response? Why, Parliament, consisting then only of the Commons, I am sorry to say, organized a society entitled 'The Corporation for the propagation of the gospel of Jesus Christ in New England.' And the preamble of the act passed in connection with this society is a very remarkable one and shows how interesting was the relationship which our ancestors bore to the Indians to whom they held out the hand of fellowship. Here it is:

" 'Whereas, the Commons of England have received certain intelligence by the testimonial of divers faithful and godly ministers in New England, that divers heathen natives of that country, through the blessing of God, upon the pious character and pains of some godly English of this nation, who preached the gospel to them in their own Indian language, who not only of barbarous have become civil, but many of them, forsaking their accustomed charms and sorceries and other Satanical delusions, do now call upon the name of the Lord—with tears lamenting their misspent lives, teaching their children what they are instructed in themselves, being careful to place their said children in godly English families and to put them to English schools, betaking to themselves but one wife and putting away the rest, and by their constant prayer to Almighty God morning and evening in their families, expressed to all appearances with much devotion and zeal of heart; therefore,' etc., etc.

"Therefore the Commons established this corporation to raise a fund in England for this purpose, and by their apostle John Elliot, completed, as early as 1663, or one hundred and forty years before the foundation of the British and Foreign Bible Society, a complete version of the Bible in the Algonquin tongue. Probably there is not a man now living who can read a word of it. Certainly there is not a vestige of the tribe for whom it was written, but it is a grand monument for its author, and it pointed the way for this Society and for the American Bible Society.

"I cannot take up any more of your time. I only wish to ask, What is it that we are working for as societies? Each for its own interest primarily, but, next to that, we have a greater and a further mission, and that is to promote and advance the cause of civilization, of order, or religion, of peace and of duty.   I believe that such occasions as this go far in the accomplishment of that mission.   How far, then, is it possible to make these two great nations policemen to keep the peace of the world? Some rely upon armies and on navies, upon armaments and gunpowder and lyddite and dynamite as the best guarantees of the preservation of peace, but sometimes these things explode when least expected.   Others rely upon the slow and tortuous processes of diplomacy, but diplomacy sometimes fails, as we have had illustrations lately.

"I believe, and I think that the British and Foreign Bible Society and the American Bible Society unite in that belief, that the only sure guarantee of peace is the moral influence of public opinion.   Let each nation and the people of each nation give their governments to understand that they are for peace and there will be no war.   I believe that if these two nations which you and I represent were to set the example, the other Christian nations would follow.   Nothing could withstand such a weight of public opinion based upon this book, which speaks always to the world for peace and good will, 'peace on earth, good will to men.'   I believe in co-operation in good work, in every good work possible, between the people of our two countries.   Why should we not co-operate in all good work, we who have one God, one Bible, one language and one destiny?"

He writes to Colonel Hay on the 11th of March:

"If nothing turns up to make me think I ought not to do so, I expect to go away for the Easter holidays, leaving Mr. White in charge from about the 23rd or 25th of March to the 17th or 18th of April. I have been in charge uninterruptedly since the middle of June and should like to get a little sunshine and fresh air.

"It seems to me that your note and the responses to it have done all that is likely to need to be done on our part at present, and it has been so successful that everyone feels that you have done a great service in the cause of the neutrality of China and of ultimate peace without a dismemberment of that great empire. I cannot foresee what questions may arise in the next few weeks unless it be an occasional question of contraband in coal or provisions, as to which we are not yet in possession of the exact declarations of Japan or of Russia, the latter of which seems disposed so far as we can learn to make the inclusion of both of those articles in contraband more general than has heretofore been allowed.

"I told Lord Lansdowne on Wednesday that unless he had reason to expect important events in the Easter holidays, I should go away, that the last time I went under the assurance that nothing was going to happen, I had hardly got away before he began to raise a bobbery about Venezuela and kept it up for two months, and I hoped that if he had anything like that up his sleeve now he would let me know and I would not go. He said he hadn't and thought there would be nothing important, possibly occasional questions of contraband. He said there was absolutely nothing in the current rumors of Russia asking for mediation, that that was quite impossible. He said that he could not learn that Russia had yet established any prize courts in the East, but I don't see why she may not do so when necessary at Port Arthur or at Vladivostok. However, I shall not go farther than Biarritz, and if anything important does turn up I can return to London in twenty-four hours."

He writes his daughter, March 16:

"It now looks as if we should get off for Biarritz on the 25th to be gone for three weeks—in search of fresh air and sunshine as you say. Meantime on Saturday next, the 19th, I am off to Edinburgh to deliver my address on 'Alexander Hamilton' that evening, and to receive the freedom of that famous city on the 21st. I am afraid the three days will be very full of junketing but I don't see how that is to be helped. * * * "

Of his adventures in Edinburgh, including the unavoidable junketing, to which he seems to have taken quite kindly, he writes:

                              "American Embassy, London.
                               23 March 1904.
"Dearest Mabel:—
" * * * 'Gian' seems to be a little under the weather —got off from a dinner last night at Lady Margaret Douglas's on the plea of a cold, as did also W. Phillips on the same ground. However she has herself a big dinner tonight to which we were all going, but W. P. has again to beg off being in bed with his cold. The fact is that he is not as tough as I am, especially when it comes to junketing, of which we had a great deal in Edinburgh. We arrived at 6:15 on Saturday evening, and after a hasty dressing and a still more hasty dinner we went to McEwen's Hall to deliver my address. The Hall held nearly 3000 people and was packed. The stu-

dents—the very same who abused the Attorney General
and the Prime Minister so outrageously a month ago
when the A. G. went to be installed as their Rector—
behaved this time like buttered angels, listened most
devotedly as did everybody else, and I had no reason to
complain of the reception which all hands gave me and
what I had to say. Then there was a students' supper,
which only adjourned at 12 out of the Scotch regard
for Sabbath hours, and there I had to speak for 20 minutes—in a very different strain of course from that of
my address in the earlier part of the evening.

"Hector Ferguson took the whole responsibility in
Edinburgh with the utmost kindness and forethought.
I stayed with his close friends the Rev. Dr. Whyte's—
most lovely people as all his friends seem to be. Sunday of course we had a very proper day and some rest,
but Monday we had to work very hard. At eleven I
was taken through the Park and through two picture
galleries. At one a luncheon at Dr. W's. with a lot of
the choicest men of Auld Reekie, at 2:30 to the Town
Hall to receive the Freedom of the City in a handsome
silver casket, to which I had to respond in another 20
minutes speech, afterwards tea & cake in the City Parlor
and another speech, then back to the Whyte's for an
afternoon reception, this time mostly of choice women—
the best in Edinburgh and of course I had to move about
in lively fashion and talk to everyone; then at 6:45 to
the Lord Provost's Banquet where my health was the
principal toast, and I had to grind out a final half hour
talk, which came rather hard. After all this, W. P. who
had accompanied me through everything, was quite
used up—couldn't sleep on the night train by which we
returned so as to be in time for the Duke's funeral

in the Abbey—took to his bed yesterday afternoon, and still remains there, but promises to be up tomorrow, and right for Paris & Biarritz on Friday. I send you cuttings from *The Scotsman* of yesterday, giving a full account of the performances of the day before. The editorial pleased me very much, and the report of my speech is very accurate. Mama has sent you *The Scotsman* of Monday which tells all about Saturday night and gives the address nearly in full.

"I forgot to say that on Sunday evening Mr. & Mrs. George H. B. Hill gave us a splendid dinner which perhaps partly accounts for W. P.'s dilapidation. You remember them for we presented them a year or two ago.

"Thanks largely to Hector I look back upon my visit to Edinburgh with the greatest pleasure, my reception on all hands was delightful.

"The Duke's funeral at the Abbey was very grand. There were no ladies present except those of the Royal Family & the Lady Mayoress, and no diplomats except the heads of Missions. So even Mr. White, Mr. Carter & W. P. were excluded. The Ambassadors were in the upper stalls in the choir—three on each side, and Benckendorff sat in the lantern where the coffin was, with the other specials. The Queen and her daughters sat opposite me on the second row of stalls and the Princess of Wales and the others on the line of stalls directly in front of me, but they were all so heavily craped that it was difficult to distinguish one from another. The music was really magnificent, as even I could tell, and when they sang 'Onward, Christian Soldiers,' and the military band struck in with the great organ, and the whole congregation joined—well, really even the Stockbridge choir in its best days could have gathered inspiration from it.

"Well, day after tomorrow we are off for Biarritz where we expect to stay two or three weeks. I have to be in Glasgow on the 19th & 20th to receive my degree there, or we might stay a little longer, and as it is, if Mama likes it, I may try to persuade her & Anna to stay a little longer. As usual she has been rooting and rummaging, turning over everything as if it were her final departure from earth, or at any rate from England—but she is very well.

"Mrs. Ladenberg lunched with us today—a good deal disturbed because they are trying to make her pay as a six months' resident in England the regular Income Tax. * * *

PAPA."

Of his address on Hamilton he says in the preface to his book of addresses in England: "Hamilton was comparatively unknown in England except to lawyers, scholars and great readers. There had been a recent rehabilitation of his fame in a fascinating work of fiction ('The Conqueror,' by Mrs. Atherton) which had been widely read in England as in America, but the real facts of the great work of that surpassing genius in upholding the arms of Washington in the war, in bringing about the convention of 1787 which made the Federal Constitution, in securing its adoption by the people, and in organizing our government under it, were not widely known and it was a great pleasure to tell this wonderful story to the students of the University of Edinburgh."

And the more pleasure doubtless, and the more suit-

able, because Hamilton was by derivation a Scotsman.

All of Mr. Choate's offerings of biographies of American statesmen—of Lincoln, Franklin, Hamilton—and
of American political history, were much fresher to the
British mind when he made them than they would be
now. Only two years after his address on Hamilton
came Frederick Scott Oliver's excellent book about him,
which compared in popularity with Mrs. Atherton's
novel.

"Hotel Victoria, Biarritz.

12 April 1904.

"Dearest Mabel:—

" * * * Our room here is a bower of flowers which
friends have sent in to Mama. We go sometimes to the
Casino—dined there one evening with Cora, Lady Strafford and her new husband No. 3, who seems an agreeable
man (of the North American Indian type). The gambling
at the Casino looked very cheap and low, and is taken
part in by very vulgar people. After the first novelty
of it, it was a most loathsome sight. At the British Club
here too they are said to play very high, and the common saying is that if you don't golf or gamble there is
no room for you at Biarritz. But there are exceedingly
nice people here. * * *

Papa."

Coming back from the holiday at Biarritz, the Choates
moved from Lord Curzon's house, which had served
them so acceptably, to Mr. Arthur Balfour's, close by
at 4 Carlton Gardens.

His letter-book for 1904 abounds considerably in regretful notes, declining to be present and furnish discourse on occasions months ahead. "It is always practically impossible," he says in one of them, "to accept any invitation for six or seven months ahead because it interferes hopelessly with my freedom of movement." Besides that, retirement from office was taking form in his mind, and he wished to be free to get away when the time came and meanwhile not to be too much tied up to stated appearances.

Another class of letters contains this passage:

"Unfortunately the rules of the service in which I am engaged expressly prohibit me from making any recommendations to office. So you will not misinterpret my silence," etc.

Another thing that occasionally engaged his attention was the provision of British orators for distinguished occasions in the United States. He was consulted as to who was most to be desired, and who was most likely to be willing to come.

Frequent in his diplomatic correspondence of this time are letters to Secretary Hay relating to the concerns of China and the protection of Chinese interests against encroachers, and recording his labors to promote the policy of the Open Door, the final acceptance of which by the European powers is one of the chief glories of Mr. Hay's service as Secretary of State. To negotiate the Hay-Pauncefote Treaty, the Alaska Boundary settlement, and the agreement about the Open Door in China, and win acceptance of his achievements from the Senate, cost Mr. Hay his life, as similar efforts fifteen years later so nearly cost the life of Mr. Wilson.

"The thing that has aged me and broken me up," said Secretary Hay in a letter of this time to Nicolay, "has been the attitude of the minority of the Senate which brings to naught all the work a State Department can do." So a long letter from Mr. Choate to Colonel Hay, dated December 23, 1904, about adding bribery to the list of crimes provided for in the Extradition Treaty, winds up with this remark:

"Perhaps you will think me too fussy on such an infinitesimal point. I hope you will. But I know how easy it is for a small minority in the Senate to object to a Treaty with England of any nature, and I have even seen that one very innocent Arbitration Treaty may be opposed, and I thought it best to be on the safe side."

The letters that follow tell their own stories.

To President Eliot

"4, Carlton Gardens, S. W.
3 February, 1904.

"My Dear Eliot:—
"In looking over the College Catalogue—which is my frequent study—I was surprised and not a little disappointed to find that a man who has rendered such long and good public service as Senator Lodge has never received the degree of LL.D. from his Alma Mater, although several other colleges have conferred that honor upon him—colleges to which he was a stranger—and I could not help thinking that if the Corporation were to recognize him in that way at the coming Commencement, it would greatly please many graduates and meet with the general approval of all.

"He will have been out of college 33 years—a long period, most of which he has devoted to honorable public service, or to very creditable literary work. His lives of Washington, Webster, and Hamilton—and particularly his editing of the works of Hamilton and *The Federalist* are valuable, and he has cherished the literary spirit through all his political labors in a way that very few public men have done. You know all about his six years in the House of Representatives˙and ten in the Senate, and what personal weight he has acquired there by sheer force of talents and character. I think it may fairly be said that no man of his age and length of service in the Senate has acquired ˙anything like the influence with that body and in the country at large that he now holds.

"I can bear personal testimony to the value to both countries of his services as a member of the Alaska Boundary Commission which lately sat in London. The result which removed from the sphere of controversy a question that might at any time have imperilled the good relations of the two countries was largely due to the tact, patience, and ability of Mr. Lodge and Mr. Root. I know that services of that character are highly valued internationally—and are generally handsomely rewarded by appropriate honors by the nation on whose appointment they are rendered.

"England has peerages and orders and honors of knighthood of various sorts to confer on Englishmen who perform such services on her behalf, and they are freely bestowed; but as we have nothing of the kind to give, it would seem that recognition by his own University would be an appropriate thing.

"I confess that I feel a little jealous of Williams and

Yale and Clarke that they have anticipated his own College in recognizing the merits of this distinguished son of Harvard. They have put it in such a position that now Harvard will be conferring more honor on herself than on him, by adding his name to the honorary list in her catalogue. I have never been very close to Mr. Lodge, and supposed that, like several other alumni of Harvard who have rendered similar but much less important public service, he had already been included in that list.

"During the two months that he was in London last year I saw him a good deal at short range, and learned to appreciate his merits much more truly than I had ever done before. It is only within the last two weeks that I found I was wrong in supposing that he had already been decorated in this way by the College, and I thought I would lose no time in writing to you about it, from my interest in Harvard College rather than, or more than, in Henry Cabot Lodge—and in the hope that a *casus omissus* might be promptly made good.

"To signalize my devotion to Harvard, and at the same time my long residence in London, I am putting a stained glass window by John LaFarge into St. Saviour's Church in Southwark where John Harvard was baptized —and in whose immediate neighborhood his early days before he went to Cambridge, were spent, and I may ask you to help me about an inscription. Though not critically accurate, may I not call him the 'Founder'? It is a grand old church, which has stood for 500 years and is good for 500 more. Thanks to you, the name of Harvard means more and more every year in England, and I thought it a good place to set up his shrine.

"I wish you could be here next summer to unveil it!

Isn't it almost time for you to come to England, and might I not hope for this some time this year?

Yours most truly

JOSEPH H. CHOATE.

"Hon. C. W. Eliot."

Harvard gave an LL.D. to Senator Lodge at Commencement in 1904.

"13 May, 1904

"DEAR RANTOUL:

"I have got positive promises from Henry James and James Bryce, and hardly less certain ones from Thomas Hardy, Mrs. Humphrey Ward and Andrew Lang, to send brief tributes to Hawthorne to be read and published as part of your proceedings.* I also asked George Meredith, but although he would have liked much to do it, he has been very ill indeed lately and cannot write at present more than to sign his name. So he asked to be excused. Having got such a full wreath of laurels for the occasion I think you will hardly need anything from me—and it would be a pity to mar the purely literary symmetry of the offering.

"I have advised them all of the change of date to June 27th.

Yours very truly,

JOSEPH H. CHOATE.

"Hon. Robert S. Rantoul."

"6 June, 1904.

"DEAR LORD ROSEBERY:

"You have no idea how popular you are in America, or what a demand there is for your presence there. To-day's mail from the United States brought both of the enclosed invitations to you to attend great banquets there, one from the Chamber of Commerce of New York,

* At the Hawthorne centenary. He was born in Salem, July 4, 1804.

and the other from the New England Society of Brooklyn, with the request that I would forward them to you, and add my word of persuasion to you to accept them, which I gladly do. I need not say that both are organizations of the highest merit and standing. The Chamber of Commerce embraces in its membership all that is most important in the commercial world there, and the New England Society of Brooklyn is composed of leading men of that city, natives of New England, and the object of their organization is to keep alive the great principles of New England history.

"Both societies would regard you as their guest going and returning and at New York, and the New England Society hopes that you will keep its invitation under consideration until you receive a special call from a representative of the Society.

"I shall be glad to forward your favorable replies.

Yours most truly,

JOSEPH H. CHOATE."

On June 29 he was present at the anniversary festival of the Printers' Pension, Almshouse and Orphan Asylum Corporation and gave the toast. He talked about printers from Caxton's time down. He distributed prizes at the Crewe Mechanics Institution, and talked about railways and tenacity of purpose. He spoke eloquently and with feeling at the unveiling of the statue of Lord Russell, of Killowen, in the great hall of the Royal Courts of Justice. He was on hand when Mrs. Choate launched the big Cunard liner *Caronia*, and replied for her when her health was drunk.

On September 9 he wrote a message to independent voters, advocating Roosevelt's re-election, which was reproduced in facsimile in the New York *Tribune* of October 24, as follows:

"A few words to Independents:

"I assume that every Republican will support Roosevelt and Fairbanks, and every Independent voter should do the same. President Roosevelt is the soundest and staunchest Independent of them all. The politicians cannot force his hand. He has seen to it that the laws of the United States should be faithfully executed, cost what it might and cut where it would, and that is his chief duty under the Constitution. His honesty, courage, intelligence and devoted patriotism have made his administration a signal epoch in our national progress and prosperity. His lofty character has commanded the wholesome respect of all foreign nations by whom he is generally recognized as the most striking figure in American life, and to-day, thanks to his strength, independence and commanding reputation, supporting and enforcing at every step the wise diplomacy of Mr. Hay, the United States occupy a more exalted position among the nations of the earth than ever before. They know him as well as they do their own statesmen, and they know that he always means what he says. American rights are universally and promptly respected, and the safety of every American citizen, on sea and land, throughout the world is assured.

"The last four years have proved that the rights of property are safe in his hands, that he is equally considerate both of capital and labor, and that he is the sworn and relentless foe of all plunderers, to whatever party they may belong. The national credit at home and abroad was never so high and secure as now; our vast national resources are promptly and honestly collected, and the purity of the civil service is secure in the hands of its foremost champion.

"Those great unfinished undertakings, which the nation has so much at heart—the construction of the Isthmian Canal, on which the development of our commerce and national power depend, and the conduct of affairs in the Philippines in their steady progress towards ultimate self-government, can be more safely entrusted to him than to any new man. Under his administration our present foreign policy, which avoids all entangling alliances and insists upon friendly relations with all other nations, will be continued, and the integrity of China preserved, so far as our national influence can secure it.

"His absolute respect for the law is a sufficient answer to any idle talk about personal government. So far as the execution of the law is concerned, the President's voice is the voice of the nation, and his utterance cannot be too strong, too prompt or too determined.

"His enlarged experience in public affairs is of great value, and his manly and honorable record appeals to all Independents, old and young, to uphold his arms, instead of attempting to strike him down, and to let well enough alone, instead of trying new and dangerous experiments with new and untried men."

At the Thanksgiving Day dinner his talk was once more about the Pilgrims as the inventors of the festival. It will be noticed that he talked about them also in his Bible Society address. For fifty years at least he made an annual speech about the Pilgrims, and his sentiment for them, always strong, and growing by expression, was very thoroughly recorded.

"15 November, 1904.
"B. Fosset-Lock, Esq.,
  Hon. Secretary.
"DEAR SIR:
  "I have your very kind note of the 12th inst., informing me on behalf of the Council of the Selden Society that I have been elected an Honorary Member of the Society, and that I shall in due course receive its publications.
  "I beg you to inform the Council that I am deeply sensible of the honor done me in electing me an Honorary Member of so distinguished a Society, for which they will accept my grateful thanks, and that I shall greatly value the publications of the Society.
                    Yours very truly,
                          JOSEPH H. CHOATE."

To President Roosevelt

"12 December, 1904
"DEAR MR. PRESIDENT:
  "Ever since the election so many people have been busy resigning my office for me, apparently without having consulted either you or me on the subject, that I have waited for the present lull in their activity before writing to you about it.
  "To ensure your absolute freedom of selection of your foreign representatives, I assume that every Ambassador and Minister now in office will tender to you their resignation before the fourth of March. It is with this view, at any rate, that I now surrender to your absolute disposition the office which, by your favor, I have held so long, and enclose my formal resignation to take effect on that date.

"I have always regarded my tenure of office as limited to the term of the President who appointed me, and for every reason my recall will now be most agreeable and welcome to me.

"I have certainly been here long enough—six years on the first of March next, and, as I have lately been happily reminded, longer than any of my predecessors since Mr. Adams. I ought to be at liberty to devote myself to my personal and family affairs, too long neglected, and I have many other things to do for which time is getting short.

"The moment is most opportune. The friendship and goodwill between the two countries, which I was instructed by President McKinley to cultivate, as my chief duty, are now apparently perfect, and are, I think, certain to remain so as long as you are President.

"With the free voice and pen of a private citizen I hope to be able to render good service to your cause at home. And so I shall await my letter of recall as a welcome summons.

"I shall be glad to know, as soon as your convenience permits, at about what date I may expect it. After so long a residence in London it will necessarily take some time to prepare for my departure.

"I shall leave no important business unfinished. There was one personal object, which I had much at heart, to complete and dedicate, while I was yet Ambassador in London, my memorial window to John Harvard in St. Saviour's Church where he was baptized.

"I intended it both as a memorial of Harvard's growing fame in England, and as a suitable gift to signalize my long residence in London. In spite of interminable delays, I still hope to accomplish it before my recall reaches me, but if not, it can be safely entrusted to other hands.

"I shall retire from the public service, Mr. President, with the most grateful appreciation of the constant kindness and consideration which I have always received at your hands.

"I remain, most faithfully yours,
                                    JOSEPH H. CHOATE."

"12 December, 1904
"To the President of the United States.

"I hereby tender to you my resignation of the office of American Ambassador at the Court of St. James, such resignation to take effect on the fourth of March, 1905.
                    Your obedient servant,
                                    JOSEPH H. CHOATE."

To Joseph Choate, Jr.

                    "4, Carlton Gardens, S. W.
                      13 December 1904.
"DEAR JO:–
" * * * Well, I am sending by this mail my formal letter of resignation to the President to take effect on the 4th of March, which I believe he expects from all ambassadors—but what is more I have written him a private letter, saying that I had always regarded my tenure of office as expiring with the term of Prest. McKinley, and giving him ample reasons for my being relieved from further service at that time. I have long been thinking that it would be best for us all that we should end our life in London with the termination of our 6th year, which will be completed on the 1st of March. It will be best

for us all to get together in New York, so that we are all looking forward with hope to the President's taking my view of it which ought to set us free from London about April 1st. I have enjoyed every minute of it, but there is a time for all things, and no more propitious time for my retirement could ever occur.

"This must be absolutely confidential between us—until the President makes it known. It is for him and not for me to announce. The newspaper men as usual have been very cross because I would tell them nothing, and have had all sorts of absurd items about me. For instance, *The St. James Gazette* last night said—'Mr. Choate in response to his suggestion that he was very comfortable in the London Embassy, has been informed that American tradition permits no third term, etc., etc.' Each word of it palpably false.

"Of course this will settle the question about the 63rd St. house. We shall want it ourselves, but of course be getting it ready to occupy in the fall, and come home only in time to go to Stockbridge for the summer. How fine that will be! Now that our minds are made up to it, I think we should all be terribly disappointed if anything happened to keep us through the season in London. * * *

FATHER."

To the Same

"American Embassy, London.
21 Decr. 1904.

" * * * You mustn't mind what the papers say about me. It all proceeds from some ingenious penny-a-liners, and I have no doubt has annoyed the President more than it has me. I have reason to know that he has never

authorized any statement whatever. He will get my letter by the *Deutschland* on Friday and no doubt will answer it in his own good time. It will be delightful not to be public property any longer, whenever that time does come. * * *
FATHER."

To the Same

"American Embassy, London.
24 Decr. 1904.
" * * * When I hear how things are going in Washington, I am very glad to be out of it. There seems to be a general scramble among Senators for the whole diplomatic list. I see that the *Deutschland* arrived at New York on Thursday so that my letter must already be in the President's hands. I told him that I had always regarded my tenure of office as limited to the term of the President who appointed me, and that there was every reason why my letter of recall would be agreeable and welcome to me; that I had been here long enough, 6 years, and as I had lately been pleasantly reminded, longer than any of my predecessors since Adams, that I ought to be free to attend to my own personal and family affairs too long neglected; that I had many other things to do for which time was getting short; that the time was opportune; the friendship and good feeling between the two countries which President McKinley had instructed me to cultivate as my first duty were now apparently perfect, and were certain to continue so while he was President, and that with the free voice and pen of a private citizen I hoped to be able to work for his cause at home, so that my recall would be a welcome summons. * * *
FATHER."

To President Roosevelt

"10 January, 1905

"DEAR MR. PRESIDENT:

"I thank you most sincerely for your very kind letter of December 24th and particularly for your suggestion that if the delay will not inconvenience me you desire me to arrange to remain in the Embassy until I can personally dedicate my memorial window to John Harvard in St. Saviour's Church.

"I shall be most happy to do so, and the delay will not inconvenience me at all. I shall accordingly make my arrangements to remain and will promptly advise you as soon as I ascertain from Mr. LaFarge at what date approximately the window which he is preparing can be completed and put in place.

"It will give me great pleasure to conclude my life in London in so graceful a manner.

Yours most sincerely,

JOSEPH H. CHOATE."

"4 Carlton Gardens,
Jan. 9, 1905.

"DEAREST MABEL:—

" * * * William has doubtless told you of my delightful letter from the President. Last night it was followed by one even more so from Colonel Hay, who said many pleasant things and that the President wished to leave the time for the acceptance of my resignation to my own convenience. So we stand exactly as we should have wished to, if it had been left absolutely to ourselves from the outset. * * *

"Notwithstanding her apprehensions Mama got through the Roberts dinner very well, and confessed that she had enjoyed it very much. There were a lot of Military celebrities there. Lord Methuen and Lady M., 'Plummer' whose name was on everybody's lips throughout the war in South Africa and Mrs. Plummer, Sir George Clarke, one of the Triumvers who reformed the War Office and Lady Clarke, Sir William Chamberlain, who has been Roberts' aide (he said he had met you) and will probably go with them to America, General Grierson, etc., etc. The only real civilians besides ourselves were Sir George Farrar and Lady Farrar. Sir George was in the Jameson Raid, and was one of the four condemned to death in Pretoria, and for twenty-four hours his wife and everybody else thought he would be executed. But next day they commuted his sentence to 15 years and afterwards gradually remitted it until they finally let him go free on payment of £25,000 fine, and today he is one of the Governing Council in the Transvaal Colony.

"The Robertses are bent upon going to America in the fall for three months, and we have claimed the first right to them in Stockbridge. Lady Roberts, to whose lot I fell at the dinner, was most entertaining with her reminiscences of her long years in India, going backwards and forwards eighteen times for the children's sake, her intense and delightful pride in her husband and her daughter, her little bottles of Bisgop's Varsallette, and digestives—and her free comments upon people and things in general. I am sure that you will like her very much and that she will be most popular in America. * * *

PAPA."

As noted before, Mr. Choate for some months had been restricting his engagements for public appearances. When it got out that he was going home, there were a great number of applications for the pleasure of his company and farewell words at farewell dinners. His letter to Sir Frederick Pollock that follows tells the story that he told to all the rest. He told it in some cases with evident reluctance, but stuck to it because he could not accede in one case and not in another without getting into trouble.

"4 Carlton Gardens, S. W.,
22nd January, 1905.

"DEAR SIR FREDERICK:

"I am very grateful to you and Mr. Bryce and the Anglo-American League, for inviting me to a sort of farewell dinner before I leave England, and if it were only the Anglo-American League I should not hesitate a moment to accept and arrange for it. But I find myself unexpectedly overwhelmed with a large number of similar invitations from public bodies, which if I were to accept them, would keep me before the footlights in the rôle of a departing Ambassador making a 'positively last appearance' week by week from now until my departure.

"Prominent among these are the Pilgrims, who are also zealous supporters of the Anglo-American cause. If I accept one I cannot decline the other, and so I have written to the Pilgrims declining their most cordial invitation.

"There are two 'Farewell Banquets'—which I must accept, and I think you will agree with me that I ought to do so—the Lord Mayor's, which has become a traditional affair, and one to which the Lord Chief Justice has invited me on behalf of the Bench and Bar of England, an irresistible command to me as a lawyer. At one or the other of these, doubtless, the chief of the Anglo-Americans will be present.

"And so I am going to presume upon the reliable friendship of yourself and Mr. Bryce to ask you to concur in my view that I ought to content myself with these two final public appearances, and to be excused from accepting the others including the Anglo-Americans who are all my friends.

"At least I ask your sympathetic judgment on this somewhat embarrassing predicament—the embarrassment of a very rich supply of earnest and devoted friends.

"If you and Mr. Bryce concur with me, I then propose to decline all the other invitations to public dinners except the two I have mentioned.

"After you have digested this most self-denying letter I shall be glad to hear from you again.

Yours most truly,
JOSEPH H. CHOATE."

Another line of correspondence in his letter-book relates to the window in memory of John Harvard that he was putting in St. Saviour's Church in Southwark. His concern about that was very great, as were also his anxieties. It was necessary to induce the church authorities to accept a window from the United States—a thing without precedent—and to accept the design of Mr. John LaFarge, about which also there were serious hitches. Mr. Choate heartily approved of Mr. LaFarge's design and had a great admiration for him as a maker of windows. He considered him the best stained-glass-window maker in the world, and wanted to have a piece of his work in England, and he wanted to have enough Harvard in the window to make it easily recognizable as a Harvard window. He succeeded in all these aspirations, but not without hard work, much thought, much correspondence, and all the diplomacy he had. Finally he had great anxieties for fear the window would not be finished and received in time for him to be present at its dedication. Mr. La-Farge was a great artist. He had in a high degree that aspiration towards perfection which makes a great artist always want to think again, and try again, and to improve his best; so whether he would finish the window by the time appointed was a solemn question. But he did do it, and that whole enterprise turned out entirely to Mr. Choate's satisfaction and happiness.

"Windsor Castle,
27 Jan'y. 1905.

"Dear Jo:—

"Mama and I have been here for two days on a visit to the King and Queen, who have spared no pains to make it most agreeable. Besides ourselves there are Lord and Lady Lansdowne, Lord & Lady Iveagh, Lord & Lady Minto, Lord Roberts and Count Metternich, the German Ambassador,—a very pleasant party. The Castle has been immensely improved since the time of the old Queen who had insisted for forty years in keeping everything exactly as it was during the Prince Consort's time, so that there was room for great change and improvement. I suppose there is no other palace in the world that has in it such a vast mass of treasures in art and everything interesting except the Vatican, which is largely inaccessible. But here everything has now been arranged and exhibited to the best advantage and the effect is magnificent. Mr. Holmes, the librarian, who has been here for thirty-five years, was at our service.

He knows the history of every object in the palace and has shown us everything, and last night the King and Queen took us through their own private rooms, and showed us their rare contents. The Queen seems to have in her bed room in glass cases all her rare and splendid jewels which are wonderful. In fact every object in the Castle seems to be of value, and in very many cases they could not possibly be replaced. On Wednesday night, the King took Mama out to dinner, and I took the Queen, and had on my left Lady Arthur Hill who came in from the neighborhood and said that you once visited them for nearly a week in Ireland. And last night I took out Lady Minto, and the Japanese Minister, Mama. The weather has been perfect and our visit a complete success. We return to London this (Friday) afternoon. * * *

FATHER."

"3 February, 1905.

"DEAR COLONEL HAY:

"Referring to your kind letter of December 28th, I have at last been able to advise the President of the approximate date at which I expect to be able to dedicate my memorial window to John Harvard, as between the 10th and 20th of May, and have accordingly, in pursuance of his request expressed in his letter of December 24th, asked him to accept my resignation at a time shortly subsequent to the latter date, whereupon I shall be glad to receive my letter of recall, so that my successor may present his letter of credence before the 1st of June, when the season begins to be most interesting.

"I am taking some little risk in this, because of La-Farge's well known tendency to delay and the similar tendency of English workmen and the ecclesiastical authorities. But it seems to me only fair to my successor not to stand in his way after the time designated. So, if I fail to get the window dedicated within the time named, I shall leave it to other hands.

"I am beset, as you may suppose, by an overwhelming number of invitations to 'Farewell Banquets,' dictated by the abounding hospitality and goodwill of the British public, from all sorts of public and semi-public and private bodies, but I have concluded to make only two 'positively last appearances'—at the Lord Mayor's Banquet, which has become traditional, and at a dinner tendered to me through the Lord Chief Justice from the 'Bench and Bar of England,' a compliment from my professional brethren which I regarded as a command,— and to decline all the rest. One of these, I think, will take place shortly before the Easter holidays, and the other shortly after. There is an intervening fortnight, as you know, during which 'everybody' is away from London.
            Yours most truly,
                JOSEPH H. CHOATE."

                "American Embassy, London.
                    4 February 1905.
"DEAR JO:—
    " * * * I doubt whether Mama and Mabel can now contain themselves till May, as our plan has been. I am to stay until I can get my memorial window to John Harvard set up in St. Saviour's Church and dedicated, which I hope can be done at some date between the 10th and 20th of May. Should it not be accomplished by the latter date I should not feel like standing in the way of my successor, but shall leave it to some one else to

dedicate. I hear that President Eliot is in Switzerland. It would be too good luck to hope for, to get him to do it. * * *

FATHER."

"DEAR MR. NOYES: "15 February, 1905.

"In response to your call in the last number of the *Harvard Graduates Magazine*, I send you the following additions to my record in the Quinquennial:

" 'LL.D., Cambridge, 1900. Yale, 1901. St. Andrew's, 1902. Glasgow, 1904. D.C.L., Oxford, 1902. President Constitutional Convention, New York, 1894.'

"The last named fact I offered indirectly for insertion in the last Quinquennial, but for some reason, which I don't recollect, perhaps because it came too late, it was omitted. But I think I am right in claiming it for insertion.

"The precedents are abundant. James Baldwin, 1745, President Const. Conv., Mass., is exactly in point, and I enclose a list of other insertions of similar 'facts' which though not strictly within the specifications enumerated in the catalogue have become established. * * *

Yours very truly,

JOSEPH H. CHOATE.

"James Andrew Noyes, Esq."

"DEAR MR. NOYES: "22 April, 1905

"If not too late, I send you for insertion against my name in the new Quinquennial catalogue, another honor that I have just received, having been elected an Honorary Bencher of the Middle Temple (Inn of Court). This is

a very ancient society, as you know, and of the highest
standing, and my election was regarded by it, and certainly by myself, as a highly 'honorable distinction.'
So it comes directly within your published rules.   In
fact it is unique, as it has, I think, very rarely been conferred.

"If you approve, I would suggest this entry:
" 'Hon. Bencher Middle Temple, 1905.'
"I shall be glad to hear from you about it.

Yours very truly,
JOSEPH H. CHOATE."

The Quinquennial Catalogue is in a way the tombstone of all Harvard graduates.   On Mr. Choate's actual tombstone there is the briefest possible record, hardly
discernible, carved on the base of a cross.   Doubtless
that is as he would have had it, but as will be seen, he
was solicitous that as much of the story about him as
could with propriety be told in the catalogue of Harvard
graduates should be correctly and completely set forth.
If anything is permanent in this life and this country,
it is the Harvard Quinquennial Catalogue.   With fair
luck that will outlast most cemeteries and will always
be easily accessible to examination by persons interested.

"American Embassy, London.
21 Feb. 1905.
"DEAR JO:—
"Mama & Mabel think it so very funny that I should
have become a member of a Whistler Society, that I
enclose a cutting from today's *Times* showing how it
came about.   I had accepted for the dinner on the posi-

tive promise that I shouldn't be called on for a speech, but they fairly got the better of me, by making me an Honorary Member on the spot. * * *

FATHER."

To the Same

"4, Carlton Gardens, S. W.
18 March 1905.

"You might call this 'Carlton Hospital' rather than Carlton Gardens in the last fortnight—for mama and I have both been down all that time with this nasty Influenza which has been very prevalent in London. I had taken Marion Hague and her father all one long afternoon through many 'historic spots' in Old London, and that night was seized with violent fever and headache which lasted many days. Mama looked after me the first day and immediately took it, and had to go to bed, and there we were with a Doctor (Harley) and two trained nurses. I advise you not to get it, as it is evidently rank poison. However we are out of the woods now, and one trained nurse leaves this morning. I was down stairs yesterday for the first time and it did me good, and am to drive out today. Mama is only a day or two behind me. It hasn't interfered with business for there isn't much now, but it raised 'Ned' with our social affairs and duties, as we had to throw over any quantity of dinners, beginning with one we were giving ourselves for the Prince & Princess of Wales. Fortunately I have but three 'functions' left and those quite a way off—the dinner to be given me by the Bench and Bar of England on April 14th, the Lord Mayor's Farewell Banquet on the 5th of May and the dedication of my window as soon as may be after its arrival. The President ac-

cepted my resignation as of the 30th of May, but I hope
to get through a few days before that so as to sail on that
day.

"My oid firm are turned out of 52 Wall St. after 40
years' occupation because the City Bank wants the
rooms for themselves, and have taken offices at No. 60,
and will give me a room for temporary shelter on my
return. Mr. Southmayd goes with them and will surrender his lifelong objection to elevators.

"Have you seen Prof. Münsterberg's new book 'The
Americans'? It is well worth reading. On p. 558 you
will find a delightful reference to your baby and her start
and prospects in life which I am sure will please you and
Cora very much, and on p. 112 a reference to me which
is somewhat overdrawn. * * *

FATHER."

At the banquet to Mr. Choate by the Bench and Bar
in the hall at Lincoln's Inn on April 14, the Lord Chancellor presided, and a very large company, which must have
included everybody of importance in the legal profession
in England who could get there, sat around the tables.
In proposing Mr. Choate's health the Lord Chancellor
called the company "a somewhat unique assemblage of
our great profession." "I do not think," he said, "I
have ever seen so many together." He spoke of Mr.
Choate as a lawyer and then as an Ambassador. He
went on to say:

"I regard an ideal Ambassador as being like one of
those beautiful machines which work so easily, smoothly,
and rapidly that you hardly appreciate that they can
be working at all. They make no noise. But occasionally
it does not depend upon the Ambassador alone. Some-

times people make imprudent speeches. That has occurred, and the Ambassador has to make everything smooth. That is a difficult thing to do. I will not detain you by what may be considered to be a description of the ideal Ambassador; but I will only say that our great guest has been so many years with us, that he has been about us and among us, and that he has never given offence to any one. When one considers what the responsibilities may be—nations like individuals sometimes get into a passion, and unless a man is able to withstand the popular voice, either of his own country or of the country by which he is surrounded, to keep both his temper and his head, the issue may be the greatest disaster that may happen to a nation—the disaster of war. What shall we say for the Ambassador who during the whole period of his residence among us has used all his great influence, an influence so great because it is accompanied by the temper and honour of a gentleman, to prevent anything like a tendency to that jealousy and hostility which from time to time will arise among nations? I cannot go on in his presence beyond saying this, that without, I think, a single dissentient voice, our guest would have been recognized to have done all that an Ambassador should do to keep the peace between two of the greatest nations on earth. It is true that once upon a time we quarrelled—we will not consider how many years ago that was—and we separated. And so did we when we were Saxons, so when we were Normans. But I do not think the practical politics of the day recognize the difference between Saxon and Norman. And so I may say that between the great country of which my friend is the representative and ours we will recognize the fact that the past is past. The dead may bury its

dead in the past, and we can only remember now that
we are kindred nations, and ought to love one another.

"And now I come to the hardest part of my task, and
that is to say farewell. I confess I love the old Greek
idiom which in one word says farewell and bids the parting friend to rejoice. We do say to lawyer, Ambassador,
and best of all, to friend, farewell, and at the same time,
rejoice. To go back to your own country and your own
home, surrounded by the holy melodies of love, to go
back with the respect of all with whom you have come
in contact, with the consciousness that you go back with
the sense of duty nobly done, with the knowledge that
in your day and generation you have advanced the ten-
dencies to peace; to go back, not like the Roman conqueror, with trophies of a successful campaign, but having won the affection and admiration of a whole kindred
people, that may indeed justify the apostolical farewell
and induce us to say rejoice, and again I say rejoice."

Then he proposed his health, and the Attorney-General
seconded it, for he said that though it was not usual to
second the proposal of a toast, this was not an ordinary
occasion. He made further remarks, but briefly, and
Mr. Choate responded as follows:

"My Lord Chancellor, my Lords, and Gentlemen,—
I may say brothers all, for I accept your presence here
to-night as a signal proof that neither time, nor distance,
nor oceans, nor continents can weaken the ties of sympathy and fraternity between the members of our noble
profession wherever the English law has reached or the
English tongue is spoken. On this spot, consecrated for
centuries—I was going to say for unnumbered centuries—

to the study and development of the law, I feel that we are gathered to-night for a veritable professional love-feast, if I can judge from the kindly words of the Lord Chancellor and the Attorney-General and from your genial countenances. No profane presence of laymen, no troublesome affairs of clients, can disturb us here to-night. We are all lawyers, except the Judges, and they, too, are lawyers who have soared in ascension robes to a higher and nobler sphere. I thank you all from the bottom of my heart. For an American lawyer who long since withdrew from the arena, to find himself the guest of the united Bench and Bar of England, supported by the presence of all that is illustrious and famous among them, is a position which only overcomes me with a sense of my own unworthiness of the compliment you have paid me. I cannot but feel that in my person and over my head you desire to pay an unexampled honor to the great country that I represent, to its Bench and Bar, that daily share your labors and keep step with your progress, and to the great office that I am about to lay down.

"Let me say a single word about the altogether too lavish compliments that the Lord Chancellor has paid me in respect to my official career in England. My task has not been the difficult work of diplomacy to which he has referred. It has all, from the day of my arrival here until now, been made absolutely easy by the spirit with which I have been received. The two representatives of this great country with whom I have had to do at the Foreign Office—Lord Salisbury and Lord Lansdowne—have made my task perfectly easy, not only because they have always practised the modern diplomacy, meaning what they say and saying what they mean, with never a card up any sleeve on either side,

but because in every single incident they have met me
more than half-way in all that went towards conciliation, harmony, and union between the two countries.
It was also easy for us on both sides for other reasons—
because the two great chiefs of State on either side, the
late illustrious Queen and the present occupant of the
Throne, his not less illustrious Majesty, upon the one
side, and President McKinley and President Roosevelt
upon the other, have all the while been determined that
the two countries should be friends; and, back of all
that, a circumstance which gave great force to everything that either has ever said, the rank and file, the
great mass of the people on either side, were determined
that nothing should happen to impair the friendship of
the two peoples. I cannot tell you how much I thank
you for your presence here to-night. I am especially
proud that the chair is occupied by the Lord Chancellor,
whose name in both countries is a synonym for equity
and justice. In spite of his thirty-five years at the Bar
and his eighteen years upon the Woolsack, he is the very
incarnation of perennial youth. Time, like an ever-
rolling stream, bears all its sons away, but the Lord
Chancellor seems to stem the tide of time. Instead of
retreating like the rest of us before its advancing waves,
he is actually working his way up stream. He demonstrates what I have been trying to prove for the last three
years, that the eighth decade of life is far the best, and
I am sure he will join with me in advising you all to hurry
up and get into it as soon as you can. He gave me his
personal friendship immediately after my arrival here,
which has all the time been growing stronger and
stronger; and, while he has been drinking at some
mysterious fountain that always renewed his mind and
his body, I can answer for it that his heart has all the

time been growing younger and fresher and warmer. I must also acknowledge with gratitude the presence of the Lord Chief Justice to-night. He, too, has graced my life in England with his friendship. His name is a household word in America. He is held in the highest esteem and honor; and I only hope that he will yield to my repeated persuasions to come over and give us a chance to show how much we like him.

"The occasion and the Lord Chancellor's and Attorney-General's most kindly words, I am afraid, will make me a little egotistical. I must disavow what they have so strongly pressed—my great prominence in the profession. I only tried always to keep my oath to do my duty by my client and the Court; but I will confess that from the beginning to the end of my forty-four years at the Bar I loved the profession with all the ardor and intensity that that jealous mistress the law could ever exact, and was always trying to pay back the debt which, as Lord Bacon says, we all owe to the profession that honors us. In my youngest days I could not resist the attraction of those historic and dramatic scenes and incidents in the lives of the world's great advocates which everybody knows. Who would not have given a year's ransom, a year of his life, to have heard Somers, in the case of the seven Bishops, in a speech of only five minutes, breaking the rod of the oppressor, winning the great cause, and at one bound taking his place, the foremost place, among the orators and jurists of England; or Erskine, the greatest advocate anywhere and of all time, when he dared to brave even the mighty Mansfield's admonition that Lord Sandwich was not before the Court? 'I know he is not before the Court, and for that very reason I will bring him before the Court.' He entered the tribunal that morning an absolutely briefless barrister, and went out of the Court with thirty retainers in his pocket and followed by a crowd of solicitors engaged in a race of diligence to see who should reach his chambers first. Who would not have given a year of his life to have heard Webster pleading before the Supreme Court of the United States for the little college in the hills, where his intellectual life began, and throwing successfully round it the shield of that most beneficent of all constitutional provisions, that no State shall pass any law impairing the obligation of contracts?

"I started in life with a belief that our profession in its highest walks afforded the most noble employment in which any man could engage, and I am of the same opinion still. Until I became an Ambassador and entered the *terra incognita* of diplomacy I believed a man could be of greater service to his country and his race in the foremost ranks of the Bar than anywhere else; and I think so still. To be a priest, and possibly a high priest, in the temple of justice, to serve at her altar and aid in her administration, to maintain and defend those inalienable rights of life, liberty, and property upon which the safety of society depends, to succor the oppressed and to defend the innocent, to maintain Constitutional rights against all violations, whether by the Executive, by the Legislature, by the resistless power of the Press, or, worst of all, by the ruthless rapacity of an unbridled majority, to rescue the scapegoat and restore him to his proper place in the world—all this seemed to me to furnish a field worthy of any man's ambition.

"The relations between the Bench and the Bar of England and those of the United States are far more intimate and enduring than I think even you can suppose. I wish you could enter any of our Courts in America anywhere between Boston and San Francisco. You would find yourself on familiar ground and perfectly at home—the same law, the same questions, the same mode of dealing with them. You would find always and everywhere the same loyalty on the part of the Bar to the Bench and on the part of the Bench to the Bar. Some things you would miss. You would miss, I think, some of that dignity, some of that picturesqueness, at least, which prevails in your own tribunals. Our barristers appear in plain clothes in Court. The Judges— some of them—wear gowns, but never a wig. I think it would be a very rash man that would propose that bold experiment to our democracy. If the Lord Chancellor had wished that our primitive and unsophisticated people should adopt that relic of antiquity and grandeur, he should not have allowed his predecessors in his great office to tell such fearful stories about each other in respect to that article of apparel. We have read the story of Lord Campbell, as given in his diary annotated by his daughter, as to what became of Lord Erskine's full-bottomed wig when he ceased to be Lord Chancellor— that it was purchased and exported to the coast of Guinea in order that it might make an African warrior more formidable to his enemies on the field of battle. We have a great prejudice against anything that savors of overawing the Court, overawing the jury; and if any such terrors are to be connected with that instrument our pure democracy will never adopt it.

"Now, gentlemen, these ancient Inns of Court, and, above all, Westminster Hall, with its far more ancient and historic associations, which have been the nurseries and the home of the Common Law for ages, are very near and dear to my countrymen, and especially to my brethren of the Bar in America. There is nothing dearer to them. They flock to Westminster Hall immediately on their arrival here; and they wish—I wish for them—to acknowledge that infinite debt of gratitude that we owe, that the whole world owes, to the Bench and Bar of England, who have been working out with untiring patience through whole centuries the principles of the common law which underlie alike the liberties of England and of America. It was the Bench and Bar of England in the Inns of Court and in the Courts in Westminster Hall, and more lately in the Royal Courts of Justice, that established those fundamental, those absolute principles that lie at the foundation of our common liberties. What are they? That there is no such thing as absolute power, that King, lords, and commons, President, congress, and people, are alike subject to the law; that before its supreme majesty all men are equal; that no man can be punished or deprived of his dearest or any of his rights except by the edict of the law pronounced by independent tribunals, who are themselves subject to the law; that every man's house is his castle, and though the winds and the storms may enter it, the King and the President cannot; in other words, and the sublime words of the great Sidney, that ours, on both sides of the water, is 'a government of laws and not of men.' Indeed, we claim these venerable structures as in large part our own. I believe that William Rufus held his first Court in Westminster Hall at Whitsuntide, 1099. Well, when John Winthrop, of the Inner Temple, went over to America to found the State of Massachusetts in 1629, those Courts, that great Hall, these Inns of Court had been as much ours as yours for hundreds of years;

so that you see we claim a very great interest, a personal and immediate, and direct right in all that has contributed to the growth and development of the law in England. You had been in these very Inns of Court, studying and teaching the law, for at least a century before Columbus made his great discovery, which opened the dawn of a new creation and put an end to the dark ages. In Magna Charta and the Petition of Right our colonies carried with them the germs of what has grown to be American law and American liberty. At the beginning there were no lawyers in America. They had an idea of a Utopia which could be carried on successfully by the help of the clergy, without them. But we have made great progress since then, and our last census shows in America more than 100,000 lawyers. I can give the exact number—104,700, of whom 1,010 are women. Now, I am afraid the Lord Chancellor, who is so conservative, would hesitate a little at the admission to the Bar of 1,010 women; but I assure him that if he will go over there and hold a Court in which they may be heard, and if you, gentlemen of the Bar, will go over there, and take retainers with them or against them, you will be so fascinated that you will embrace every opportunity afterwards of repeating the experiment.

"Now, our Declaration of Independence, which the Lord Chancellor seems to have a little doubt about, our Constitution of the United States, which he has no doubt about, are only the natural sequence of Magna Charta and the Petition of Right. Our Revolution only followed suit after your Revolution of a hundred years before. We stood for the same principles, we fought the same fight, we gained the same victory. Our Jefferson and Franklin and their associates in declaring independence, our Washington and Hamilton and their associates in organizing the Government of the United States and setting its wheels in motion, were only doing for us what Somers and his great associates had done for you in 1688. Now you will not be surprised that in these fateful events, which meant so much for the welfare of the world, and in which the lawyers took a very great part, these Inns of Court contributed their *quota;* and that there were five of the signers of the Declaration of Independence who had been bred to the law in the Middle Temple, and three of the framers and signers of the Constitution of the United States who had been bred in the same Inn, and one of them was afterwards nominated by President Washington as Chief Justice of the United States. So you may well imagine with what delight I was informed a day or two ago that I had been made a Bencher of the great American Inn, the Middle Temple. I do not think any American lawyer has ever had such a success as that. They may have won more cases, they may have got more fees, but they never have been made Benchers of any of the Inns of Court. In fact, this incident, so touching to my heart, has almost changed my mind. I have a great mind not to go back to America, but to remain here and resume the practice of the law where those five signers of the Declaration and those three signers of the Constitution left off 125 years ago. I should like to cross swords and join conclusions with some of these distinguished Benchers of the four Inns of Court who grace these tables to-night. I do not know what my brethren of the Bar at home would say, but I think they would say, 'If you have achieved such a success as that make the most and the best of it at once.'

"Well, there is no difference between American law and liberty and English law and liberty. I should like to mention two responsibilities which have been thrown upon the Bench and the Bar in America in a greater degree than here. One is that on the Bar the whole burden of legislation from the beginning has been thrown. In a country like ours, where the executive and the legislative departments are kept asunder by impassable constitutional barriers, it is justly considered, and has always been considered, that, for making and amending and expanding the law, the men best qualified are those who are already skilled in the law, and so from the beginning the majority of lawyers in Congress and in each one of the Legislatures of our forty-five States has been uniformly maintained.

"And then upon the Bench there has been thrown another very great responsibility, growing out of our peculiar form of government, exercised by all the Judges and culminating in the unique power of the Supreme Court, to which the Lord Chancellor has referred, to set aside, to declare null and void, any Act of any Legislature or of Congress itself which comes in conflict with the provisions of the Constitution. I believe it has been exercised by that Court about twenty-four times in the case of Acts of Congress, and something like two hundred times in the case of State enactments, and it has been the balance wheel upon which our complicated and dual system of government has turned. There we have over every foot of the soil of our great territory and over every living being within it two distinct and independent Governments, each supreme and absolute in its own sphere and working in absolute harmony because of this harmonizing function of our great tribunal.

"I said a little while ago that perhaps you excelled us in your tribunals in dignity, in the control which the Court exercises, and ought to exercise, over the Bar. It is all illustrated by a single difference of phraseology. In America we say that the counsel try the case and that the Judge hears and decides; but, if I understand your common parlance here, the Judge tries the case and the counsel hear and obey. That is where we have got a good deal to learn from you. It is exactly as it should be. But do not believe for a moment that there is any abdication on the part of our tribunals, from the Atlantic to the Pacific, of the functions and authority that belong to the judicial office. If anybody should go over there and try it on he would find that he was very much mistaken indeed. There is an example set by that august tribunal to which I have referred. No Court could be looked up to with so much reverence; no Court, I think, receives the homage and deference, not only of the community, but of the Bar, in such a signal way as that; and the influence of its example is widely extended, and other tribunals follow as they may. Now, gentlemen, I must not occupy any more of your time. I cannot express the overflowing feelings that are welling up from my heart at this moment when I find myself thus honored by the most illustrious men of the Bench and Bar in England, and that such words of affection for me should have been spoken on every side. I can only thank you again and again. Let me tell you of what one of my predecessors said—I think many of you knew him—himself a very great lawyer, Mr. Phelps. Before I left America to come and take up my office here he called upon me and he said, 'Mr. Choate, the best nights that you will have in England are those that you will pass with the Bench and the Bar.' 'The lawyers,' said he, 'are the best company in England, and I advise you to lose no opportunity of cultivating their friendship. You certainly will have your reward.' My Lord Chancellor and gentlemen, I have faithfully followed his advice and I have my reward to-night. No one ever had one more rich and generous. I shall carry the memory of it with me as long as I live, and I think I shall be attracted by the love of my professional brethren to visit these shores as often as I can."

"American Embassy, London.
15 April 1905.

"DEAR JO:—
"I send you from today's *Times* a full account of the Dinner given me last night by the Bench and Bar of England, perhaps the greatest honor I have ever received. Also, the same paper's editorial upon it. * * *

FATHER."

To His Wife

"4, Carlton Gardens, S. W.
17 April 1905
"I got William to enclose to you Mr. White's letter, knowing that you would be glad to hear from a competent witness who had seen it that Canonica's bust of me has turned out well in marble and is an amazingly good likeness. * * *

"This evening I had a long call from Sir Wm. H. Russell and Lady Russell—the old war correspondent of *The Times*. He seems very old and infirm although only 85, the age of Lord Wemyss and John Bigelow about. With the aid of two sticks and a man to put on his hat and button his coat he just can crawl across the floor. But he talked still very interestingly about old times & men. * * *

J. H. C."

At the farewell banquet given by the Lord Mayor at the Mansion House on May 5, there was another very distinguished gathering, headed by the Archisbhop of Canterbury, the Prime Minister, the Duke of Wellington, and Lord Lansdowne. Mr. Choate's health was proposed by Mr. Balfour, who said of him among other things:

"Since he has represented here the country with which we are most closely joined together with ties of blood and friendship, he has seen us in those six years pass through many phases, he has seen us mourning and rejoicing, suffering disaster and victorious. I do not know what impression he may have formed of the men of his blood upon this side of the water, but we, at all events, have formed our estimate of him and have had opportunities of forming it. He came here as others among his predecessors have come, with the ability and the wish, not merely to be the representative of one great State at the Court of another great State, but as one who was ready to take his part in that portion of our public life—thank Heaven, no small portion—which is unconnected with party politics. In that portion he has played his part, not merely worthily, but with brilliancy and distinction. We thank him for all he has done in many parts of the country to show how close are the common interest and the common ties which bind together the two great halves, the great fragments, of the Anglo-Saxon race. He belongs to that profession

whose mission is that of the peacemaker—I do not allude to what perhaps he would regard as his profession
in life—namely, that of the advocate and brilliant lawyer. I do not know that the word peacemaker is one
that would be most appropriately applied to that particular profession, which has so many other distinctions,
but not, I think, that one; I allude to the profession to
which the six years I refer to have been devoted—that
profession of which the very trait is, or ought to be, that
of smoothing away the difficulties and misunderstand-
ings, all the small causes of friction which, left neglected,
may in the body international produce the most dis-
astrous effects, as they do in the human body lead from
small causes to great diseases. But he has been much
more than the diplomatist, and I hope he will carry away
from this country much more than merely diplomatic
ideas. He represents, and worthily represents, a country which is bound to us by ties far more permanent
than those of interest, far deeper than those which are
born of common objects which may unite, and do unite,
nations of different culture and race to attain some common end. I do not think the matter could be put more
happily than it has already been put tonight by Sir Henry
Campbell-Bannerman, when he reminded his audience
that however much the original Anglo-Saxon race, to
which the Ambassador belongs, might have been modi-
fied by successive immigration of men from all parts of
Europe, that nevertheless the civilization has always
been, is, and must always remain, of the type common
to the dwellers in Great Britain and her self-governing
colonies, and to the United States of America, common
law, common literature, an identity of view on matters
religious, a common method of dealing with all new prob-

JOSEPH HODGES CHOATE.
From a photograph by G. C. Beresford, taken in London in 1903.

lems, a common outlook upon the world—these are things which we did not acquire for ourselves, but which we inherited and which we cannot dissipate. I do not say that the Governments of the world, looking back upon the last century, have always shown themselves wise in dealing with their international relations, I do not know that the official leaders have always done their part in developing what should be a common sentiment, but a common sentiment survives in spite of what the official leaders may say or may do, and I am glad to think that as time goes on and as one decade follows another, so old bitternesses are lost in historic dust, old causes of difficulty diminish or vanish altogether, and then emerges slowly but surely that feeling of a common brotherhood which is the surest prospect, as I venture to think, of international peace and of international progress. You, Mr. Ambassador, have contributed in no small degree during your tenure of office to this happy and healthy growth of sentiment, and may it be the privilege of our children to look back over a long line of your successors to an ever-increasing development of sentiments, of emotions not to be formulated easily in words, not finding their true or best embodiment in formal treaties, but each stronger than any treaty or any instrument devised by man, binding together indissolubly through all time the two great liberty-loving sections of one race in the interests of peace, in the interests of progress, and in the interests of a culture which may learn, and will learn, from nations of every race and language, but which must through all time maintain a separate individuality of its own. In the name of this great and distinguished company I beg to drink your health, to wish you all happiness in the future, and to assure you that though you have been drawn to us from your original home to what I trust I may call your second home, you have left many friends behind you, many who look back with affection and respect to your career here; and this is no formal or official expression of our sentiments, but one which goes straight to the heart of every one of us."

Mr. Choate replied as follows:

"My Lord Mayor, Mr. Balfour, my Lords and Gentlemen,—Certainly this is the crowning hour of my life. At any rate, it is positively my last farewell benefit upon the English stage. To be received and fêted by the Lord Mayor of London, who holds the most unique and picturesque office in the kingdom, who bears upon his breast the badge which his predecessors in direct succession have worn for more than seven hundred years, the Chief Magistrate of this wonderful City, the centre of the world's commerce and the seat of the British Empire; to have my health proposed and my obituary pronounced by the Prime Minister, who bears upon his ample shoulders all of this great globe which the British drum-beat encircles, supported as he is too by such a number of possible Prime Ministers of the future, all ready and willing in the fulness of time, with consummate self-sacrifice, to relieve him of this great portion of his duty; to see present also so many members of that august but occult body, the Cabinet, who labor in secret, but to-night for my sake have come out into the full glare of the bright electric light; to be honored by the presence of the Foreign Secretary with whom I have had such delightful intercourse, Lord Lansdowne, from whom no secrets are hid; and then to find that so many of the famous men of England of all professions, parties, and opinions

have come here to-night as my friends—I could look
almost every man in this company in the face and claim
him almost as an old friend—I do not dare trust myself
to speak at all about it. I can only thank the Lord Mayor
for his magnificent hospitality, and you, all my fellow-
guests here, for your inspiring presence. I am sure that
you will indulge me, before I say the fatal word 'Farewell,' in a few words in response to what has been so
eloquently said to you by the Prime Minister. Altogether too much credit has been attributed to me for
the happy, the delightful relations that now exist between our two countries. If I have contributed in the
least degree to maintain and preserve what I found already existing, the last six years will be the proudest
of my life.

"But, gentlemen, the real credit of this happy state
of things belongs not to me or to any Ambassador, but
it belongs to the two men who are responsible, and have
now for some years been responsible, for the conduct of
our relations, no longer foreign relations—I mean Lord
Lansdowne and Mr. Hay. The diplomatist who should
try to pick a quarrel with Lord Lansdowne would be a
curious crank indeed; because he would have to pick it
all himself; Lord Lansdowne would be no party to it.
And, happily, so it is with Mr. Hay. Never were two
statesmen more happily matched, for the noble game
that is entrusted to them. When the noble marquis
escapes from the *ennui* of Downing street and the tire-
some visits of Ambassadors, to his beloved retreat in
the extreme southwest of Ireland, he finds himself in
the next parish to the United States, with nothing between us and him but fresh air and salt water. And I
think I have noticed that he catches and reflects the
breezy influences of that close neighborhood. At any

rate, I have always found that my best time for dealing with him on American questions was when he returned refreshed and invigorated from that near approach to the Western World. Always, the policy of the Foreign Office, so far as I have observed it, has been one of fairness, frankness, justice and simple truth, and I hope that he has found our State Department the same.

"No single man can claim exclusive credit in this happy result. You all know how constant, how unceasing your gracious Sovereigns and our high-minded Presidents have always been in the same direction. I wish to say here to-night that I have never been called into the presence of his Majesty the King or of his illustrious mother that I did not find them full of expressions of sympathy and friendship for the country that I represent. I well remember the last interview that it was my honor to have with your late illustrious Queen. It was immediately after a frightful conflagration had occurred in America, where many lives were lost. She knew all about it, she had studied all its details, and was as full of sympathy and sorrow as if the disaster had occurred in her own dominions. And as for his Majesty, the King, why, his instinct for peace is so unceasing, his genius for conciliation so perfect, as he has been showing to the world in this very last week, that it will be impossible hereafter as long as he lives for any of the other nations to quarrel with his own people.

"I have been asked a thousand times in the last three months, 'Why do you go?' 'Are you not sorry to leave England? Are you really glad to go home?' Well, in truth, my mind and heart are torn asunder by conflicting emotions. In the first place, on the one hand, I will tell you a great secret. I am really suffering from homesickness. Not that I love England less, but that I love America more, and what Englishman will quarrel with me for that? There is no place like home, be it ever so homely, or, as the old Welsh adage has it, 'east and west, hame is best.' My friends on this side of the water are multiplying every day in numbers and increasing in the ardor of their affections. I am sorry to say that the great host of my friends on the other side are as rapidly diminishing and dwindling away. 'Part of the host have crossed the flood, and part are crossing now,' and I have a great yearning to be with the waning number. And then, on the other hand, to make a clean breast of it in this family party, I am running a great risk, if I stay here much longer, of contracting a much more serious disease than homesickness—I mean Anglomania, which many of my countrymen regard as more dangerous and fatal than even cerebro-spinal meningitis. To a young man it is absolutely fatal, but to one who has well-nigh exhausted his future, the consequences are not quite so serious. It was wisely said by one of the Presidents of the United States that he would not trust a Minister or an Ambassador in England more than four years, because those English would be sure to spoil him, and you have done your best to spoil me—not as the children of Israel spoiled the Egyptians, by taking from them all they could lay their hands upon, but by heaping on my undeserving head all the honors and compliments and benefits that you can lay your hands upon. And so it is hard to say whether I am more glad or more sorry, or on which side of the water I shall leave or have the largest half of my heart. Mr. Balfour has spoken of the advantages that I have had in studying the English people, and he wondered what sort of impression I should carry home. Well, I shall carry, in the first place, the most delightful personal memories—memories of exalting and enduring friendships formed, of many happy homes visited, of boundless hospitality enjoyed.

"But I shall carry away something better than that. I shall carry away the highest appreciation of those great traits and qualities which make and mark your national life—the reign of law absolutely sovereign and supreme in all parts of the land; individual liberty carried to its highest perfection, perfected by law and subject to it; that splendid and burning patriotism which inspires your young men when their country calls to risk life and all they hold dear for her sake. I recall that lofty stanza of Emerson applied to our young men when they responded to a similar call:—

> " 'So nigh is grandeur to our dust,
>   So near is God to man;
>   When duty whispers low—"Thou must"
>   The youth replies, "I can!" ' "

I shall carry with me the recollection of that splendid instinct for public life which animates and pervades those classes here from whom public duty is expected, and the absolute purity of your public life which is the necessary result. There are so many other things that I witnessed here. I wish I could spend time in recalling more of them.

"One thing that has struck me from first to last here in England is the loyal devotion of all the people to the integrity of the Empire, conforming, as it does, exactly to our fundamental idea of American life that everything must be sacrificed, everything else must be sacrificed if necessary, to maintain the sovereignty and integrity

of the Republic. I came here believing that you were a
cold and phlegmatic people, not capable of those mercurial outbursts of emotion which sometimes carry away
my own countrymen and those of other nations. But
I have lived here long enough to change my mind and
to know you better. I have seen you, as Mr. Balfour
has said, in all the vicissitudes of peace and war, under
the strain of a tremendous anxiety and apprehensions
of disaster, and in all the exultation of victory. I found
that under your cool exterior, your serene repose of manner, the hall-mark of the English gentleman, which other
nations may well envy, you carry hearts as warm as ever
inspired the enthusiasm of any people. I was brought
up to believe that work, hard work, was the end and
aim of life—that that was what we were placed here for.
But on contemplating your best examples I have learnt
that work is only a means to a higher end, to a more rational life, to the development of our best traits and
powers for the benefit of those around us, and for getting
and giving as much happiness as the lot of humanity
admits.

"Six years ago I came among you an absolute stranger
upon a mission wholly new to me, but from the moment
I landed I was no longer a stranger. All doors were open
to me, endless hospitality was showered upon me, and
I learnt that I had really some useful work to do here.
In these days of cables and wireless communications,
when the Foreign Office of each nation is brought into
actual presence in the capital of every other, an American Ambassador who confined himself to official duties
would have very little work to do. I was instructed by
President McKinley to endeavor to promote the welfare
of both countries by cultivating the most friendly rela-

tions between them; and in obedience to that instruction I have gone to and fro among the English people, coming in close contact with them, studying them at near range for the purpose of discovering the distinctions and differences, if any, that exist between us. I have endeavored to make them better acquainted with my own country, its history, its institutions, its great names, for the purpose of showing them that really the difference between an Englishman and an American is only skin deep, that under different historical forms we pursue with equal success the same great objects of liberty, of justice, of the public welfare, and that our interests are so inextricably interwoven that we would not, if we could, and could not if we would, escape the necessity of an abiding and perpetual friendship. I have no doubt now, and can have no doubt, about the permanence of the peace which now exists between us. War between these two great nations would be an inexplicable impossibility. We have got along without it for the last ninety years; we shall get along perfectly well without it for the next nine hundred years—absolutely so.

"The gravest questions have arisen during this protracted period of peace, questions which other nations might have made causes for war, and we have settled them all without a single exception by resort to the peaceful mode of arbitration, to the principle of which Senate and people are all equally committed. You must not be troubled by hearing of any domestic discussion as to how this happy result of leaving every question that may arise between us to final settlement by arbitration can best be brought about. In the practical application of the principle we have never yet failed in the past, and we shall never fail in the future. Of course, as you all know, there are questions which are not capable of arbitration, but no such questions are possible, as it seems to me, to arise between your nation and ours. Our good understanding is now complete and perfect; our interests are more interwoven than ever before; our knowledge of each other is greater and closer than ever before, and every year and every day it is growing closer. It means very much that our multitudinous visits to your shores have been responded to in a single season by return visits of such men as the Archbishop of Canterbury, the Bishops of Hereford and Ripon, Lord Dartmouth, Mr. Bryce and Mr. Morley; and, if I am rightly informed—if I am not mistaken—in the event of any change of Government the retiring Ministers would follow their example, and they would find in the capacious bosom of our broad Republic the rest for which they were seeking, and the new life and inspiration which would bring them home for the next rebound. And I really believe that, if you follow the advice of his Grace and these returned statesmen, a visit to America might be made hereafter an absolute qualification in the education of a British statesman.

"Our literature on both sides is filled and saturated with our good understanding. The most recent eminent historian of Great Britain exhausts the power of eulogy in dwelling upon the merits of those arch Republicans, George Washington and Alexander Hamilton, and even of Benjamin Franklin, who snatched the lightning from the clouds and the sceptre from tyrants. And it has also been discovered what we always knew—that my predecessor, Mr. Adams, who stood here like a rock for the interests of his country in days most perilous to our peace, has really proved to be in the end the best friend of both countries, as Mr. Herbert Paul, in his last volume, for which I thank him, declares him to have been. He says that at Geneva he saved the arbitration from collapse and the two nations from falling apart, and he boldly suggests that he is entitled to have a monument at Westminster as well as at Washington. I thank him for that. Then, on the other side you have heard a good deal, and I have heard a good deal, of the rancor and bitterness that had grown into the American school-books, especially the school histories, bringing down to present times the hard feelings of our former conflicts; but Mr. Goldwin Smith, whose name you will all respect as an historian, in his very recent address before the American Historical Association, declared that, having heard a great deal about this vice in the school histories in use in America, he made a collection of our school-books of the present day and examined them, and he expresses the positive belief that there is very little in them which could give offense to any reasonable Englishman.

"Then you heard what my successor, Mr. Whitelaw Reid, who will soon be with you, said recently in New York. Let me read it to you, for it is a very good introduction of him to this audience. He said that international good will 'after all is no longer a subject of much concern. We do not continue to worry over an object of national or international desire when it has already been attained. We are content to enjoy it.' The good will between your country and this already exists. Never at any stage of our history has it been so generally taken as a matter of course on both sides of the Atlantic. And let me say here that you will find my successor—you will recognize him as a life-long advocate of friendly relations between England and our own country. He will

come among you as an old friend. You have received
him before on several most distinguished and brilliant
missions. His experience and diplomacy, his knowledge
of affairs, his versatility are well known, and I am sure
that you will give him a good old-fashioned, hearty,
British welcome.

"Now, serene and secure as our peace is, I am not
so foolish as to indulge the hope that it will never be
disturbed. Untoward events will happen, unfortunate
things will be said, something or other will happen that
will for the moment disturb the serenity of our peaceful
relations. And how are these threats of disaster to be
avoided? Standing here by the side of your predecessor,
eight years ago, Lord Salisbury said that there was nothing in the traditions of Government, nothing in the ten-
dencies of official life, which was any danger, if any existed,
to good relations. 'Take care,' he said, 'of the unofficial
people, and I will see that the official people never make
any war;' and he went on to speak of that public opinion
which dominated Governments then, and which has since
grown to dominate them still more. If any such unhappy occurrences do arise, we are to be tided over them
by public opinion and by that great exponent of public
opinion and guide of the public conscience—a high-minded
and patriotic Press on both sides of the Atlantic. If the
Press does its best to minimize such untoward events
and to keep the people cool till sober second thoughts
come we shall all be glad; but if they stir up the embers
and fan the flames and pile on the fuel, they may get up
a conflagration which will tax all the international powers
of the fire brigade commanded by Lord Lansdowne and
Mr. Hay to extinguish.

"And now why waste a night in words when I only

came here to say a single word? I bid you, and through you the people of England, farewell with infinite regret, carrying with me the most precious memories and the best opinions and a mind enlarged and improved by my six years here, having learned to take a broader and a happier view of our relations and the possibilities of our two peoples than I had before; and I end as I began, by thanking the Lord Mayor for his boundless hospitality and for giving us this splendid occasion for the interchange of friendly sentiments between two great and friendly peoples."

He writes to Secretary Hay on May 23:

"I have today presented my letter of recall, and immediately afterwards lunched with the King. I cannot tell you how light-hearted I feel at having gotten rid of all responsibility, and Carter already begins to stoop under the weight of it. For the first time in six years and four months, I am no longer tongue-tied, but can say what I please about anything and anybody."

On the same day befell the dedication of the Harvard memorial window at St. Saviour's Church (Southwark Cathedral). What Mr. Choate said on that occasion tells the story of the window and records his own feeling about it; to wit:

"My Lord Bishop, I may be permitted to state in a few words my object and purpose in presenting the window to the Cathedral. I desired to signalize my long residence in London by an appropriate gift which should be in itself emblematical of the deepseated and abiding relations of friendship which happily unite our two countries. As a loyal son of Harvard, I thought that nothing

could be more fitting than a permanent memorial here
of the principal founder of Harvard University. John
Harvard was born in this ancient borough, close by the
end of London Bridge, and baptized in this venerable
church in 1607, almost three centuries ago. Educated
at Emmanuel College in Cambridge, where he spent
eight years, during at least four of which Milton was at
Christ's, he and Milton received substantially the same
nurture and discipline, and must often have been thrown
together. At any rate, he imbibed something of the
same spirit as Milton, for his contemporaries speak of
him as a scholar and pious in his life. Seeking larger freedom of thought than could be found in the London of
that day, he made his way to Massachusetts, and there,
within two years of his arrival, he died, prematurely, as
it then seemed, but in the fulness and perfection of time,
as is now manifest; for, finding the infant colony
struggling without means to establish a college in the
wilderness, in the first decade of its settlement, he be-
queathed to its foundation his library and half of his
considerable fortune, and, what was better still, his name,
which has now become so illustrious. The colonial record
is quaint and touching:—'After God had carried us safe
to New England and we had builded our homes, provided necessaries for our livelihood, reared convenient
places for God's worship, and settled the civic government, one of the next things we longed for and looked
after was to advance learning and perpetuate it to posterity, dreading to leave an illiterate ministry to our
churches when our present ministers shall lie in the dust.
And as we were thinking and consulting how to effect
this great work, it pleased God to stir up the heart of
one Mr. Harvard (a godly gentleman and lover of learn-

ing then living among us) to give the one-half of his estate
(it being in all about £1,700) towards the erecting of a
college, and all his library. After him another gave £300,
others after them cast in more, and the public hand of
the State added the rest. The college was by public
consent appointed to be at Cambridge, a place very pleasant and accommodate, and is called according to the
name of its first founder, Harvard College.' It assumed
in its arms, as you will see in the window, a double motto
—*Veritas*, truth, a word broad enough to embrace all
knowledge, human and divine; and, what meant the
same thing, *Christo et Ecclesiæ*, to Christ and his Church,
that the supply of godly ministers might never fail.

"And now, after the lapse of three centuries, the little
college in the pathless wilderness has become a great
and splendid University, strong in prestige and renown,
rich in endowments, and richer still in the pious loyalty
of its sons, who supply all its wants upon demand with
liberal hand. It is not unworthy to be compared with
Oxford and Cambridge, those ancient nurseries of learning from which it drew its first life. And the name of
John Harvard shares the fame which mankind accords
to the founders of States. From the beginning until
now it has occupied the foremost place in America as a
radiating source of light and leading. In all the great
movements of progress by which the United States have
advanced from that little handful of storm-swept immigrants on the Atlantic coast to the Imperial Republic
of to-day, Harvard University and its sons have had
their full share; and without disparagement to her
younger sisters, who are many and great, it may truly
be said that, as she was first in time, she has always been
first in position and influence; and especially in the mat-

ter of education, which is and always has been the chief industry of America, she has always led and still leads the way. So considerable have been the contributions of her sons to the public and social and intellectual life of the nation that, if all other books and papers were destroyed, its history could be fairly reproduced from the Harvard University Catalogue, and from what is known of the lives of the *alumni* there registered. And if you ask if she is still true to her ancient watchwords *Veritas* and *Christo et Ecclesiæ*, I can answer that, in our own time, in a single quarter of a century, she has sent forth Phillips Brooks to be a pillar of Christ and the Church, and Theodore Roosevelt to be a champion of the truth, and thousands more who in humble spheres follow in their footsteps and share their faith and their hope.

"Thus the name of John Harvard, unknown and of little account when he left England, has been a benediction to the new world, and his timely and generous act has borne fruit a millionfold. Coming back to the very beginning of things, we are here to-day to lay a wreath upon his shrine. I hope that this memorial, which the Dean and Chapter have kindly consented to accept from my hands, will long remain for Americans to come and see the very spot where one of their proudest institutions had its origin, and to remind all Englishmen who visit it how inseparable we are in history and destiny. I hope, also, that it may tend to keep alive the kindred spirit between the Universities of the two countries; for Harvard is just as surely the offspring of Cambridge and Oxford, and the own daughter of Emmanuel, as old England is the mother of New England. In the earlier period of the colony we had one hundred teachers from Oxford and Cambridge, and of these seventy were from Cambridge, and of these again twenty were from Emmanuel. So long as ideas rule the world let all the Universities of both countries stand together for truth, and with one voice let them say to the youth of both lands, 'Take fast hold of instruction. Let her not go, for she is thy life.' I am under deep obligations to the Dean and Chapter for consenting to receive and cherish this gift, and to Mr. LaFarge, the distinguished artist, for the noble manner in which he has designed and executed it."

On May 29 Mr. and Mrs. Choate called at Buckingham Palace and said good-by to the King and Queen, and on the next day they sailed for home.

CHAPTER IX

PRIVATE CITIZEN AND PUBLIC SERVANT

WELCOMED HOME BY THE PILGRIMS AND BY THE UNION LEAGUE CLUB
—LAW PRACTICE—POLITICS—DINNERS—PUBLIC SERVICE—THE
SECOND HAGUE PEACE CONFERENCE—LETTERS FROM HOLLAND—
HIS OWN ACCOUNT OF THE CONFERENCE'S ACCOMPLISHMENTS—MR.
SCOTT'S ESTIMATE OF MR. CHOATE'S PART IN IT—OTHER COMMENTS
—MR. CHOATE'S OPINION OF "ALLIANCES" IN 1916—SUPPORTS
TAFT FOR THE PRESIDENCY—FAMILY CORRESPONDENCE—ADDRESSES
ON CHARLES F. McKIM, FLORENCE NIGHTINGALE, AND MARK TWAIN
—LINCOLN CENTENARY—DINNERS AND SPEECHES—LORD KITCH-
ENER'S VISIT—PUBLISHES ENGLISH ADDRESSES—IN COURT—MR.
SOUTHMAYD'S DEATH—EIGHTIETH BIRTHDAY—GOLDEN WEDDING—
BACKING PRESIDENT WILSON—AN OCTOGENARIAN'S DAY

A large, distinguished, and lively company, including
several Ambassadors, Lord Roberts, Mr. Bryce, Lady
Lansdowne, and a score or more of others, saw Mr. Choate
and his family off from Euston Station on May 30, 1905.
He got to New York on the 8th of June and was welcomed on the 9th at a great dinner of the Pilgrims of the
United States at the Waldorf-Astoria, with Bishop Potter
in the chair. The Pilgrims should not be confused with
the New England Society. The Pilgrims were of much
more recent origin, with branches in New York and in
London, and apparently with the general purpose to
promote amity between the United States and Great
Britain. It was an amusing dinner of course, with Bishop
Potter and Mr. Choate both in excellent form. The
Bishop told how when Mr. Choate was riding with a
young woman in the Strand she asked him if he was not

Bishop Potter. That, he said, was the turning-point of Mr. Choate's life. Mr. Choate said he was once told he looked like Bishop Potter, and when he blushed, his informant said: "Oh, yes, sir; the likeness is wonderful, only the Bishop never looked half so clerical."

The more substantial part of Mr. Choate's address, not including this chaffing, is in the volume of his "American Addresses." He gave some account of his stewardship, speaking of the two Presidents that he had served under and of the two Monarchs, Queen Victoria and King Edward, with whom his office had brought him into relation. He also spoke of the "two great and difficult questions which threatened to disturb, and did in fact disturb, the perfect harmony which ought always to prevail," and which had been forever disposed of and set at rest. Those were the matters of the Alaska Boundary and the Hay-Pauncefote Treaty. He spoke also of the need there was of providing a house for the American Ambassador in London, and forthwith it was proposed at the dinner to raise a fund for that purpose and subscriptions were offered; but nothing came of that, and of course the obstacle to providing permanent residences for our Ambassadors is not the cost, nor any scarcity of funds, but the difficulty of persuading Congress that it is a desirable thing to do.

Four nights later there was a dinner for him at the Union League Club, where there was much pleasant discourse, especially from Mr. Root.

Mr. Choate never retired from the practice of law. He took law cases after his return from England and continued to take them, but he never again spent himself in professional work as he had done before he became Ambassador. In a letter written about a month before he left England, in reply to a request that he should accept a retainer in an important case, he wrote:

"After fifty years of hard work I feel that I am entitled to a holiday and to lighter work hereafter. So I have long ago resolved not to plunge into the rough and tumble of the profession as I was always ready to do. At the same time I shall hardly be content to do nothing, and an occasional argument and acting as counsel out of Court would suit me better than to be idle.

"I haven't seen much about Mr. ——'s controversy, but I imagine it will involve great detail, and heaps of figures which were always my particular aversion, and are more so now than ever."

The day following his letter he cabled that he would accept a retainer when he got home.

So he did in a measure go back to professional work, and one saw him down-town and coming for his luncheon to the Down Town Club as in times past, but his most important calling in these later years of his life was to be a public institution, responsive constantly to appeals for speech or service for causes that seemed to him to deserve his help. When he got home from England he was seventy-four years old. As has appeared, he went on going to dinners and making discourse, which never ceased to be acceptable and never at all diminished in charm. In this year that he got home William Travers Jerome ran on an independent ticket for re-election as District Attorney because the regular party nominations for that office were not satisfactory. Mr. Choate pitched in ardently to help on Jerome's campaign.

He spent the summer in Stockbridge, and in October

one finds him coming to town again. He was the guest, along with General Horace Porter, of the Chamber of Commerce at luncheon on October 17. On October 21 he was the guest of honor at the dinner given by the Lotos Club. Writing to his daughter the next morning he says:

"Behold me in New York the morning after the Lotos dinner, up at sunrise and ready to take the 9.31 train on the Harlem which reaches State Line at 2, where I hope to be met by the motor.

"I enclose a very scattering account of the dinner from the morning *Sun*. There was a great deal of fun and good feeling, and if they wouldn't 'lay it on so thick' it would have been quite as enjoyable to me as it evidently was to them. But moderate praise and eulogy seems to be impossible here. I warned them against the killing pace at which everybody in New York is moving, and held up the example of the English courts and lawyers in working never more than eight weeks on a stretch and then having a vacation of ten days or a fortnight besides their ten weeks in the summer."

In that same speech, as reported in *The Sun*, he spoke of Mr. Hay, who had died, as one of the men whose names would stand imperishably in the annals of the American people, in the history of diplomacy, and in the history of the world. He also said: "While I was in England I grew vain and proud of my country, when all the people surrounding me were growing prouder every day of the people who were descended from the same stock with them. The longer I stayed away the prouder I became of the land that gave me birth, and now that I have returned and studied the things I have seen, I believe it occupies the most promising position in the world."

On November 1, at Carnegie, Hall he made a speech for Jerome that is still delightful reading. He was one of those who spoke at the meeting on November 13 in the United Charities Building in memory of Mrs. Josephine Shaw Lowell. A fragment of what he said in speaking of her, as a newspaper reported it, is worth transcribing:

"You know our own dead often exercise a very much more potent influence over us than any of our living associates. Time cannot loosen their hold on heart and mind. In one sense they never come back. In another and actual sense they are always coming back, especially in our hours of peril. We gain more support from them than from any living associate.

"Just as we hear distinctly the voice of a friend in Boston or Chicago over the telephone, and can tell whether it is a joyful or a sorrowful voice, so through the long distance telephone of time we hear voices with equal distinctness. In dreams—if they be dreams—we see the forms of our own dead. In danger we feel the support of their loving hands."

He writes from Stockbridge to Mrs. Choate, November 29:

"Yesterday I spent a good deal of time in reading over Effie's letters to Nellie Joy—or part of them, for they cover a great many years. In truth they give a very detailed narrative of our whole happy family life in those years, and they must be carefully gone over, and arranged in order of date. She did lead a very happy life until that last illness set in. There is a lovely lock of her hair cut off in 1879. I think it must have been when she had the scarlet-fever—which must be somehow set and preserved. The letters show her fine character and excellent intelligence and her devotion to us all. She tells many stories about Jo which I had quite forgotten and which are very funny—his devotion to Santa Claus at Christmas time, that Jo really believes in Santa Claus and thinks he lives down the register. So he called down there what he wanted, and they, she and Mabel, replied from below. So he thought his calls were answered by Santa Claus himself."

There was a dinner of the Chamber of Commerce on November 1, and he and General Horace Porter were speakers at that, and again they both appeared at the St. Andrew's dinner on the 2d of December.

On December 22 he came once again to the dinner of the New England Society and told his recollections of what it was in 1855, when he first joined it. That discourse, also included in his published addresses, contains the story of the presence of Doctor Holmes and old John Pierpont at that dinner, and of how Doctor Holmes seemed to Doctor Pierpont not upstanding enough for the cause of liberty, and how the old antislavery minister, John Pierpont Morgan's grandfather, set him right.

Throughout the winter, occasions kept calling to him, and he responded to some of them. He talked to the Radcliffe alumnæ on January 13; he spoke for Tuskegee on January 22. He went to Ottawa as the guest of the Canadian Club on the 1st of February, and made a speech there.

On March 13 he delivered an address, included in his published addresses, before the Bar Association of the City of New York about James C. Carter, who had died about a year before. On March 29 he appeared at a meeting in behalf of the blind; and so on, and so on.

In due time he got back to Stockbridge and writes to his daughter from there:

" * * * I have just been motoring to New Marlboro —an excellent ride, with M—— —— *and Togo,* who did himself great credit and behaved very well. M—— says that —— and —— did not make any great progress. Although every facility was given them they did not exhibit any very serious symptoms. 'But M——,' said I, 'do you know the symptoms?' 'Oh, yes,' said she, 'I think I do.' 'Well,' said I, 'but I fear you only know them *objectively,* not *subjectively.*' 'Ah,' she replied, 'I have felt them myself to some extent.' And so, and so, and so, we whiled away three hours on the road to New Marlboro and back. * * * "

Perhaps it was at Stockbridge, perhaps before he got there, that he did what was for him an unusual thing in writing an introduction to the posthumous novel, "The Dream and the Business," of Mrs. Craigie, whom he had known well in England and who had died since he left there.

In October, 1906, he was in New York again, and writes on the 4th of that month from the Fifth Avenue Hotel to Mrs. Choate:

" * * * I had a delightful present today from Mrs. Jim Sterling. In looking over her husband's papers she found the letter which you wrote to him on the 10*th of July,* 1861. You can imagine what it was all about. It was a long and very dear letter, and perhaps if you are good I shall let you see it on my return."

On October 16 he writes to her:

" * * * Today after filling my engagement at the
dentist's I have spent mostly at the Club, mooning what
I should say at the Cooper Institute meeting tonight
and am ready for them only somehow I don't feel quite
so enthusiastic about such things as I once did. * * * "

Not quite so enthusiastic at seventy-five, but still
very much in the ring. The political issue that autumn
concerned judges and whether a Murphy-Hearst ticket
should be elected. That was doubtless the occasion of
the Cooper Institute meeting, as it certainly was of a
big meeting at Carnegie Hall on October 24, where Mr.
Choate was the leading speaker.

He appeared for the American Sugar Company on
November 20 in a trial about rebates. He presided and
made an introductory address (included in his published
addresses) at the Carl Schurz memorial meeting on
November 21, and helped out the Natural History Museum on December 20 at a ceremony of acceptance of
busts of eminent citizens that had been given to it. One
finds him on January 16, 1907, delivering an address (included in his published addresses) before the New York
State Bar Association at Albany on the English Bar,
and on February 3 making an address on Lincoln under
the auspices of the Board of Education at the Cooper
Union, telling his audience how it was in that same place
that he first heard Lincoln speak.

A little later at a Chamber of Commerce meeting he
pleaded to safeguard the Adirondack forests, and pleaded
again on April 3 in court to defend the railroads against
the Public Utilities Bill.

PRIVATE CITIZEN AND PUBLIC SERVANT 317

Then he goes to Europe as first delegate to the Second Hague Peace Conference, and there are letters again.

To His Son

"On Board R. M. S. *Adriatic*
30 May 1907.

"DEAR JO:—

"After a very fine voyage we have just left Cherbourg for Southampton and expect to be in London by eight o'clock all much improved by the voyage and very well. So far as I can gather from the London papers which came aboard this morning, the programme for the Hague Conference is not settled yet and Sir Edward Grey said in the House of Commons yesterday that 'as at present advised' the Conference would open on the 15th of June. Our Government had not prepared its instructions when I left but perhaps that was because the Secretary of State (Mr. Root) had spent the week at New Haven delivering law lectures. I still think that the immunity of private property at sea will be the one important question. Whether England is prepared to yield the position she has held so obstinately and come in to our view, that *all* private property at sea except contraband and violating blockade ought to be exempt from capture and destruction, I hope to learn when we get to London. It seems so manifestly for her interest, that I hope she will. * * * "

To the Same

"Delegation of the United States of America to the Second Peace Conference at The Hague, 2 August 1907.

" * * * Our Conference is beginning to move a little more rapidly, but I have no idea that we shall be able to get away from here before Sept. 1st. We have a strong hope of getting through our plan for a permanent and continuous Court of Arbitration at The Hague, for which I made the opening address yesterday, and if we do that I shall feel that the work of this Conference will compare well with that of the First, and that we shall by no means have come here in vain. I hope to get a printed copy of my address tomorrow and to send it to you. We have necessarily had a great deal of junketing but I think it is about all over now. Last week on the invitation of the Belgian Government we made a journey to Bruges—one of the most picturesque and mediæval of the cities hereabouts, and were treated to the show of the Tournament of the Golden Fleece, an excellent reproduction of the days of Chivalry, and were received at a State luncheon in a grand old Stadt House. As the excursion lasted from 7 in the morning till midnight, you can judge that we are all very well. Tonight our Delegation gives the last of its dinners to our fellow delegates, four dinners of 50–80–60 & 90 guests respectively —all of which have been quite successful. Then we are to have two private dinners of 24 each to return the civilities we have received from people here. * * * ”

(August 4.) “ * * * The Queen Mother's birthday was celebrated day before yesterday, chiefly with noise and Chinese lanterns. The lady in whose honor it was done, stayed out of town to avoid the uproar, but the people here are very easily amused, as ordinary entertainments which are found in other places, seem not to exist here. * * * ”

(August 29.) “ * * * We are now in the critical days of the Conference which will determine what mea-

sures of importance are to go through. I think we shall
save the agreement that force shall not be resorted to
for the collection of contractual debts until an arbitration has been had or refused—the International Prize
Court of Appeal, and some general arbitration agreement however weak, and some agreement as to the necessity of a Permanent Court of Arbitration and as to its
Constitution, even though it be found impossible to agree
upon a mode of distributing the Judges which may have
to be left to the Nations or to another Conference. On
the whole, we are doing pretty well. * * * "

To His Wife

"I have been so busy from the moment you left, as
hardly to know that you were gone. We seem now really
to be trying to make up for the time lost last week, and
everything is humming. Yesterday we got through our
Court project, in the shape of a recommendation to the
Powers to adopt the project which we have been elaborat-
ing with so much care, and to establish the Court upon
it when they have arranged a plan for the selection of
Judges. It was by no means all that we wanted—but
Germany & Great Britain turned against us on our plan
of electing Judges by a vote of the nations, being afraid
that it would result in their being left. But it will do—
and is a tremendous advance on the situation in the last
Conference, when the idea of such a Court was scouted
as an impossibility.

"Today, in the forenoon, the forty-five delegates came
to a *unanimous* vote in favor of one resolution about
the next Conference, and that we regard as quite an
achievement—and this afternoon we spent three hours

on the dreary subject of submarine mines without making much progress. * * * "

To the Same

(Sunday evening.) " * * * Yesterday I gave up our rooms engaged on the *Kronprinzessin Cecilie* and am writing to the White Star and the North German Lloyd for later dates. What a bore that we cannot find out when this blessed Conference will end! I think now it may be about October 10th. But there are quite a number of difficult questions yet to be settled or smothered. * * *

"Speaking of hats. I saw an excellent selection in a shop window in Harlem which might suit you well and save you much trouble.

"I think you would have enjoyed the Queen's party, as everybody was there you know. The Prince has little sense of humor. When I told him that I had said to Her Majesty that if we stayed here much longer I should apply to become a Dutch subject, he seemed to think a minute and then said, 'What would you want to do that for?'—which I thought was good."

To the Same

(Tuesday evening.) "This is the 24th of September and this morning I awoke at quarter past six, and was wide awake at once, for just at that minute forty three years ago we heard that first little cry which made such a revolution in our lives, and was the beginning of so much joy & so much sorrow. Perhaps you didn't hear it just then. Ah! If he had lived what a difference it would have made—and how much we should have leaned upon him as we grow older—but his fine life & character will be a joy forever."

To the Same

(Sunday evening.) "This is my last hour at The Hague and I feel as if another long chapter in my life had closed. Nothing remains of the American Delegation except Mr. Hale and Col. Blanchard who go to Paris tomorrow. * * *

"Yesterday and today I have been out all the time, walking yesterday morning on the beach and the promenade at Scheveningen, and going out as far as the Monument which I had never visited before. * * * In the afternoon I explored Delft on foot, going there by train —one gets but little idea of the quaintness and picturesqueness of the old place by simply driving through in a motor, but I walked through the oldest part of the town and found old gateways dating in 1600—a wonderful old City gate with turrets which must have been built before that, arches and bridges which must have antedated William the Silent, and canals whose ancient *smell* testified that they were older still. On the whole it was all well worth an afternoon's excursion. In the afternoon the entire remnant dined at the Hills'* whose indefatigable kindness holds out to the end.

"Today I persuaded Mr. Hale to accompany me to Delfts-Haven to see the place from which the Pilgrim Fathers coming down from Leyden, embarked on the *Speedwell* to join the *Mayflower* at Southampton. * * *

"I see that the London papers, who have always been in an illhumor about the Conference, are doing their

* David Jayne Hill, American Minister at The Hague.

best to decry its work, but by & by when they have had time to compare the situation as we left it with the situation as it was left by the First Conference, they will do us better justice. * * * "

To His Daughter

"The Hague, 19 Oct. 1907.

"We are certainly going home at last, to my infinite relief. Today the Conference adjourned sine die—after a meeting at which the dullest possible speeches were delivered by Mr. Loo, Nelidoff, Beaufort, VonTets, Isudzuki, Triana and Kahn, and every one was so pleased when it was all over. This morning we signed the Acte Final as it is called, and I took a walk in the woods. Then I have our passages home—yours, Mama's and mine, Margaret's, Osborn's and Sydney's, and discharged all my indebtedness to the servants, by giving our sandy haired waiter £20, who immediately handed it to the headwaiter, and both immediately deluged me with thanks. I told the chambermaid that Mama's gift was only part of what she was to have, and am to hand her ten florins more before I go, or thereabouts. Then Mr. Malloy's funds take care of all the staff of the head porter and all that business is out of the way.

"But my greatest achievement was yesterday getting Harper and the motor off. It goes by the *Minnehaha* on Saturday, and he by the *Frederick the Great* on Sunday and will get to N. Y. two days in advance. They gave him a first class ticket for a 2d. class fare, $60., and he went off apparently very happy. The greatest difficulty was in getting it from here to London, and he couldn't possibly have done it but for the help of the Doctor with the impossible name at the Company's office here, and of Mr. Feterich, the U. S. Despatch agent in

London. It went from Rotterdam to London by the Batavia line. Its case was waiting for it at the *Minnehaha* and Mr. Feterich sent his expert down from London to help Harper get it off, the same man who had helped him land it in May. In Rotterdam the Dutch people at the steamer made every possible trouble. They never heard of such a thing as shipping a motor the same day it arrived in Rotterdam. It must wait and become absolutely cool, etc., etc., etc., etc. The Doctor kept the wires hot all day, and at last just 15 minutes before the boat sailed, he got a despatch saying that it was safely on board. It had to be laden on the *Minnehaha* today; hence the need of despatch. As I have got no telegram from them to the contrary, I know it is all right.

"Almost all the European Delegates are off tonight. The more distant ones, including ourselves, are to sign the various conventions tomorrow, and I have my ticket for stateroom on the Flushing boat Sunday night. Today I sent farewell flowers to Madames de Grovestine, de Schloezer and Boreel, and have charming notes from them.

"Hale has been very good to me. He took me to dinner at the Club last night and dines with me tonight. The Club has not dissolved in tears after all. It sat up nearly all night last night.

Ever your loving   PAPA."

To the Same

"The Berkeley Hotel,
Piccadilly, W. Oct. 20. 1907.

"I arrived here
on the Flushi-

night we passed by the Hook of Holland—an excellent boat with a sound sleep all the way. * * *

"I lunched at Dorchester House and then went to the Potter-Cary wedding with the Carters, and to a reception at Minnie Davenport's house in Montpelier Square, met Nellie Joy, and several other old friends.

"Tonight I have had —— and her husband to dinner. He seems to be a masterful man and most agreeable and I think she has found her match. She never knew him until two months ago, and was married after an engagement of six weeks. She seems very happy, and I should think everything promised well. It is his second marriage—his first wife of whom he spoke freely was a St. Louis woman.

"I have sent Osborn off to see his mother and sisters who live in Bedfordshire, and he is to return on Wednesday. He seemed much delighted when I proposed it to him.

"On Wednesday I am to dine with my brother Benchers of the Middle Temple, their annual dinner to the Benchers of the *Inner* Temple.

"I found another great diplomat on the boat, Charley Richardson, Secretary at Copenhagen. He goes with us on the *Cecilie* to America on leave. I asked him if he was married. He said—No, but he hoped to be very soon. 'What,' said I, 'are you engaged then?' But he said no—so the field is open. London is empty and very delightful, and I wish you were here. * * * "

There is a good deal more to tell about The Hague Conference in 1907 than is told in Mr. Choate's letters. As said, he was the head of the American Delegation, which included General Horace Porter, David

Jayne Hill, Minister at The Hague, Rear-Admiral Sperry, General George B. Davis, William I. Buchanan, James Brown Scott, an accomplished expert on international law, U. M. Rose, and Congressman Richard Bartholdt. As for what was accomplished, let Mr. Choate himself tell about it. He did so in two lectures delivered at Princeton University in 1912, which were published with notes and an introduction by Mr. James Brown Scott, but closer to the event was the story as he told it in an address on Washington's Birthday, 1908 (less than six months after he got home), on University Day at the University of Pennsylvania, when he received an LL.D. and was the chief speaker of the day at the Academy of Music in Philadelphia. In his address he talked about the Conference and a good deal about President Roosevelt, who had sent him there. Paying respect to the day and the occasion, he considered these topics from what he believed would have been Washington's point of view, taking note of the growth and increase in power of the United States to a point where, he said, "if this country is preserved in tranquillity for twenty years longer, it may bid defiance in a just cause to any power whatever." He spoke of the Panama Canal, which he was sure would "appeal most strongly to the aspirations of Washington's great American heart," and of the cruise of our fleet around the world which Roosevelt had ordered, and which also, the speaker thought, would have gratified Washington. He went on about The Hague Conferences as follows:

"Let us recur to our original text from the Farewell Address: 'Cultivate peace and harmony with all nations.'

"It was on that errand that we were sent to The Hague with instructions t⌐

the hand of our great founder. Though these have never yet been made public, I may be pardoned on this occasion for quoting a single paragraph, to show in what a pacific spirit our President through his eminent Secretary of State (Mr. Root), can instruct his emissaries sent on peaceful missions.

" 'In the discussions upon every question it is important to remember that the object of the conference is agreement and not compulsion. It is important also that the agreements reached shall be genuine and not reluctant. Otherwise they will inevitably fail to receive approval when submitted for the ratification of the powers represented. Comparison of views and frank and considerate explanation and discussion may frequently resolve doubts, obviate difficulties and lead to real agreement upon matters which at the outset have appeared insurmountable. It is not wise, however, to carry this process to the point of irritation. After reasonable discussion, if no agreement is reached, it is better to lay the subject aside, or refer it to some future conference, in the hope that intermediate consideration may dispose of the objection.

" 'Again, each conference will inevitably make further progress, and by successive steps results may be accomplished which have formerly appeared impossible. You should keep always in mind the promotion of this continuous process through which the progressive development of international justice and peace may be carried on and you should regard the work of the second conference, not merely with reference to the definite results to be reached in that conference, but also with reference to the foundations which may be laid for further results in future conferences.'

"It was in this spirit that we went and labored—and with surprising results in the way of progress.

"I am aware that widespread misapprehensions have existed as to the work of the conference, and I gladly avail myself of this opportunity to correct some of these, and to give you a hasty glimpse at least of some of the valuable results achieved.

"Because we did not do everything that was expected, it was asserted that we did nothing. Because in many things we did not reach final and definite results, but left them, as we were instructed to leave them, for future conferences or intermediate diplomacy to carry on, the world was told that there were no results.

"It seems to have been forgotten that we were not a Congress or a Parliament, entitled and bound to force through measures for which a majority might be obtained, but strictly a conference, met as Franklin said in the Federal Convention—not to contend, but to consult, in a friendly and mutually yielding spirit, on questions of general concern to all, but on which interests and opinions might radically differ, and which could only reach conclusions with substantial unanimity.

"It is only by comparing the situation in which each important question considered had been left by the first conference with the position in which it was placed by the action of the second, that any just idea can be formed of the advance or progress made in each, and in this view I may be pardoned for stating, in respect to four or five of the measures which we were instructed to advocate, their relative situations before and after the conference.

"First, there was that great American idea of making commerce free from the perils of spoliation by war—the immunity of ene___ merchant ships in case of war. For more than a hundred years the United States had advocated this, ever since Franklin in the negotiation of our Treaty of Peace with Great Britain in 1783, had tried unsuccessfully to have it incorporated as a cardinal article of that convention.

"At the first Conference in 1899, although presented by our government in an able memorial signed by the whole delegation, and a powerful address by Ambassador Andrew D. White, it was refused a hearing on the technical plea that it was not embraced in the programme, although to the common mind it seemed to be as much so as many other subjects that were considered and acted upon—and it was referred to the next Conference. There, however, it was fully and fairly discussed, and for some weeks intelligently considered and finally adopted by a vote of two to one—twenty-two nations to eleven— Germany alone, of the great military nations, was with us—the others vigorously and consistently opposed on the openly avowed ground that they would not give up the right to strike at the most vulnerable point of their enemy on the outbreak of war. It cannot be doubted, however, that the moral effect of the vote of such a large and emphatic majority of the nations will go far to dissuade future combatants from the exercise of the right, or to lead them to agree together not to exercise it during the war—and the way is now open to the twenty-two nations who voted for the suppression of the right to enter into general or separate treaties agreeing to abandon this relic of barbarous warfare.

"Next, an International Court of Appeal in Prize was agreed to by an actually unanimous vote of all the nations. Everybody knows how prone all national courts of prize in every country are to decide in favor of their own captors, sitting as they do in the territory of a belligerent, and in the very heat of conflict. It is unnecessary to tell you how American neutral commerce has suffered from this cause from the time of Washington down to this day. As we expect generally to be neutrals in all the future, as we have been generally in the past, the establishment of this court—the first real international court ever assented to by express agreement of all the nations—is an immense boon to American interests. It was brought before the Conference for final adoption as the joint proposition of Great Britain, Germany, France, and the United States, with a scheme prepared for the constitution and organization of the court, its powers and procedure, and the mode of selecting its judges, all of which met with universal consent.

"Then there was our proposition which was introduced and conducted with such skill and tact by General Porter, that in the case of ordinary public debts founded upon contract, claimed to be due from one nation to the citizens of another, force should not be resorted to in any case for their collection, until arbitration had been offered and refused, or if accepted only in case its award had not been complied with. This proposition had no particular relation to our Monroe Doctrine, for it applied to all nations alike, great and small, debtor and creditor, European and American, but it does put an effectual barrier in the way of blockading a debtor State, or seizing its territory or revenues, as a means of compelling payment of its contractual debts, until arbitration has been had or refused—and will greatly tend to the peaceful settlement of all such controversies.

"And who will say ᵗʰᵃᵗ ᵗʰⁱ

ward? Finally, the treatment by the Conference of
the great question of arbitration—arbitration the only
substitute yet discovered for the arbitrament of war in
international disputes—marked a still further advance
in civilization.

"In the First Conference in 1899, the very idea of a
general agreement of arbitration of such a nature had
been abandoned as an impossibility. But now from the
time of the introduction of the proposition by us on the
15th of July until the early days of October it was debated with great ardor and interest, but with uniform
good nature—debates in which almost every nation took
part—and being brought to a vote in the first commission to whose care the question was intrusted, it was
adopted by a majority of more than four to one—thirty-
two to thirty-five being in the affirmative on the several
clauses of the proposition, and five to eight in the nega-
tive. This decisive vote in a Parliamentary body would
have finally settled the question. But ours was a Conference only, and not a Parliamentary body, and here
our instructions came in, not to press any measure to
the point of irritation, and not to force a reluctant consent which might be repudiated by the ratifying powers.

"Although it was proposed that only consenting nations should sign under the ægis of the Conference, leaving it for others to come in afterwards or stay out as they
pleased, yet the five dissentients resisted so stubbornly
that fears were entertained of serious discord if the matter
were further pressed, and it was generally agreed to go
no further, but to adopt instead a rather colorless vote
adopting the principle of general arbitration, and recognizing that there were cases that should be so disposed
f   But on this substitute we abstained from voting,

on the ground that it was a decided retreat from the advanced position to which the great principle had been carried by the previous vote upon our carriage of the measure.

"But who can deny the tremendous advance made on this momentous subject since it is now open to the thirty-two nations that upheld our proposition to enter into general or special treaties to carry it into effect, or that this great weight of international public opinion will ultimately persuade the dissentients to come in?

"In the same connection our project for the creation of a permanent international Court of Arbitration, to which all controversies of an international character might be voluntarily submitted at the option of the parties for settlement, after being fully debated was adopted by general consent, it being agreed with substantial unanimity that such a Court should be established, and a constitution for its powers, organization and procedure was submitted to the constituent powers, with a recommendaton that the Court be established as soon as the powers could agree upon the number of judges and the mode of their selection.

"It was upon this last feature that the Conference found itself hopelessly divided—the method that had been unanimously adopted for the Court of Appeal in Prize, for a graded distribution of the judges by years among the different nations, in some proportion to their relative importance, giving to the eight great powers each a judge all the time in the prescribed period of twelve years, and the others graded periods for eleven years down to one, as in the case of Panama, was now rejected by all the smaller powers, who claimed that as they were equal in sovereignty, and had equal votes in the conference, they must have an equal judicial voice in this Court of Arbitration. The greater powers could not agree that technical equality of sovereignty made substantial equality of power, and so this knotty question was left for the powers to settle and establish the Court as I have no doubt they will do in the quieter atmosphere of diplomacy.

"We struggled hard to bring all the powers to consent to some method of an election of judges, even going so far as to offer for ourselves to run the risk of being left out of the court, as the result of such election, but England and Germany who had stood loyally with us throughout were unwilling to take that risk.

"When it is remembered that on the First Conference no progress whatever was made with this project, the advance accomplished is most notable.

"From the days of Washington until now arbitration has been with the government and people of the United States the favorite method of settling all international controversies, and we have resorted to it habitually, and there can be no reasonable doubt that in good time the court and the agreement for which we were so urgent will be established by general consent.

"And, last of all, a resolution was unanimously adopted which secures the meeting of another Conference to carry on the good work, without waiting for any particular power to call it, and the preparation of its tentative programme by an international committee who are also to propose a scheme for its organization and procedure.

"Judge, then, from these acts accomplished and these advances made, whether the Second Peace Conference at The Hague was a nullity, or whether it did its full share to advance the cause of international justice and p⸺ ⸺⸺ What I claim is that in what it did, and what it refrained from doing, it was in direct conformity with the principles of the Farewell Address, and that Washington himself, could he have had cognizance of its proceedings, would have given it his cordial support."

In that address Mr. Choate told pretty much all that was necessary to give one an idea of what the Conference accomplished, but did not throw any more light than he could help on his own part in the accomplishment. As to that, Mr. Scott's introduction to the Princeton lectures is helpful. Mr. Scott points out that a union of a loose sort, as distinct from a political union, does exist between the nations that compose what we call society, that the very expression "society" implies such a union. He said that the purpose of the Hague Conference as defined by Léon Bourgeois is to make of that loose society a society of law, that to do that there must be universal assent of the nations to an international system, the acceptance by all of them of the same conception of law and precise application of these accepted principles to all international relations in peace and in war. He goes on:

"Supposing, however, an agreement upon the principles of law which should regulate the conduct of nations in their mutual intercourse, we know that differences of opinion are sure to arise between nations, as between individuals, regarding the interpretation and application of the law. Therefore, there should be called into being international tribunals for the interpretation and application of principles of law, just as national tribunals exist for like purposes. Mr. Choate devoted his energies to the creation of two such tribunals, the International Court of Prize and the Court of Arbitral

Justice. Through his timely intervention and conciliatory attitude in the question of the prize court, he was able to adjust apparently irreconcilable differences. He generously places the compromise to the credit of the American Delegation, but it was in fact his personal achievement, and the fundamental agreement upon the principles of an International Court of Prize is his contribution to the establishment of that Court. But the Prize Court deals with questions arising out of a state of war. It is essential to the ordinary administration of justice between nations that an international tribunal exist for the decision of controversies arising in time of peace, now fortunately the normal relation between states. Therefore, Mr. Choate urged upon the Conference, in season as well as out of season, the creation of a truly permanent court composed of judges 'acting under a sense of judicial responsibility,' to quote the happy phraseology of Secretary Root's instructions. After weeks of doubt and uncertainty, a project of thirty-five articles regulating the organization, jurisdiction and procedure of a truly permanent court of arbitral justice was adopted by the Conference, with the recommendation, as stated by Mr. Choate, that the court be established when the Powers had agreed, through diplomatic channels, upon a method of appointing the judges. This is also a triumph with which Mr. Choate credits the American Delegation, but the official acts and documents of the Conference tell another story, and history will count Mr. Choate as among the founders of the International Court when it has been established.

"But a law would be of little importance and international tribunals would be little better than empty courts unless there were an agreement by the nations to observe the principles of law in their mutual relations and to submit to the determination of the courts disputes which arise concerning either the existence or application of principles of law. Therefore, acting under the instructions of Secretary Root, Mr. Choate proposed a general treaty of arbitration which pledged the nations to submit to arbitration differences of a legal nature and especially disputes concerning the interpretation or application of international treaties or conventions, reserving from the obligation to arbitrate disputes, which although of a legal nature, involve the independence, vital interests and honor of the contracting parties. After weeks of discussion and heated debate in which the leading delegates participated, the proposed treaty was defeated, primarily through the irreconcilable opposition of Germany. If Mr. Choate's intervention in the discussion of the Prize Court can be cited as an instance of gentle persuasion and of gracious and happy phrase, his addresses on the subject of arbitration glow with emotion and the intensity of conviction."

The despatch of the correspondent of the Paris edition of the New York *Herald* from The Hague on August 19 speaks of the critical condition at the Congress the day before, when the American proposal for a permanent court came near being wrecked, but was saved by the German proposition about Prize Court judges. It speaks of the effort to get something worth while out of the Conference, which up to that time had not done very much, and goes on to say:

"A delegate said to me today, 'We are more than ever convinced today that Mr. Choate holds the whole Conference under his hat. He has acted as a big, broad-minded man, setting aside all matters of trifling details, and ever alive to a large, comprehensive view of the situation. Baron Marschall von Bieberstein has been splendid, whole-souled and admirable in the way in which he assisted and backed him up. You can compare Mr. Choate at the present moment to a man alone in a churchyard. He stands with his projects well and alive, while so many others have been buried, and he is very near the gate. The Americans have given their assistance in all directions whenever asked. They have no "axes to grind." They have, so to speak, thrown out planks all around, to try and save others floundering about in troubled waters.' "

Mr. Strong in his book about Mr. Choate quotes the political editor of *Gil Blas*, Comte de Saint Maurice, as saying of Mr. Choate:

"He is the *enfant terrible* of the Conference. He seems aware, neither of the grandeur of the mission intrusted to the delegates, nor of the personal majesty of their excellencies. He is barely a diplomat. He it is who, with an air of innocence, inserts into a discussion a few cold words which effectively shatter the grandiloquent bubbles of his colleagues. He it is who unsmilingly emphasizes some imposing puerility. It is he, always he, whose brief logic brings back to earth again discussions which have drifted into the pacific ether. What superb balloons he has thus pricked. What pretentious aeronauts has he brought to earthly realities.'

The next Hague Conference was to have met in 1915. By that time the effort to save the world from war had met with a very considerable setback. It was very much as though the patient whom the doctors were called to consult over had died. In the Great War restraints such as the two Conferences had so laboriously devised were very much like cobwebs in the path of a mad bull. Europe relapsed back into first principles. Inexpert people now, when they think of the Hague Conferences, wonder if anything is left of value of all that they contrived, and whether the new quest for world peace will follow the paths on the Hague map, or whether new pathfinders will blaze a new trail. What Mr. Choate himself would have thought about it if he had lived to see the war through, and what he would have thought about the League of Nations, it would be extremely interesting to know, but is hazardous to surmise. There is a letter of his to Mr. Moreton Frewen, dated from Stockbridge, June 30, 1916, which touches a little on these questions. He said:

"My Dear Mr. Frewen,

"I read your article on 'The Monroe Doctrine and the Great War' with great pleasure. But I find it far from easy to *agree wholly* with anybody or anything connected with our relation to the War. I can't agree with you that the Monroe Doctrine had much to do with bringing on the War; nor with Taft and Murray Butler that we should enter into a League to enforce Peace, which I regard as only another name for a League to make more war; nor with Eliot that we should enter into a League *permanent and offensive and defensive* with the Entente Nations to fight Germany and her Allies, because I think that would divide the world into two alliances ready to fight each other as they were before this horrible conflict began; nor with (Earl) Grey for a Federation of pretty much all the Nations.

"I am heart and soul for the Allies, as I believe most of my countrymen are, and I am sure they are going to win by putting Germany down. But I don't think that any of these questions can be taken up for serious consideration until that is accomplished and we see what there is left of the Nations engaged in the War. I hope there will not be much left of Germany or Austria and nothing of Turkey in Europe.

"I consider Wilson's idea that we may be called in to help arrange the terms of Peace as simply ridiculous. The Nations that are carrying on this War will settle the terms of Peace for themselves and will want no aid from us.

"As to Alliances, I still strongly incline to the opinions of Washington and Jefferson, that the true policy of this country is to form no Alliances Offensive and Defensive of a *permanent nature* with any Nation. If this was sound policy when we were an infant Nation, certainly it must be so now when circumstances have made us the strongest of all.

"You must take a great interest in our Election now pending, etc., etc.

Ever truly yours,

JOSEPH H. CHOATE."

This letter is interesting, but it only makes one the more curious to know what Mr. Choate would have thought of the League of Nations. So far as concerned the United States, everything happened after June 30, 1916. We got into the war, and our help in arranging the terms of peace ceased to be ridiculous.

But to return to the year 1908:
It was the time for choosing candidates for President.

Mr. Choate came out for Taft. The other candidate most considered by the Republicans was Mr. Hughes. Mr. Taft was nominated and duly beat Mr. Bryan without much trouble. It was after election that Mr. Choate, back in town from Stockbridge, wrote to his daughter (November 11, 1908):

"* * * Mr. Southmayd appeared at the office yesterday *in a yachting cap*, like Elbridge T. Gerry's—much to the amusement of everybody. He wouldn't sell his place in S. to anybody on any account, and he hopes that when he dies it will burn down with all its contents, so that nobody else can ever use his things."

To His Daughter

"8 East 63rd St.
19 Jany. 1909.

"* * * Yesterday and today I am spending some of the time that I expected to have in Washington in weeding out my Library—and am sending today 30 vols., most of them big ones, to the Astor Library which will make my shelves quite easy, and give me room for more. It is wonderful how many books one accumulates that are too good to give away, and not quite good enough to keep.

"William Phillips went back Sunday night. His promotion has been quite wonderful, as he has been advanced at one leap from a 'messenger' in the State Department at $900 a year to 3d Assistant Secretary of State with the same salary as Mr. Bacon, $4500. I think he will 'make good.' His two years in China, in spite of the typhoid fever, prove to have been a good investment. He seems to be *persona gratissima* at the White House. * * *

"I made him a special messenger to the President

(Roosevelt) in my place, to present an invitation from the
Pilgrims to accept a Banquet after the 4th of March and
before he sailed for Africa, to allow his old friends in New
York to give him a greeting and a send-off. I thought if
anybody could persuade him William could, but he telegraphed me last night that although he worked upon
him with all his might he persisted in declining. The
President seems to be having a bad time just now and
will continue to do so, I think, to the end of his Term.
All the hostility that he has been so studiously storing
up in Congress for seven years is now coming back upon
him. * * *

FATHER."

Mr. William Phillips had been private secretary to Mr.
Choate in London and the Ambassador had broken all
his rules in recommending him strongly to the President
and Secretary of State for retention in the diplomatic
service. Hence Mr. Choate's pride in his success.

To the Same

"Sixty Wall Street,
5 Feby 1909.

" * * * I've had quite a busy week. Monday night
Mama and I went to an illustrated lecture on Lincoln at
Mr. John S. Kennedy's which proved to be most interesting, and of course I had to say a little about Lincoln
there.

"Tuesday I devoted to Albany and the State Charities which was constant work from the time I arrived
until half past ten at night, for we had two long meetings
—a tea which I like least of anything I know. You
stand and receive and perspire freely and shake hands

without regard to the beauty of the shakee, and utter vapid nothings, and then there was a dinner of the workers which was not so bad. But I got back from Albany in time to attend the *Staats Zeitung* Dinner to our old acquaintance Count von Bernstorff which was really a fine affair, although being at the Manhattan Club, where they are not in the habit of giving big dinners, it dragged so that it was 10½ before the speaking began and I didn't get home till midnight. But I was very glad to go as we always liked von Bernstorff, and he has come to his Ambassadorship very early and after some valuable service. Mr. Bigelow even was at the dinner, but went home at 10:30. * * *

FATHER."

Nineteen hundred and nine was the year of the Lincoln Centenary. McClellan was the Mayor of New York, and there was a Lincoln commemorative meeting at the Cooper Union on the 12th of February, at which the Mayor and Mr. Choate made addresses, and Doctor Lyman Abbott furnished the oration.

To His Daughter (at Miss Tuckerman's in Washington)

"8 East 63rd Street,
Sunday, 18 April, 1909.

"What a lovely day this must be in Washington, for it is much the finest we have had here, and Washington just at this time is about three weeks ahead. This morning Mama and I took Jo and Cora in the motor over the new bridge and on to Prospect Park and Coney Island and as Cora had never seen these before she was much delighted, and we all enjoyed it very much indeed. At

Coney Island there were quite a number of people in bathing in the ocean, which I thought required much courage or much crankiness. Mama was much interested and had to disembark and lean upon the sea wall and watch them and smell the sea breeze, which was most refreshing.

"This afternoon they were here with the children, and while they were here Carrie Dahr and her boy came in. Then all three de Gersdorffs came in, so that we had altogether a children's party that you would have enjoyed very much. Mama had provided a lot of floating toys— ducks, geese, alligators, turtles and goldfish and a steamboat which when Jo wound it up would sail 'round the bath-tub, so we had a bath-tub party in Mama's bathroom where it seemed that Marion and Helen would fall in and be drowned.

"Walter Nettleton also came in later, and said he was waiting to hear from you and Emily (Miss Tuckerman) what you and especially she think about the Golf Club plans, now that she has got the Old Dwight Place. I congratulate her on that purchase. I think it must be called the Stockbridge Spinsters' Sunny Home. What a delightful point from which to watch the games.

"I went to Mrs. Robinson's dinner. It proved to be not *Mrs.* Robinson's at all, but her husband * had invited a few of us, Mr. Gilder, Mr. De Forest, Mr. Wheeler of Columbia College—only 8 in all to meet Prof. Meyer late of Oxford, now of Liverpool, University, a noted archæologist who is here to study the Cesnola Collection, of all things in the world.

"As I went up the steps of 84 Irving Place, it all at once came back to me that on the 24th of Septr., 1864, I

* Edward Robinson, Director of the Metropolitan Museum of Art.

went up the same steps and in at the same door to announce to the Leupps (our bridesmaids) the birth at quarter past six that morning (and it wasn't much after noon then) of our first child, our dear Ruluff.

"I ran up to Albany on Wednesday at 8:30 on the Empire Express, lunched at the Ten Eyck, appeared in the afternoon before the Judiciary Committee of the Senate, trying to defeat the effort of the Public Service Commission [for more power] over the Railroads of which they have too much already. It was quite interesting, and I think we got what we went for. I got back home at ten o'clock. * * *

"Aunt Mary was here this afternoon looking pretty well, but Uncle William was laid up with a headache and couldn't come with her. I told her he works too hard—men as old as he is ought to work only by fits and starts. We are all right for a short run, but not for a Marathon race, like our old (horse) Major."

To the Same

"Stockbridge, Mass.
22 July 1909.
" * * * Do you see that our old friend, M. Léon Bourgeois, is President Faillieres' first choice for prime minister in place of Clémenceau? The papers seem to think he will decline on account of his health. But he is so ardent and patriotic that I believe he will accept, and will make a fine premier. * * * "

Charles F. McKim, the architect and senior partner in the famous firm of McKim, Mead & White, had built Mr. Choate's house in Stockbridge and had helped him with his John Harvard window in St. Saviour's Church in Southwark. Mr. Choate knew him very well and appreciated him very highly. With great propriety, therefore, Mr. Choate was chosen to deliver the address at the McKim memorial meeting at the New Theatre in New York on November 23, 1909. The address is included in the volume of the "American Addresses," and is the kind of address that we would all like to have made about us if anything was necessary to be said. Another address included in the same volume was that on Florence Nightingale, spoken on May 18, 1910, at the fiftieth anniversary of the founding of the first training-school for nurses in New York. At that time Miss Nightingale was still living, but the address is just as good as an obituary, very kind, very appreciative, and she must have had the satisfaction of reading it.

In December, 1909, the American Economic Association celebrated its twenty-fifth anniversary, and Mr. Choate presided at a great meeting of its members in Carnegie Hall on December 27. He defended New York to the visitors against the charge of giving up to mercenary things.

The Pilgrims of the United States gave a dinner on January 11, 1910, to Henry White, Mr. Choate's associate in the Embassy in London and afterwards Ambassador to France, and of course Mr. Choate was there to pay a tribute to him.

His seventy-eighth birthday came along on January 24, but two days later he was arguing in court before Judge Ray in the suit against the Metropolitan Securities Company to recover two or three million dollars. He made a very lively appearance in that suit and was freely quoted in the papers. General Kitchener came to these

States for a visit in April, and Mr. Choate was active in the hospitalities, public and private, offered him. There was a dinner at the Waldorf, given by the Pilgrims, at which Mr. Choate presided.

He writes to his wife on June 14:

"MY DEAREST & ONLY ONE.

"I am so sorry that I cannot be with you tomorrow to celebrate your birthday—but must postpone the celebration till Saturday & Sunday. The day is a very precious one to me—and has been since 1860 when I first found it out—and that is exactly 50 years ago, when your winning face was framed in the simplest of summer bonnets in black & white. I wish I had it in black & white now. Well after tomorrow our combined 50 years will have increased to 150, and on the whole we have much, very much to be grateful for. In spite of all the drawbacks our lives together have been most happy, and for one I should like to live them all over again. * * * "

To the Same

"Metropolitan Club, New York.
Wednesday evening, June 22, 1910.
"Everybody calls it hot—and it is—but I have been very comfortable all day, lunching and dining at this Club—dining on the roof in cool breezes and looking down upon the rich foliage of the trees in Central Park.

"I was down town all the afternoon and am happy to say that my principal piece of business—the settlement of the Securities case—seems to be progressing.

"On my way up I saw a tremendous crowd at 5th Avenue & 22nd St. filling the entire street. As it proved they were simply waiting for Roosevelt to come out of Scribner's, and when he came there was a rush and a crush, and a hurrahing as if King George V. were coming, so that with difficulty he could get into his auto, and then it took two blocks before two mounted policemen could get him free from the crowd. All the same he evidently enjoyed it immensely. * * * "

To the Same

"The Arlington, Washington, D. C.
14 December 1910.
" * * * Our meeting .was an interesting one and it seems difficult to devise ways of spending the income of such a vast sum as ten million dollars for the 'promotion of peace'—and the Trustees will have to study many interesting questions. * * * "

A meeting evidently of the Carnegie Endowment for International Peace, of which he was a trustee and vice-president.

Mark Twain died in that year of 1910, and there was a meeting in memory of him at Carnegie Hall, at which Mr. Choate's contribution prompted this remarkable outburst of admiration in the *Brooklyn Eagle* of December 2:

"Probably the finest example of oratory seen and heard in this country since the death of Wendell Phillips, occurred at Carnegie Hall on Wednesday evening, when Joseph H. Choate literally conversed with his audience, without a single gesture, about the late lamented Samuel L. Clemens, 'Mark Twain.' Every judge of natural oratory with whom I have spoken unites in declaring it to have been the sublimity of all that the human voice and the physical frame are capable of imparting to a listener and a beholder. Taken altogether, Mr. Choate's address was the most excellent thing of the kind New York has known. It was a living, tender and truly sympathetic eulogy of the dead humorist, without a trace of humor or a word of flippancy." *

His book of addresses made in England, under the title of "Abraham Lincoln and Other Addresses in England," was published in the fall of 1910 and brought out interesting reviews both in this country and abroad.

He appeared in April, 1911, for the Missouri, Kansas & Texas Railroad Company against the United States Government in a matter of land claims that involved about sixty million dollars' worth of property. A little later in June he was counsel for the Widow Watt in a matter relating to the division of her husband's estate, and his reappearance in the Supreme Court of New York, where he had practised so long, excited general interest and newspaper remarks.

To His Daughter

"8 East 63rd St.,
23 May 1911.

"I have just come from the opening of the Public Library, which was a great event. Mr. Bigelow was in fine form, and conducted the whole proceedings, but unfor-

* As reported in *The Tribune*, December 1, 1910, Mr. Choate began by saying: "We are certainly not gathered here to mourn for Mark Twain. There is no doubt that in those two last lingering years of his he would have welcomed the fateful reaper at any time. When he heard of Gilder's death, he said: 'Ah, no such good luck comes to me.' This audience is, rather, a tribute to his character, to his signal triumphs, to all he did to make men happier and better. I believe in the last thirty years no man has done more or as much in this direction as he."

tunately we could not hear a word that he said. Mr. Rives read a good plain discourse giving the history of the Library from the beginning, and there were brief addresses by Park Commissioner Stover, Mayor Gaynor, Gov. Dix and President Taft, who could be heard by everybody and made much the best speech. But not a word was said about Dr. Billings who, I think, is the man entitled to the most credit, or of John Cadwalader who has labored very hard for the last fourteen years to bring about this great result—while of course your friend Andrew Carnegie had to come in several times for a round of applause for the heaps of money he has given for the building of twenty or thirty branch libraries, but I think that Billings and Cadwalader enjoyed being let alone quite as much as Carnegie liked the applause.

FATHER."

In July, 1911, Mr. Southmayd died, a departure which came very near Mr. Choate. His letters to his family are full of jokes about Mr. Southmayd, who belonged on one side of him to comedy, but what Mr. Choate really felt and thought about him appears in the address he read on May 14, 1912, before the Bar Association of the City of New York. It is one of the most interesting papers that have been written by a lawyer about a lawyer. He told of Mr. Southmayd's amusing side, what he called his quaintness, but also pictured his character and his great accomplishments and ability and devotion as a lawyer so that the portrait stands out for admiration.

Speaking of him as one of the great lawyers of his time who commanded the unbounded confidence and esteem of all the leaders of the profession, he told of his origin, his early schooling, which was finished "at the unripe age of twelve and a half because his teacher announced to his astonished father that he had taught the boy all he knew," and how he was taken over by Judge Elisha Hurlbut, who invited the father to send the boy to him and he would try to make a lawyer of him. So, starting in the office of Hurlbut and Johnson, "although he thus began the study of the law at a very tender age, he found it most congenial and buckled down to it in earnest. He seems to have had no tuition, outside the office at any rate, except what he may have got by attending Court; but he had wonderful powers of concentration and made such progress and so rapidly mastered the law that, at seventeen, he came to be known in the office as the 'Chancellor'; and the story goes that when clients called they were apt to find the two masters in the outer office discussing public questions, and they would say: 'Do you want to talk politics? Here we are. But if you've come on law business you will find the Chancellor inside.' "

Furthermore, speaking of Mr. Southmayd's connection with the firm of Butler, Evarts and Southmayd, of which Mr. Choate became a member, he said:

"During the whole period of his connection with it, until he retired at the age of sixty, in 1884, Mr. Southmayd was the mainstay of the whole concern. If there was a knotty point of law or practice to be decided, a difficult will, trust or contract to be drawn, an important opinion to be prepared, it was almost always left to him, and he always succeeded—he would never give in till the problem was solved; and as he was known to be always at his desk, clients at all hours flocked about him for advice, which is, I think, the most responsible and difficult part of our whole professional work. And then, too, in consultation he was invaluable. You can imagine what a resource it was to Mr. Evarts or to myself, coming down from Court at the close of a protracted and exciting day, to talk over with him puzzling and unexpected questions that had arisen and get the benefit of his cool and quiet judgment."

His story of Mr. Southmayd's connection with the income-tax case has already been told in this book.

January 24 (1912) was Mr. Choate's birthday, and he was eighty years old. The newspapers very generally remarked upon it and said pleasant things. He stayed at home all day to celebrate it and had a family dinner in the evening. John Bigelow had died and it was a sentiment virtually undisputed that Mr. Choate had succeeded him to the position of First Citizen of New York.

The New York Genealogical Society had made him an honorary member, and a reception given to him at the Society's hall was pretty much a birthday reception. He talked there about Lincoln and Grant, giving his own memories of both, as the Society had requested. Ambassador Reid was at the meeting and contributed remarks which included some allusion to Mr. Evarts, and that lured out of Mr. Choate's memory the famous story of his going up with Mr. Evarts, then Secretary of State, in the State Department elevator in Washington, which was packed with young men who wanted jobs in the diplomatic service, and of Mr. Evarts remarking to him that it was the biggest collection for foreign missions he had ever seen taken up.

As has been remarked, Mr. Choate seldom told stories in his speeches. Such stories as get into speeches are usually narrations of what some one else has said. As a rule Mr. Choate said things about which other people made stories, and so it was with Mr. Evarts, whom he quotes.

In February Mr. Choate was at the dinner given to
John A. Mitchell, of *Life*, on the thirtieth anniversary
of that paper's birth.

He writes to his wife on June 12, from his office in
town:

"Until an hour ago I have been very busy about the
business on which I came down, and have also done nearly
all my errands, reserving for tomorrow the dentist (from
whom I had to beg off today), the oculist, and running
the Harvard dinner, which promises to be a very great
affair. You will imagine me sitting for three hours with
T. R. on my left hand and introducing him to our loving
brethren."

This dinner was the dinner of the Associated Harvard
Clubs, at which about fourteen hundred alumni sat down.
Evidently he was going strong, treating himself with
consideration, but not with any excess of indulgence.

The great event of the year in Mr. Choate's life, and
in Mrs. Choate's life, was the celebration of their golden
wedding on October 16, at Naumkeag at Stockbridge,
a great occasion, greatly celebrated, in which there was
a high degree of public interest. The newspapers of
the day told about it faithfully. The invitations, which
had 1861–1911 in gold figures at the top, said that Mr.
and Mrs. Choate would be at home on Monday, the
16th of October, from three until six o'clock, at Naumkeag, Stockbridge, Massachusetts. That was the central
event of the entertainment. Hundreds came to the reception—the neighbors from Stockbridge, Lenox, Pittsfield and thereabout, and many from farther away. Besides that there was a great family dinner on the night

of the 15th for fifty relatives and near family friends, and there were presents—a good many—an inevitable accompaniment of a wedding-anniversary celebration, and in the case of a golden wedding where golden presents are most suitable, rather a serious detail. In people at the golden-wedding time of life the desire of accumulating things is likely to have grown faint, particularly if they are things that need to be carefully kept; but of course when people have a golden anniversary, they must take what comes.

By way of making an outgoing current to offset this golden stream that came in, on the wedding-day morning everybody employed on the place, men, women, and children, got a golden coin from Mr. or Mrs. Choate, who met and greeted them all on the piazza at Naumkeag.

The dinner the night before—it was Sunday night—is recorded as a very notable social event in the Berkshire Hills. The Springfield *Republican* says that the cake was about three feet high and that Mrs. Choate cut it with a golden knife. The most difficult thing of all on such an occasion is to have what needs to be said, said acceptably. On this occasion the necessary remarks were made, for the most part, by Mr. Choate.

He got back presently to every-day life, and we find him giving President Taft all the backing he could in the arbitration treaties which he was trying to get through the Senate.

Late in the year a movement began for the celebration of the hundred years of peace between Great Britain and the United States, following the War of 1812. In connection with that there came up discussion of the Panama Canal tolls, which the British Government con-

MRS. CHOATE (1915).
From a photograph by Hollinger.

sidered discriminative against foreign shipping and not in accordance with the Hay-Pauncefote Treaty. That matter was earnestly disputed for nearly two years. Meanwhile Mr. Wilson had been elected President and came into office on the 4th of March, 1913, and promptly took a firm stand against the tolls and succeeded after a long fight in getting the law that instituted them repealed. It was of course a matter that interested Mr. Choate very much indeed, the more so that he had so much to do with the Treaty. We find him making what *The Times* called a "brief, vigorous, impassioned speech" before the Pilgrims (on February 4, 1913) on the situation created by the Panama Tolls Act. He ridiculed the notion that there was, or could be, any substantial difference of opinion as to the meaning of the Hay-Pauncefote Treaty. "If ever two men," he said, "deserved the gratitude of their respective nations, and each of the other's nation, those men were John Hay and Lord Pauncefote, perfectly plain, straightforward men who believed that it was their part to say what they meant and to mean what they said, and to express in perfectly clear English what was in their own minds. And when they said that the ships of all nations should have free and equal passage through the canal without any discrimination whatsoever, they meant just that. They lived and died without ever once suspecting that their words were capable of any other meaning than was borne on the face of them."

It was at this same dinner of the Pilgrims on their tenth anniversary that there was given to Mr. Choate, the president of the society, a gold-and-silver salver, bearing bread and salt, the traditional Pilgrim fare.

Repeatedly Mr. Choate urged the repeal of the Canal

tolls. He spoke of it before the Chamber of Commerce
on February 14, and again in Washington in opening
the Fourth Conference of the American Society for the
Settlement of International Disputes, when also he urged
the delegates to help about convening the Third International Peace Conference at The Hague. It is notable
how much the promotion of world peace was on his mind
in the later years of his life, and how constantly he spoke
and worked to promote it. From the time he went to
London to the end of his life, he was dedicated to that
purpose. At the Second Peace Conference he had worked
to provide for the calling of another conference in 1915.
Now he pressed it upon attention that the third conference should be called.

He seemed in good health in the summer and wrote
to his wife:

"Metropolitan Club, New York.
17 June 1913.
" * * * Today has been very hot, as last night was—
but last evening I dined upon the roof here and found it
delightfully cool, and this morning at breakfast I found
the wind blowing across the Park so cool that I had to
have the window shut, yet since then I believe the thermometer has crept up to 90°. This did not prevent my
putting in quite a good day's work; viz., the oculist's,
the dentist's, to Howard's to get a little present for
Josephine (I narrowly missed seeing dear Mabel at the
dentist's—she was to come at half past two), to the hat-
ter's, to Brooks's to get a wedding suit, to Arnold &
Constable's, to *The Tribune* office to see young Mr.
Reid to get him to induce his mother to take your place
as Chairman of the Woman's Centenary Committee, to

Stetson's office to inquire about his wife who was operated on for cataract last Saturday (both eyes) and was glad to find she was doing well, to Jennings' office to inquire about his fine boy, a Junior at Yale who was one of the victims of the R. R. accident at Stamford—arm and leg both broken, but they *hope* he will get perfectly well—'*sure* about the *leg*, but not quite about the *arm*,' but they have got him down safely to the Presbyterian Hospital where his chances will be much better than at the one in Stamford—then to Morgan's office to attend to a little matter of business and to see Mr. Davison who has just had his vacation and Jack Morgan who is soon to go—then to my office to meet Mr. Delafield and one of the officers of the Museum of Natural History to discuss their new Pension Fund Scheme—an hour with Mrs. Nicoll dictating a long letter to Mrs. Reid, and others shorter, and signing many checks—several sessions with Mr. Bickford about the phraseology of my will—to lunch with Jo where we met Douglas Robinson who said his wife nearly died a' laughing when she read the account of the people who went with the Peace Conference to Oyster Bay, myself, Carnegie & Alton B. Parker, but he couldn't explain to me how such antipodes as Sulzer and Roosevelt could get together in support of the Governor's queer measures—after lunch more letters, until it was time to walk to the subway in time to get to the last meeting of the Governors of this Club for the season—and then you will naturally say with Pepys 'home to bed.' But no! I am going home to take off those wet clothes and dress for another dinner on the roof, where perhaps I may meet some pleasant friends, and perhaps not. * * *

J. H. C."

A tolerably full day for a man of eighty-one, topped off by a letter of some length in his own hand and the declaration of purpose to get into dry clothes and dine on the roof. Roofs are not favored, as a rule, by octogenarians as places to dine.

To His Wife

"Metropolitan Club, New York.
11 Sept., 1913.

"I changed my mind and came to the Metropolitan Club, where, for a wonder, I found a very good room, a corner room looking out on the Park.

"On the way down I found myself sitting by Admiral and Mrs. Dewey, which not only shortened my journey, but materially lengthened my life, so that I am now expected to live to *102*. At any rate Mrs. Dewey said that I ought to be ashamed if I didn't, for God had given me a right start and I ought to help God all I could. It was chiefly by the constant use of lacto-bacilline now used in liquid form, that all this was to be accomplished. The Admiral, who is to be 76 in January, showed up as a signal proof of the magic of this wonderful remedy. But Mrs. Dewey was not quite so successful, though a very earnest advocate of the system. She was leaving Pittsfield because every day she stayed there she suffered from neuralgia. 'But,' said I, 'have you tried anything for it?' 'Oh, yes,' she said, 'I have tried everything for it except leaving, and now I am trying that.' The lacto-bacilline combined with aromatic spirits of ammonia—for both of which I have full directions—is to save me from all bodily harm.

"Mayor Gaynor's death has simply stunned everybody, and nothing but good is heard or read of him, which is all right. Everybody who doesn't want Tammany to rule in every department will have to vote for Mitchel whether they like him or not. Still I greatly fear that Tammany will win."

(Saturday morning.) "I got through all right in Washington and home at ten last night and found your special delivery letter. You did not tell me that you were going to discharge four servants at once. I thought it was only the cook. Why so secret?"

That autumn of 1913 he went to a meeting of the Bar Association at Montreal, whither came also Lord Haldane and Maître Labori, the defender of Dreyfus.

To His Wife
"60 Wall Street.
13 Nov., 1913.
"Our meeting of the Peabody Trust today went off as usual. But it was a little gruesome, for the two Trustees who sat on my right and left were wheeled in in chairs by their nurses and were both a little incoherent. We must wind up before the rest of us get that way. It looks as though we should have to hold only one more annual meeting."

The Peabody Fund *was* wound up, not because its trustees became incoherent but because its work as a separate institution was finished.

President Wilson's stand on the Canal-tolls matter doubtless warmed Mr. Choate's heart towards him, but there were other matters in which he watched him closely and took thought for him. The Mexican question, be-

queathed by President Taft to his successor, continued
to rest heavily on public attention, and Mr. Wilson's
policy of watchful waiting was criticised with great energy, but at the banquet at the Waldorf-Astoria Hotel
on November 20, to celebrate the one hundred and forty-
fifth anniversary of the Chamber of Commerce, Mr.
Choate broke out with unexpected remarks.

"Well, what," he said, "is the most stirring question
today that agitates the hearts of the American people?
Its name has been mentioned several times, but it really
is Mexico. What are we going to do with Mexico, or
what is Mexico going to do with us? I should like very
much to discuss the policy of the United States of America in regard to Mexico. I think I could occupy the whole
evening with that if I only knew what that policy was.
At best, there is only one man who knows what that
policy is, and he very wisely keeps his own counsel and
won't tell. And I am not sure that even he knows. I
am not sure that we are not all drifting with him at our
head from day to day, and even from hour to hour, waiting, like Micawber, to see what may turn up.

"It is a very trying situation; it is a very dangerous
situation; but one thing I know, and for one thing I appeal to the heart and head of every gentleman present
in this chamber tonight, that in this trying situation
there is but one duty for all of us, and that is to stand
by the President of the United States.

"You may call it diplomatic business; you may call
it Executive business, but it is fair to assume that the
President is in possession of information vastly superior
to that which even all of the members of the Chamber
of Commerce of the State possess. He knows what he

is talking about. He knows what he is aiming at. One thing we are sure of, that he is for peace; that he is for preserving peace at all hazards, and that by no act of his shall this nation be plunged into a destructive and dreadful war. He is entitled to support from us without regard to party and without regard to creeds. We must stand by our President through thick and through thin, and we shall come out right in the end."

The following month Mr. Choate fell ill. This first serious illness he had ever had began with a severe attack of angina pectoris, which was followed by other troubles. It kept him abed for two or three months, and it seemed for a while that he could not recover, but he would not let go, and being strongly disposed to continue in this life, he got very much better, and when the war came along his immense interest in that seemed to reanimate him altogether. It was this illness, that he speaks of in the beginning of his autobiography as the "long confinement to my room and bed for the first time in more than eighty years," that induced him to dictate those memoirs. He writes to his daughter as he was getting better:

"8 East 63rd Street,
22 Feby. 1914.

"DEAR MABEL:—

"No, I can't let even Miss Logan (his stenographer) come between me and my only daughter, and am writing you as you see, with my own hand. * * *

"When I came in just now I found the card of Mr. & Mrs. Fredk. W. Vanderbilt had just been left. They have just got back to New York from their yacht-week, and I should like very much to have seen her and heard all about that. Probably she called to see you, but possibly me, for she and I have one common point of interest because her father was one of my earliest clients, and was so pleased with the way in which I tried a very dangerous case for him, that after he paid my bill, he sent me $500 as a present, and in token of his great satisfaction.

"We are jogging along as well as we can without you. I seem to be gaining every day, and the Doctor now comes only once in four days. This morning he agreed that I should go and preside at the next monthly meeting of the Century on the 7th of March. * * *

FATHER."

CHAPTER X

THE GREAT WAR

AUGUST, 1914—HIS HEALTH—HIS CONNECTION WITH CLUBS, MUSEUMS, AND OTHER ORGANIZATIONS—MEETINGS, DINNERS, AND COMMITTEES—A VISIT TO TORONTO—ELECTION—THINGS MOVE—WAR DECLARED WITH GERMANY—SPEECHES—THE VISITING COMMISSIONS —A HARD WEEK WITH THEM IN NEW YORK—THE END

All of a sudden, in the cheerful world in which Mr. Choate, improved in health, was concerned with manifold activities mostly agreeable, the tocsin sounded with a terrible and momentous clang, and hell began to break loose. He writes from Stockbridge about it to his daughter, in letters that run through the first half of August.

"Stockbridge, Mass. 2 August 1914.

"Dear Mabel:—

"I suppose that like all the rest of the world, you have spent the afternoon in reading this terrible war news which is turning the whole world upside down. If we lived anywhere but in America, if we were Germans or Russians or Austrians or Frenchmen, I suppose that at this moment Jo and George and Arthur and the De Gersdorffs and all the rest of our young men friends would be shouldering their muskets and marching to the nearest rendezvous to join the army. For that is just what the horrid word 'mobilization' means. There is a capital cartoon in one of the papers today representing Youth strapped to the mouth of a cannon, to which the old

Austrian Emperor is just setting a flaming torch, and that is just what War means.

"I cannot help thinking, however, that when these great armies get face to face and begin to count the terrible cost, they will find some way out, and Peace will come again, which all the Nations so sorely need. * * * "

(August 3.) "We are still doing little but reading the war news which seems to me to be worse than ever this morning. Those Germans are a little too smart in trying to steal a march upon both France and England. But they will be come up with, I think, for they seem to be driving Great Britain, against her will almost, to side actively with France and Russia—to keep her promises to them, and when they find themselves really arrayed against the three great powers—Germany & Austria must give way and find some way out. The papers this morning say that Austria on Saturday expressed her willingness to accept Sir Edward Grey's proposal of a conference.

"You are so near to Hog Island now that you may possibly find out about the Choate Farm there,—who owns it and whether it is for sale. * * * "

(August 5.) "Mama showed me your very nice letter received this morning giving an account of your various wanderings about the coasts of Massachusetts. You must have had a great frolic in spite of all these horrible wars. Now that England has fairly engaged with the rest of the Nations against Germany, I suppose it has got to be fought to a finish, and don't see what is to prevent a final stop being put to the arrogant pretensions of Germany which are always disturbing the world. But perhaps now, finding pretty much all the rest of the world arrayed against her, she will call a halt. * * * "

(August 6.) "We were much appalled this morning to read of the dying condition of Mrs. Wilson and that all his prodigious labors of the last few months have been done with this dreadful fate hanging over him. I hope he will be persuaded now to let Congress adjourn and take the real rest which he so much needs. * * * "

(August 7.) "Dr. Peterson came up today in spite of the heat and gave me a thorough overhauling. As I expected he pronounced me much better in all respects, and thought that after about three days more of rest, I could begin to move about and be practically well. * * *

"The war news is terrible—and doubtless will be so for many days. The poor German people who do not want war at all are being sadly abused by their rulers who certainly have been behaving as badly as possible. * * * "

(August 11.) "You say nothing about Essex or Hog Island or any of the Choates in that direction, so I suppose you haven't been there. I imagine that the Choate Farm on Hog Island remains much as it was a hundred years ago. Dr. Bentley who visited it in 1819 says in the Fourth Volume of his Diary which has just come out, 'Oct. 6. We went for amusement to Patch's beach. * * * Here we had only low places on the Marshes. We reached Patch's Beach, having passed farms which were in the possession of the heirs of the Choate family, etc. Choate and two other farmers live on Hog Island, celebrated for its *Mutton, Butter & Cheese* beyond any land in Essex.' So I imagine you in your old age raising sheep on Hog

Island, and running a dairy farm, and I think Kitty would like to join you there. But I think you would have to give up a good many of your present amusements. * * * "

(August 12.) " * * * I haven't got my freedom yet, for I suppose Dr. Southworth who was to call today is waiting to hear from Dr. Peterson who has apparently to decide. * * * "

(August 16.) " * * * You press your inquiries about me. Well, at this moment I feel as well as ever I did, but expect ups and downs until this trouble is wholly cured. You know how long it took and how it tried our patience before, and I think it is sure to come all right before long. Yesterday I drove (in the Victoria) through the Warrin Woods—and it did me much good. So you see I am not quite such a close prisoner as I have been. * * *

FATHER."

To His Wife

"Metropolitan Club
Nov. 6, 1914.

"Before going to the Round Table dinner I must give you an account of the last twenty-four hours.

"We arrived on time and I deposited myself at this Club, just in time to dress and go to the dinner and business meeting of the Board of Managers of the Century, from which I returned in time to go to bed at ten o'clock. This morning I called up Dr. Draper and proposed to come down to his office, but he had already left for an early call in 57th Street and from there came here to see me. He put me through the usual course of inspection and inquiry and pronounced me splendidly well, and fully approved of my going through the program for which I came. Mr. Cunliffe Owen called at 12.30 in a taxicab to take me down to the meeting and lunch of the executive committee of the Pilgrims, where I spent a very pleasant hour, then to Wm. Wheelock's office to see about No. 10, which is in their hands for leasing."

In the letter above he speaks of two institutions that had been part of his life for many years, the Round Table and the Century Club. The Round Table was a dining club. There are few allusions to it in his letters because the Round Table dinners were in the winter and belonged to town life, of which the letters here quoted give a very brief record. The Century Association along with the Art Museum and the Natural History Museum, the Harvard Club and the Union League Club are included in the list given by Mr. Root in his address on Mr. Choate before the Bar Association of the City of New York. "At the age of thirty-five," Mr. Root said, "he was President of the New England Society in New York, the organization which for more than a century has done honor to the history and spirit of his race. At forty-one he was President of the Union League Club, that Institution created in the darkest days of the Civil War to promote, encourage, and sustain absolute and unqualified loyalty to the Government of the United States. He was President of the Harvard Club, of the Law School Association, of the Century Association. For forty years before his death he was a Governor of the New York Hospital. He was President of the New York Association for the Blind. He was President of the State Charities Aid Association. He was one of the incorporators of the Metropolitan Museum of Art, and one of its Trustees for the forty-seven years which followed its organization in 1870; and for many years before his death he was Chairman of its Law Committee, and a member of its Executive Committee, and Vice-President. He was one of the incorporators and during all its existence a Trustee of the American Museum of Natural History. He was an active Trustee and the Vice-President of the Carnegie Endowment for International Peace. He was Vice-President of the Society for the Judicial Settlement of International Disputes. He was a member and Chairman of the Sub-Committee on Elections of the Committee of Seventy, that Committee which roused the honest citizenship of New York to the rescue of the City from the shame of the Tweed Ring control. He was Honorary President and an active coadjutor in the National Defence League, which did so much to arouse the patriotic people of our Country to realize the deadly peril to their liberty of possible German military domination, and to make them understand that the time had come when American Institutions must be defended again by force of arms, or must perish."

Yet Mr. Root's list is doubtless incomplete. For one thing it does not mention his connection with the Peabody Fund for Southern Education of which he speaks in the letter of November 13, 1913.

Mr. Choate's connection with these various boards and institutes was by no means perfunctory; especially to the Art Museum and the Natural History Museum he gave long attention. Mrs. Choate had had much to do with starting the Brearley School in New York, and he was always interested in that and was to be depended upon to help it by counsel, speech, or in other ways.

When the school moved from 44th Street to 61st Street and into the new building, Mr. Choate responded to the call to come and speak at its celebration (November 26, 1912) in the new school, and told that day about the beginning of it and its history since. James Croswell, the head master, said: "He came down to my apartment (on 34th Street) in a cab to see what was expected of him and discuss what he should say." That was quite characteristic of the way he dealt with such duties.

To His Wife

"Metropolitan Club, New York.
Nov. 7, 1914.   Saturday Evening.

"Dear Saint—

"'I do admire of woman-kind but one,
  And you are She my dearest dear,
  Therefore it shall be done—
  That is to say, I'll write you every day. * * *'

"No great events have happened today, except that I went to Brooks's and ordered some new clothes—a blue serge suit '*like the last*,' and a handsome overcoat. But alas! when they came to take my measure, I was found to have lost 1½ inches round the chest, and 2 inches round the waist—and if this goes on there will not be much left of me by and by. * * * "

To the Same

"Metropolitan Club
November 9, 1914.

"I see my way clear now to come up tomorrow morning in the train which leaves here at 8.51 and gets to Stockbridge I think at about 1.30. But I shall have to come down on Thursday afternoon because the Carnegie Peace Foundation meets for its annual meeting here on Friday at ten.

"I got through the two Museum quarterly meetings (Trustees) a few minutes ago. The Art Museum has got the Altman Collection ready to open next week, and the Riggs Collection (armor) is well under way. We had a very full meeting of Trustees, including Mr. Frick, who looked as well as ever in spite of all the bad reports about him.

"So the other Museum was well attended, and the only serious question in both Museums is how the rapidly increasing cost of maintenance shall be provided.

"I just met Bishop Greer in the reading room of the Club who looks wonderfully well after his hard work, but he was not dressed in khaki like the Bishop of London."

To the Same

"Metropolitan Club
November 28, 1914.

"The Century meeting last night was most agreeable, as I had the pleasure of meeting many old friends, but I was sorry not to find Uncle William who seems not to have returned to the city, and the Club apparently has no charms for either of the de Gersdorffs. I suppose Carl was at the football game which Harvard appears to have won in great shape. Silas Brownell was there and gave a good account of his family, and President N. M. Butler, who has quite forgotten his prophecy, by which on his first return he gave the Kaiser's army fifty days to be starved out, and so end the war. But I'm afraid that fifty weeks will hardly do it.

"Tomorrow I have the Art and Natural History Museums' quarterly meeting, and after that I know of nothing else to detain me."

To His Daughter

"8 East 63rd Street, 3 February 1915.
"I enclose a splendid article from today's *Sun*.* It is copied from yesterday's *Evening Sun* where it appeared as an editorial. It shows how much remains to be done before the Germans are put down. * * * "

The *Lusitania* was sunk on May 7, 1915. Some consequences of it appear in the next letter, especially Mr. Bryan's retirement on June 8, because Mr. Wilson's *Lusitania* note was too strong for him.

To the Same

"Stockbridge, Mass. 13 June 1915.
" * * * I ought to be in two places on Tuesday—in New York at the Conference called by the National Security League of which I am Honorary President, and at Albany to attend the 700th anniversary of Magna Charta, but I have considered discretion the better part of valor, and setting one off against the other I go to neither. * * *

"What do you think about Bryan? He has certainly done the State some service at last, by taking himself out of the State Department, where he has been much worse than useless.

"The Germans, so far as we can guess, seem to be

---

* The article he speaks of was evidently one of the early war pieces by Frank Simonds, whose war editorials brought him great reputation.

taking the President's last note in a kindly way, and I have no fear of any war between us and them. * * * "

(June 16.) " * * * I asked Mama yesterday whom we should ask for the Fourth of July, and she said emphatically 'Nobody.' But that is what her first impulse is always, and I don't despair of having a house full, as of course we ought to have. * * * "

(June 21.) " * * * Commencement week has drawn all the young people to Cambridge, but they don't care to stay for Commencement itself which comes on Thursday, and are all to return that day. If I had known how cool it was to be, and how well I was to be, I should have been there myself to open the great Widener Library— a great event in the History of Harvard. * * * "

To the Same

(June 24.) "Commencement today at Harvard is not a scorcher after all, and I am very much disappointed not to be there. But I have the new Quinquennial Catalogue which arrived this morning and that is something. I find that Jo has corrected his name since the last Edition and reappears as Joseph Hodges Choate, 1897, and no doubt Sandy will appear in the same way in or about 1933 & keep up the line. In the new way of entering honors in the Catalogue I am glad to see both Carl and Jo recorded as 'm. c. l.' *magna cum laude*, but George de G. & Charley Choate have not even 'l.' Still what difference does it make, for Charley who apparently did nothing in College has beat them all in the race. * * * "

(June 30.) "Mama has been driving like a steam-engine ever since you left us, 'getting ready for the meeting of the Garden Club,' she says. I thought the house was all ready. But you never saw such an upheaval—men and women in all directions moving things from one place to another and turning them upside down and back. Hilda and Lily being initiated as upholsterers and my secretary entirely appropriated to write notes inviting outsiders, and yesterday I was sent all the way to Lenox to buy eight cents' worth of hooks and rings with which to hang up Mr. Beaman's piece of tapestry in the hall. Mrs. Alexander Sedgwick and Mrs. Arthur Swann called this morning, but she could only shake hands with them on arriving and departing, appearing with hammer and tacks for that purpose. Really, as I have often told her she is a 'very remarkable woman.' * * *"

(July.) " * * *—— writes me that he has had to cut out parts of my article about —— contributed to ——, and no doubt he has largely spoiled it, poor as it was. That is why I hate to give anything to any magazine or review—the liberty they take in mutilating what is sent to them. So, when I was in England —— came and begged me to let him have my address on the Supreme Court for publication in the ——, and when it appeared he had cut out about a third of it, and what I considered the most important part. Of course I shall not give anything more to ——.

"The German Foreign Office seems to be merely 'putting off' our President and makes no answer as yet to his second note. I think the Kaiser would like to give a conciliatory answer so as to keep on good terms with us, but is afraid of his own military clique. The report is today that the President is demanding an answer straightaway—without any more 'ifs' 'ands' or 'buts.' I hope so. I have been reading up on Richard H. Dana and find C. F. Adams's Life of him very interesting reading. It brings up many public events of my early years the details of which I had wholly forgotten. * * * "

(July 19.) " * * * Mr. Whitridge sails for England again this Saturday to be gone till October, but I am afraid that in the meantime there will be no very good news about the war for him, or for anybody, although he thinks, as I do not, that the Germans are very near the end of their possibilities. I think they will last a great while yet, and I only wish the President would end his parlez-vous-ing with them and give them plainly to understand that unless they give a prompt and favorable answer, our diplomatic relations with them must come to an end. I thought at one time that this would be a more serious matter, because we are giving all parties, French, English, and German, so much help through our Embassies at London and at Berlin, especially at Berlin, but my impression is that, if Gerard is recalled and Bernstorff sent home, as he ought to have been long ago, that business can be very well attended to by Consuls, who will still remain, although the Embassies may be closed. * * * "

On September 28, 1915, he writes to his wife from Toronto, where he had gone to receive an honorary degree:

"It is all over! We arrived on time at a little before ten last night, and were met by Sir Edmund [Walker],

who quickly brought us to his home in his motor. The
rest of the family were already in bed, having married
off the youngest son at half-past two in the afternoon.
So we were allowed to go to bed at once, which we were
very glad to do.

"This morning Lady Walker appeared—a very bright
and pleasing person, full of fun and charm.

"This forenoon we devoted to exploring the city, and
a delightful city it is—no sky-scrapers or apartment
houses, but a house for every family. At one we lunched
at the Club, with the gentlemen who were to present
the candidates for degrees, and went at three to the convocation, where that ceremony was gone through. When
all had been presented they insisted upon my speaking,
which I did for about fifteen minutes, and the large audience seemed to be in full sympathy with what I had
to say. We take the train for home at 9.30 tomorrow
morning."

To His Wife

"Metropolitan Club
September 30, 1915.
"I arrived here very safely last night at ten o'clock,
none the worse for wear. Only sitting still for twelve
hours was a little tedious. Jo took very good care of
me, and for that matter so did everybody else. You
would have been surprised to see how much they tried
to make of me. I enclose cuttings from two of yesterday's Toronto papers, which I am sure will amuse you.
Sir Edmund and Lady Walker entertained us most hospitably, and I have asked them to stop over at Stockbridge on one of their trips to or from Toronto to New
York, a journey of which they seem to make nothing.

They have four sons and three daughters, all married but the youngest son and the youngest daughter, and thirteen grandchildren. He is at the front and she is waiting for some man who is good enough for her to appear."

About this visit to Toronto there is a letter from Sir Edmund Walker, whose hospitalities Mr. Choate so much appreciated. He was chairman of the Canadian Peace Centenary Association, that undertook the celebration of the hundred years of peace between the United States and Great Britain. He was also chairman of the board of governors of the University of Toronto, which before the war had the largest attendance of any university in the British Empire. When the war interfered with the preparations for the centenary celebration about which he had several times conferred with Mr. Choate, it occurred to him that the celebration might properly be undertaken, in a way, by the University of Toronto, which should commemorate the hundred years of peace by giving honorary degrees to a number of eminent Americans. So the governors determined to hold a special convocation of the university, and the degree of LL.D. was conferred on six citizens of the United States, with Mr. Choate at the top of the list.

To this honor Mr. Choate made response for himself and his companions. As to that, Sir Edmund says:

"I was fearful that Mr. Choate, having received countless honorary degrees, might in a few graceful words have merely thanked us, in which case, in view of the war situation, the international aspect of the event would have fallen rather flat. But the moment his clear, strong voice was heard I felt sure he would say something worth while, and to my great delight he made the first, great, pro-ally speech delivered in North America. Next day I wondered whether he would have spoken as fearlessly in New York as in Toronto, and you may imagine my pleasure when at the Anglo-French dinner he delivered practically the same speech somewhat enlarged and much more outspoken."

On behalf of the recipients of the degree, Mr. Choate said:

"I am ordered by the highest authority to speak for a few minutes and pronounce the benediction which will bring these exercises to a close. I was set upon this morning by a great body of the reporters of Toronto, and I was struck with their wonderful gallantry and dash, and thought they ought to be in the trenches, and for a moment I wished they were. They wanted to know what I was going to say this afternoon, and I was obliged to tell them that during a long lifetime I had cultivated the habit of speaking without saying anything. So they got nothing out of me.

"I am a neutral and therefore my tongue is nationally tied, but I can say for myself that wherever men are fighting for liberty and justice and civilization I am in full sympathy with them. Perhaps it is only fair for me to say that I believed that of the one hundred millions of my countrymen at least ninety millions are in full sympathy with me.

"It is a wonderful thing that two great nations living side by side, who for forty years before had been squabbling all the time, and in those forty years had fought two wars, one of seven years' and the other of three years' duration, were able afterwards to live together in peace for one hundred years. When I went to The Hague as the delegate of the United States in 1907, to attend the second Peace Conference, all nations of the world, great and small, were living in peace with each other.

> " 'No war nor battle's sound
> Was heard the world around.'

We sat four months cheek by jowl with the Germans, the Austrians, the Turks, and all other outlying nations. We all thought that we had done something at the end of the four months to advance the cause of peace, to prevent the breaking out of war, and, if war must come, to mitigate the horrors of war. Well, it seems that our success was only for the moment, it was only transient. Everything we did at that conference, every provision that we enacted for the purpose of preventing war or mitigating its horrors, has been trampled upon and violated, and all our agreements have been torn into shreds of paper and thrown to the winds.

"I am often asked what is going to be the end of all this. Is it a fact that a century of united labors on the part of all the universities of the world, including this great University of Toronto and the McGill University have all been for nothing? Has civilization been thrown to the winds? Has liberty been entirely forgotten? Has justice ceased to be respected among men? And what is to be the end of all this? Well, by and by peace will come. We do not know when or how, but it will come, and the work of the universities will have to be resumed with greater ardor and, I believe, with greater success than ever before. I should like to recommend the motto of my own University of Harvard for general acceptance and as a guide of conduct for all the universities of the world. That motto is 'Veritas,' the Truth. Harvard has flourished under that watchword for nearly three hundred years. There is only one thing that can hold civil society together. There is only one rule which can hold the nations of the world together in peace, and that is the law of good faith, and nobody knows it better than the men who are fighting in the trenches on your side and on the other side.

"I have little confidence in, although much sympathy with, all the schemes that are on foot for promoting peace, but it is no use crying 'Peace, peace' when here is no peace and no possibility of peace—no possibility of peace until the authors of this awful war are brought to a condition where their adversaries and the whole world can see that hereafter they will obey our rule, the rule of good faith, the rule of keeping contracts, the rule that when they make a treaty they must stand by it, whether it is to their interest or not, and put an end forever to this awful theory which they have propounded and which they have acted upon during the last twelve months: that whenever their interests required they could throw all treaties and contracts to the winds.

"When war broke out, the idea prevailed in some malignant minds that the British Empire would fall to pieces, that Canada, Australia, and New Zealand, and other British dominions beyond the sea, great and small, would go each its own way; but instead of that, when the first blow was struck, when Belgium was invaded, the British Empire proved to be more closely united and more impregnable than ever before.

"When we heard how your strong young men were marching to the fight, when we heard of their great and

gallant achievements, when we heard how freely they
laid down their lives in this cause of liberty and justice
and civilization, our hearts bled with yours, and the
people of the United States were actually in full sympathy with you. Of course there are a few—shall I say,
malignants? I do not wish to use any offensive words,
but we have many millions of men of foreign descent,
one-half of them on one side and one-half on the other.
But if we should go to war with you against an unspeak-
able enemy—I do not want to mention its name—I think
nineteen-twentieths of all those people would stand by
our flag, the Stars and Stripes. I wish in closing to express for myself and on behalf of all my colleagues on
whom you have bestowed the signal honor to-day our
deep sense of gratitude and our high appreciation of the
honorary degrees conferred upon us by this great university. We wish also to acknowledge the generous enthusiasm with which your Canadian committee joined
with us and the British committee in the programme for
celebrating the Centenary of Peace, and to express the
confident hope that peace between your nation and ours
and our common mother country may last forever."

After the convocation there was a reception, and in
the evening a dinner at the York Club, and there, Sir
Edmund says, Mr. Choate told of some of his experiences
as Ambassador in England. Sir Edmund's diary records
that he spoke much of King Edward, saying that he was
the most human man he had ever known, and recalled
how when the time came for Mr. and Mrs. Choate to
leave England, the King invited them to lunch at Buckingham Palace, and after lunch said to an equerry:
"Where are the grandchildren?" The grandchildren
were produced and King Edward said to the present

Prince of Wales, then about ten years old: "This is my friend Mr. Choate, who is going back to America, where his home is; I wish you all to make your best bows and to say good-by to him." And so the Prince of Wales made a pretty bow and the others tried to imitate him, down to the youngest who squatted on the ground in his petticoats.

To His Daughter

"8 East 63rd Street, May 13, 1916.

"For a wonder we have got our flag out today, and now I think Osborn will take pride in putting it out on every holiday.

"Mother and I have spent *the whole forenoon* watching the preparedness procession which was a great success. Do I say *'was'*? It had really only been going for two hours when we left at twelve to come home for lunch. Indeed, we had not intended to see it at all. But only to go down 5th Ave. as far as they would let us go, to see the decorations which were very fine. The police would have stopped us at 34th St. But fortunately we took our *'police card'* with us, and although it had expired *in* 1914, that made no difference. They let us pass on until we got to the reviewing stand at the Worth Monument opposite Madison Square, which we reached just as the head of the procession was in sight—on the minute at 10:30. So we got out of our car and were immediately surrounded by any quantity of 'Committees' who gave us the best seats & just opposite those of General Wood & Mayor Mitchel who were just alighting from their carriages 'to review.' General Sherrill & his aides immediately passed, then almost an hour of City Employees—among whom George Ward, Park Commissioner, was conspicuous. Then half an hour of Dry

Goods & Woolens & Worsted trades, then Theatres & Fine Arts led by Jim Barnes in fine style. At this point the Mayor sent his Secretary across to invite us over to join his party, which was very pleasant as our seats on the West Side had become blazing hot in the sun. Mrs. Wood & Mrs. Mitchel were there and of course we enjoyed them. After sitting with them awhile we started home for lunch, although they had invited us to go with them to the Aldine Club, somewhere in the neighborhood, but —— was to be here. We were escorted across to our car by two stalwart policemen who found it for us. But on the way we had to stand for a great group of Kodakers who would take us in spite of Mama's remonstrances. So if you see two very horrid looking pictures of us in tomorrow's Sunday papers, you will not be surprised. Of course we had to run the gauntlet of a lot of reporters who insisted on knowing 'what I thought of it all,' and you will probably find some very crude views, mostly theirs but attributed to me, in the same papers. You will easily account for it. * * * "

To His Wife

"Metropolitan Club, New York.
Nov. 6, 1916. Monday evening.
"MY DEAREST AND ONLY—
"We arrived safely and on time and much rested by the long still ride. The only man in our car that I knew was Mr. French, and I was much disgusted to find from his talk that he seemed to be for Wilson, said that Hughes and the Republicans had made a great mistake in abusing him. * * *
"I judge from the accounts in the evening papers,

that both Hughes and Wilson are to be elected. It will be a relief tomorrow night at this time to begin to receive the returns and to know how New York State has gone for I imagine that will go far to determine the whole. I shall vote before breakfast as usual, and enjoy the rest of the day in quiet at the Club."

To His Daughter

"Metropolitan Club,
November 7, 1916.

"I voted before breakfast this morning as is my wont. But there were a good many before me, so my ballot was No. 60. But they put me at the head of the line because I had voted for Fremont & Dayton in 1856, and then I had to be introduced and shake hands with a young gentleman who was now voting for President for the first time in his life. * * *

"On the way up in the stage I called at the Savoy on M. de Sillac who was at the Hague with us, a sort of attaché, I believe, to M. Bourgeois, and is now here on a mission from M. Briand, Premier & Foreign Secretary, to find out the drift of opinion here about the League to Enforce Peace. I told him that if they would leave out the 'Force' I could support it, but I could not agree that the United States should bind itself to be punished by all the other members of the League if it differed from them; e. g., the Monroe Doctrine.

"We hope to hear who is President before midnight. * * * "

So he voted for Hughes, and the election, after considerable hesitation, went against him. And presently things began to come along and in spite of the election and what hopes of his, if any, it may have withered, the things that came were the things he wanted. November 6 the British liner *Arabia* was sunk without warning in the Mediterranean. On November 29, Washington protested against Belgian deportations. On December 6 Lloyd George became Prime Minister of England. On December 12, the Germans made a peace offer, refused, December 30, by the Allies as "empty and insincere." On December 20 went out President Wilson's peace note, to which Germany replied on December 26 and the Allies on January 10. On January 22 the President addressed the Senate, telling them his ideas of steps necessary for world peace. On January 31 Germany announced unrestricted submarine warfare in specified zones. Three days later, February 3, the United States severed diplomatic relations with Germany and dismissed Ambassador von Bernstorff. On February 26, President Wilson asked authority to arm merchant ships and did arm them by announcement of March 12. On March 27 Minister Whitlock and the American Relief Commission were withdrawn from Belgium, and on April 6 the United States declared war on Germany. It took five months to go from election to war.

How Mr. Choate felt about it appears in the letter following to Earl Grey, which was published in the London *Times* of May 30:

"8 East 63rd Street, April 7, 1917.
"DEAR LORD GREY:
"Your delightful cable came to hand on the 5th, immediately after the President's Message delivered in person to Congress, which, as you say, has swept all clouds from our sky, and before it had culminated in

MR. BALFOUR AND MR. CHOATE RIDING UP FIFTH AVENUE, MAY, 1917, AT THE TIME WHEN THE BRITISH MISSION WAS RECEIVED.

the declaration of war by Congress and its proclamation by the President.

"At last Americans at home and abroad can hold up their heads with infinite pride. The whole nation is now lined up behind the President, and I think that you will hear no more about doubt or hesitation or dissent among us. I think that we may now forget all the past, and let bygones be bygones, and accept the President as our great leader for the war; and we must give him credit for one signal result of his watchful waiting, and that is, that he was waiting to see when the whole nation would be wrought up to the point which has now been reached, so that he could safely announce to the world our alliance with France and Great Britain without any practical dissent.

"I say alliance, because that is justified by his noble utterances. We must stand together now until victory is won, and I think that victory will be greatly hastened by the entrance of the United States into the conflict. As you know, I have thought from the beginning that, while for the time being we might better serve the cause of the Allies by remaining neutral and supplying all that we could in the way of arms and munitions, and I am happy to say some men, as our neutral right was; that nevertheless when by entering into the war with all our might and with the aid of all our boundless resources, we could help to bring it to an end in the right way by the complete suppression of Prussian militarism, and the triumph of civilization, it would be our duty to do so. That time has now come, and I am happy to think that our great nation has acted upon the same thought, and has been really true to all its great traditions.

"We can hardly be expected to send over any large

expeditionary force at the outset, but I think that we can muster a division of something like 20,000 or 30,000 men, seasoned for war, under competent leadership, who shall carry our national flag alongside of those of Great Britain and France, without much delay, and I think that you will agree with me that nothing would give so much new inspiration to the war-worn veterans of your great country and of France and carry so much dismay into Germany as that would.

"I hope also that our Navy, which is fairly well ready, will be able to open the way across the Atlantic for our own vessels and those of other nations to carry food and munitions to your aid, and it is needless to say that we can and will furnish much-needed credit to both your nations in support of our common cause.

"You have no idea of the very rapid advance of public sentiment in favor of this cause in the last few months. In November Mr. Wilson was elected upon the rallying cry of 'Keep us out of the war,' but the defiant and impudent conduct of Germany since that day has really awakened all America to the true nature of the contest, and we must stand together until that contest is won.

Ever affectionately yours,

JOSEPH H. CHOATE."

Mr. Choate's activities immediately increased. The mayor selected him as the leading citizen of New York to act as chairman of the committee to receive the French and English Missions that arranged a visit to this country immediately following our entrance into the war. Evidently it was on the business of this committee that he went to Washington, as appears in the letter following:

To His Wife

"1624 Crescent Place, N. W.
Washington, 19 April 1917.

" * * * Last night we had a dinner of ten including the British and French Ambassadors and their wives, Senator Lodge, Lady Maud Cavendish, daughter of the Duke of Devonshire, who is here on a visit with the Spring-Rices, and Mr. Paton of Princeton, one of the Carnegie Trustees. * * *

"At the State Department everybody is worked to death. Nothing has been heard yet from either the French or British Missions but the latter is expected on Saturday or Sunday. They will probably come separately to New York which will keep my Committee very busy. The British are bent on business as you may suppose, and how the State Department with its feeble force— weak in numbers I mean—will be able to handle Mr. Balfour with his great company of supporters—twenty in number—I don't know. The Secretary thought that they would want to have a quiet time both here and in New York. But the French come here for more sentimental purposes and will want to 'see New York' and have the people see Joffre and Viviani—a wish which will be loudly responded to by our people. Last evening we had a visit from the Chief of Police, who wanted to view the premises as they are to be specially guarded during their stay in this house—sentinels at the entrance and at each of the four corners of the grounds, flash-lights to light up the whole establishment outside and in at a moment's notice and secret service men without number—the Government means to take no risks. * * * "

What followed, followed fast.

On April 25, in New York, he spoke to members of the Associated Press, and said (in part), as the New York *Times* reported him:

"Now before I sit down let me say a word about our great President, for he is entitled at every step to the applause and support of every American citizen, man, woman, and child, and I believe he has it.

"Some of us in the past have criticised the President. Some of us long hesitated and doubted. Some of us thought that watchful waiting would never cease. But now we see what the President was waiting for and how wisely he waited. He was waiting to see how fast and how far the American people would keep pace with him and stand up to any action he proposed.

"From the day the President appeared before Congress and made that wonderful address of his—one of the greatest State papers in the affairs of the United States since the formation of the Government—from that moment all doubt, all hesitation, all unwillingness was banished from the minds of all the people and he is now our chosen leader for the great contest.

"By no possibility can we have any other or think of any other, and we must uphold him through thick and thin from now until the end of the war."

On April 30, 1917, he spoke, at a dinner at the Harvard Club to General Wood, who was going abroad. His last speech at that club was on May 4 at a huge stand-up meeting of two thousand men of all colleges, held in Harvard Hall in the interests of the Officers' Training Camps. The hall was packed with men standing, and some one was addressing them when, as is related, the officers of the meeting suddenly noticed Mr. Choate appear on the outskirts of the crowd and stand watching the proceedings. He was brought in by a side passage to the speakers' end of the meeting and made a speech which as usual every one could hear and with which every one was inspired and delighted. As to that, a Harvard Club note of this address runs:

"Whenever and wherever he spoke, his wonderful voice, like the vibrant notes of a great organ, carried without effort to the furthest corners of the hall, and he could always be heard even when younger men shouted in vain. His voice, like his beautiful clear handwriting, never failed him. To have heard him once was never to forget him. His tall figure, somewhat bowed in later years, his massive head with its thick, gray hair, his humorous smile, his sallies of wit, his occasional swift sarcasm, his earnestness when wrong demanded denunciation or right merited praise, his fine and lofty patriotism, his resonant voice—all gave him a power to charm and sway men rarely equalled."

On April 21 the British Mission, headed by Mr. Balfour, arrived in Washington. On April 24 the French Mission, Marshal Joffre and M. Viviani, arrived there. In due time they came back to New York. As chairman of the committee to receive them, Mr. Choate had met each of the commissions as it landed at the Battery, had accompanied each in its procession through the streets of New York to the City Hall, where with the mayor he had greeted them in turn on behalf of the city, and had then escorted each to its residence in New York. When they came back from Washington he met them again, and spoke at every luncheon and dinner given in honor of each of them and in particular at the memorable dinner given by the City of New York to the commissions jointly on Friday, May 11, 1917, when the speakers were M. Viviani and Marshal Joffre for the French Mission, Mr. Balfour for the English Mission, the Mayor of the City of New York and Mr. Choate.

In welcoming Mr. Balfour and the British brethren at the City Hall on May 11, Mr. Choate said:

"Mr. Mayor, Mr. Balfour; Your Excellency, and Gentlemen of the Commission:—During the six happy years that I spent in England when I was sent abroad for the good of my country, I remember that from first to last, in every emergency that arose, you stood like a rock for the friendship between England and the United States. And in all that long career, public career, with which you have illustrated the history of your country and of the world, it was to you that we were constantly indebted for untiring and abiding friendship to the United States. When we entered into a war, not for our own benefit, but for the benefit of emancipating a struggling little nation, the smallest, I believe, of all the nations, we were indebted to the British Government, over which you had a controlling hand, that no interference was allowed between us and the objects of our efforts.

"It has always been the ambition and the hope of the people of the City of New York, whom I have the honor to represent for a few minutes now, that this friendship between our two countries might be perpetual and never disturbed. We were just beginning to celebrate the completion of an entire century of absolute peace between England and the United States when this horrible war that is now upon us broke out. We are disused from war. We do not exactly know how to carry on war, according to the modern methods, and it is our great delight that you have come with your able body of experts that accompany you to show us how to enter into the war, to show us what to do, and especially what not to do. I am sure we can rely upon your constant advice for that.

"We hesitated, we doubted, we hung back, not from any lack of sympathy, not from any lack of enthusiasm, not because we did not know what was the right path; but how to take it, and when to take it was always the question. I feared at one time that we might enter into it for some selfish purpose, for the punishment of aggressions against our individual, national, personal rights, for the destruction of American ships or of a few American lives, ample ground for war; but we waited, and it turns out now that we waited wisely, because we were able at last to enter into this great contest, this great contest of the whole world, for noble and lofty purposes such as never attracted nations before. We are entering into it under your lead, sir, for the purpose of the vindication of human rights, for the vindication of free government throughout the world, for the establishment by and by—soon, we hope, late, it may be—of a peace which shall endure and not a peace that shall be no peace at all. Fortunately we have now no room for choice. Under the guidance of the President of our choice at Washington, we stand pledged now before all the world to all the allies whom we have joined to carry into this contest all that we have, all that we hope for, and all that we ever aspire unto. We shall be in time to take part in that peace which shall forever stand and prevent any more such national outrages as commenced this war, and have continued it, on the side of Germany. Already we have been only thirty days in the war, and it has had a marvellous effect upon our own people. Before that there was apathy, there was indifference, there was indulgence in personal pursuits, in personal prosperity; but today every young man in America and every old man, too, is asking, what can I do best to serve my country? Mr. Balfour, during your brief stay among us, you will be able to answer that question."

On the evening of that day at the dinner to both commissions at the Waldorf Hotel, he spoke again, and it was in that address that he said that when Congress declared war on Germany, "for the first time, after two years and a half, I was able to hold up my head as high as the weight of eighty-five years would allow."

On Friday night was the dinner at the Waldorf. On Saturday night Mr. Choate gave a dinner at his own house for the visiting commissions, and after it they all went to the Red Cross meeting at Carnegie Hall, arriving at a quarter to eleven and returning home at one o'clock. On Sunday morning, May 13, Mr. Choate went with Mr. Balfour to church at the Cathedral of St. John the Divine, where there was held a very remarkable service (with Bishop Brent as preacher). Of these two days Dr. Nicholas Murray Butler, who was one of the guests at the dinner at Mr. Choate's house on Saturday evening, said two days later, as quoted in *The Herald:*

" 'Two incidents of those days will never be forgotten by those who witnessed them. Sitting in his own library after dinner on Saturday evening last, surrounded by a small group of intimate friends, he enlisted Mr. Balfour, Professor Bergson and some of the rest of us in a discussion of immortality. His questions were half quizzical, half serious, but they drew out an interchange of brilliant thought and sparkling wit that will always be memorable.

" 'Again, on leaving the Cathedral of St. John the Divine, after the stately service on Sunday morning last, Mr. Choate bade farewell to Mr. Balfour with these last words: "Remember, we shall meet again to celebrate the victory."

" 'These were the last words Mr. Balfour heard him speak,' said Dr. Butler, 'and they were the last words any of us in the surrounding group heard him speak. They were prophetic of the greatness of his spirit and of the confidence of his soul.' "

On Monday morning Mr. Choate complained of a pain around his heart and his doctor, Doctor Draper, came to see him, found he had caught cold, and advised him to stay a-bed for two or three days. In spite of that advice Mr. Choate gave attention to important questions that had come up during the visit of the war envoys and conferred about them, but he cancelled other engagements that he had made for the day. Later in the day he complained of being uncomfortable, but it was not until ten o'clock that night that he said to Mrs. Choate: "I am feeling very ill. I think this is the end." At half past eleven, May 14, he died.

What a magnificent consummation of a famous career, a career worldly in many of its efforts and details, but always at the pinch subject to the control of the Puritan conscience that would fight for righteousness when the call came! The call had come to him to serve with his last strength, his last breath, a cause that his mind and his heart both accepted as the cause of humanity. To meet it he marshalled his powers as a general marshalls his worn battalions for a final drive to victory. Sparing nothing, reserving nothing, putting into his task all his practised talent and all the prestige of sixty years of conspicuous and applauded achievement, he did what was wanted of him; did it with a voice still eloquent and winning and with energies still responsive to his will, and when the task was done, and he felt the end was coming, accepted it as something foreseen.

That was more than courage, more than patriotism, more than pride. In its essence it was religion. It was a giving up of the remnant of life that the world might be saved. By what was almost a miracle, the same chance was offered to him when past fourscore that had come and was to come to youths of twenty. And he embraced it as eagerly as any of them, and with a fuller understanding of what it meant. What he had the heart and mind and power to do in the last week he lived is in a way a justification of all his life. There was no petrifaction in him anywhere. His physical heart was damaged. He had had angina, and knew that any extreme effort was very dangerous to him. Parts of him had stiffened no doubt by age, but there was no stiffening of his power to give himself. He still loved his neighbor, his country, mankind, and still could die for them all.

It is most interesting that the talk at dinner at his house the last night but two of his life should have been on the immortality of the soul. Of that talk Doctor Butler told in an address (June 7, 1917) at a meeting of the New York Chamber of Commerce. Relating how he had been at the dinner when, surrounded by a group of intimate friends, among them Mr. Balfour and the French philosopher M. Bergson, Mr. Choate drew them into discussion of immortality, Doctor Butler said: "As I think of it now it seems almost as if that charming

MR. BALFOUR AND MR. CHOATE APPROACHING THE STEPS OF THE CITY
HALL ON MAY 11, 1917.

spirit, so rich in experience, so full of service, so crowned with applause and honor of men of two worlds—that that spirit had a prescience that it was soon to go; and feeling so confident of a life that was to follow, was quizzically anxious to know what those who were younger had to say about it."

The news of Mr. Choate's death brought messages of condolence to Mrs. Choate from the President, the King of England, and a great number of other mourning friends. His funeral was at St. Bartholomew's Church on May 17, and was conducted by Bishop Brent and Doctor Leighton Parks. The church could hold but a small part of those who wished to attend. The various organizations with which Mr. Choate was connected were represented. The pall-bearers were Mayor Mitchell, the British Ambassador, Mr. Henry White, President Lowell of Harvard, President Butler of Columbia, Mr. F. R. Appleton, President of the Harvard Club of New York, Mr. Robert DeForest, President of the Metropolitan Museum of Art, Judge Ingraham, Mr. Charles Lanier, Mr. Lewis Cass Ledyard, Mr. J. P. Morgan, Mr. John G. Milburn, Mr. Frank K. Sturgis, Mr. Francis Lynde Stetson, Mr. Charles H. Tweed, and Assistant Secretary of State William W. Phillips.

He was buried at Stockbridge in the beautiful family burying-place adjoining the old cemetery, where are the graves of two of his children.

The Pilgrims, an international organization of which Mr. Choate was president, held services in his memory in St. Margaret's Church, Westminster, London, on May 21, when the Archbishop of Canterbury delivered an address, and on May 31 at Trinity Church in New York, where an address was made by Doctor Manning.

CHAPTER XI

HIS LIFE REVIEWED

THE HARVARD CLUB MINUTE—THE UNION LEAGUE CLUB MEETING
—MR. DEPEW—THE CENTURY MEETING—MR. ROOT—MR. BRYCE—
MR. BALFOUR—COLONEL ROOSEVELT—PRESIDENT ELIOT—MR. STET-
SON—MR. ROOT'S ADDRESS BEFORE THE BAR ASSOCIATION OF THE
CITY OF NEW YORK—THE NEW YORK STATE BAR ASSOCIATION MEET-
ING—JUDGE CLEARWATER'S REMINISCENCE

Mr. Choate's death befell at a thrilling time when
there was more going on than living Americans had ever
had to deal with. He had been a part of the great performance. When he dropped, every one stopped to take
notice and think about it. The newspapers had immediately a vast deal to say, and said it, but besides that
there came and continued to come very thoughtfully
considered estimates of his career from persons highly
qualified to deal with it.

Many bereaved societies put their feelings on record
in minutes. So, following a description of Mr. Choate's
activities after his return from England and an enumera-
tion of some of the public duties he undertook, the minute of the Board of Managers of the Harvard Club offered by Mr. Byrne (May 23, 1917) goes on to say:

"It was to this great and commanding figure that
our Board always called on occasions at all out of the
ordinary—when eminent men were our guests, when
the Associated Harvard Clubs met in New York—and
frequently in the ordinary life of the Club when fresh
enthusiasm was to be aroused or devotion to Harvard

or to country was to be fanned into a brighter flame:
and the call was never in vain. He responded generously,
joyously and successfully. Everyone went home from
a meeting at which he spoke with a warmer heart, a more
courageous spirit and brighter hopes. Many told him
so; and he knew therefore that he had accomplished
what he wished, for his wish was always not that younger
men should be awed or dazzled by him, but that they
should like him and get from him something that would
cheer and inspire them. That which made it easy for
him to have his wish was the same thing which made it
difficult for anyone to envy or belittle him. It was his
kindness of heart and goodness of character. 'Let his
life be kindness, his conduct, righteousness, then in the
fulness of gladness he will make an end of grief.' He
made an end of grief for himself, for he was a happy man,
and for us too he made an end of grief whenever he was
with us.

"Lord Morley begins a chapter on the Last Years of
the Life of Gladstone with these words of Dante:

"' * * * And the noble soul is like a good mariner,
for he, when he draws near the port lowers his sails and
enters it softly and with gentle steerage.'

"After Mr. Choate had lived fourscore years, such a
picture must have pleased him as it passed now and then
before his eyes. But surely never again after the in-
vasion of Belgium, for from that moment he was a young
man once more, not only in the amazing vigor, but in
the immense scope of the labor which he performed without cessation to the end; he had work to do and what
might happen to him in the doing of it he did not care.
That work was to help to arouse his country to the danger
in which freedom was and her duty to help to save it.

In the last weeks of his life he knew the work was done; for he saw America preparing a great army to fight for democracy, which without her aid he had feared would go down in ruins. He had never been happier, never more proud of America. She was once more the Goddess of his youth; and as he looked into her eyes, open now to all her dangers and all her duties, shining with the light of faith in the justice of her cause, she was to him as half a century ago to Lowell, 'O, beautiful, my country.' "

The day following, May 24, 1917, at a special meeting of the Union League Club, Judge Hughes presided and there were addresses by him, Mr. William D. Guthrie, Mr. Charles E. Rushmore, and Mr. Chauncey M. Depew; all deeply felt, enlivened with reminiscences, and helpful to understanding of Mr. Choate's qualities. Mr. Depew spoke in particular of his practice of public speaking at dinners and on all sorts of occasions, and out of his own similar experience found an interesting reason for it. People had wondered that so hard-worked a man as Mr. Choate should spend so much strength, as it seemed to them, in exertions that might have been avoided. Mr. Depew's theory was that after-dinner talk was to Mr. Choate not so much an exertion as a change of occupation that amused and rested him.

"Many years ago," said Mr. Depew, "Mr. Choate was elected president of the New England Society in New York, and continuously re-elected. After a little, his annual address became an event for its wit, humor, and audacity. Its free handling of important personages and current questions made an opportunity to attend the New England dinner the most sought-for privilege of the year.

The occasion grew into national importance; men of the highest distinction and position gladly accepted invitations. It was a free platform, and the broadest discussion was invited, providing it was not too long. Sumner came there with his ponderous periods and stately eloquence, and Roscoe Conkling was there at his best. So were Presidents and ex-Presidents of the United States, and with them great journalists and educators, but on these occasions, some of which were historic, the master mind was easily Joseph H. Choate.

"Mr. Choate believed with me, that the mind is fresher and more capable of grasping the questions arising in one's vocation or profession, if there is relief in some other direction. We both found that in after-dinner speaking. For over forty years, many times during the season, we were on the same platform."

To a meeting of the Century Association on January 19, 1918, in memory of Mr. Choate, Mr. James Bryce (Viscount Bryce) wrote:

"No American ever did more to make more close and more tender the ties of affection that bind Britain and America together. No envoy ever left more friends, or warmer friends, behind.

"I can never forget the serene dignity and sweetness of his old age when, at Stockbridge, in the calm softness of an Indian summer, his friends gathered round him and Mrs. Choate, rejoicing to pay their homage, on the occasion of the Golden Wedding, to a life that had rendered such noble service to two great countries; and beside the memory of that softly declining day I place in thought the sunset that came five years later, when, after welcoming the representatives of England and France, he passed from among us happy in the knowledge that that for which he had so earnestly hoped and striven had been achieved, and that his country had taken her stand as the champion of right and liberty in the greatest cause for which nations have ever fought."

Mr. Balfour wrote:

"I had the pleasure of Mr. Choate's friendship during the whole period of his Ambassadorship in London, which happened to fall within the time when I was Leader of the House and Prime Minister, and I was, therefore, brought into close touch with him not only in the sphere of private life, but in that of great international transactions.

"He was admirable both in his warmth of heart and his quickness of perception, and his humour made him a delightful companion; while in public affairs, his directness, his high sense of honour, his power of effectively expounding his own case and of rapidly grasping the case of those with whom he was dealing, made him a diplomatist of the first rank.

"Let me add that, beneath all the passing subjects of international interests, and sometimes of international difficulty, which from time to time occupied the attention of his Embassy, he perceived with unerring clearness the fundamental unity of ideals and of character which bind together America and Britain.

"Next to his own country, I believe he loved mine, and by his personality, not less than by his exertions, he earned the gratitude of the old world as well as of the new."

Colonel Roosevelt was one of the speakers, and said in course of his remarks:

"Mr. Choate while Ambassador to England rendered two types of great service. In the first place he was the kind of Ambassador who achieved the good-will so strikingly shown to-night, so strikingly proved to-night by the letters of Balfour and Bryce. That is no small service in itself. It is a curious thing that the ninety years' period during which—well, I don't know that it is so curious a thing; it is a lamentable thing; I will put it that way— that the ninety years' period during which Great Britain ingeniously showed toward America a hostility which usually irritated without cowing, has been succeeded by a fifty years' period during which the average American demagogue has sought publicity by being ill-mannered toward England; and under such conditions the service rendered by the men of the calibre of Choate as Ambassador are in themselves of great consequence to this country; of such consequence that we cannot afford to ignore them in our estimate of the worth of any Ambassador.

"In addition to this, however, Mr. Choate played a great and distinguished part in connection with three international matters of the highest consequence: the Alaska Boundary, the open door in China, and the Panama Canal. The open door in China was one of those diplomatic triumphs necessarily ephemeral, because it could only be permanent if backed by force; and we chose to delude ourselves into the belief that a 'scrap of paper' was of more permanent consequence than events proved. Nevertheless, it represented a real —a temporary, but a real—diplomatic gain of great consequence, and Choate and Hay share the honor, not unequally, of that achievement."

A letter from President Eliot reviewed Mr. Choate's ancestry and life, and found in him "a fine type of nineteenth-century American manhood, and a shining example to that of the twentieth." Mr. Francis Lynde Stetson spoke at some length of him as a lawyer. "He was the head and heart," he said, "of much more than our bar. All honored him and those admitted to his intimacy loved him. In sincerity and love his own tribute to Rufus Choate may be repeated of him: 'Emerson most truly says that character is above intellect and this man's character surpassed even his exalted intellect and controlling all his great endowments made the consummate beauty of his life.'"

For the completest estimate of Mr. Choate as a lawyer we go to Mr. Root; to his address before the Bar Association of the city of New York, read at the Choate Memorial Meeting on December 20, 1917. Setting forth briefly the leading facts of Mr. Choate's life, Mr. Root went on:

"The forty-three years which elapsed between admission to the Bar in 1856 and the Embassy to Great Britain in 1899 were filled by the work of the pure lawyer. Neither business nor recreation nor politics nor any other interest diverted him from a continual and amazing activity in the trial and argument of causes. He was never an attorney. Circumstances and natural adaptation placed him from the beginning altogether upon the court rather than the office side of that line which exists in the nature of things between the duties of the barrister and the duties of the solicitor, and made him an advocate.

"He was wise and resourceful in counsel, continually called into conference for opinion and advice, for the direction of conduct and avoidance of litigation; but the main business of his life was conflict at the Bar. In all branches of the law, civil and criminal, common law and equity, military, ecclesiastical, patent, probate, marriage and divorce, constitutional, international, before juries, judges at *Nisi Prius*, arbitrators, courts martial, statutory committees and commissions, in all tribunals where judicial functions were to be exercised, up to the Supreme Court of the United States, his potent voice was heard asserting and maintaining rights for more than sixty years. He achieved the most brilliant and distinguished success. He was the delight of juries who yielded gladly to his charm, and the pride of courts who felt the dignity of their office enhanced by his appearance before them. His discussion of great constitutional questions strengthened the foundations of our free institutions. His shining example was an inspiration to the Bar and the despair of emulation.

"The law reports presented continually accumulating evidence of the most substantial basis of a lawyer's reputation, for the reports of causes argued by him supported the judgment of those who heard or read the arguments that they exhibited a wide range of sound learning, extraordinary discrimination, capacity to divine crucial questions, and power of effective presentation. The reports gave evidence also of an extraordinarily high proportion of success in the causes tried and argued, continuing through so long a period of years as to be conclusive proof of the possession of those solid qualities of advocacy which alone command enduring success. This great preponderance of success in litigation was notwithstanding the fact that for so many years of his life his conspicuous merit as an advocate brought to him great numbers of difficult and doubtful cases, in which the parties sought to overcome a probability of defeat by superiority of counsel. As the generations of the profession passed, traditions gathered about the path he had traversed,—stories of his great achievements, of brilliant attack and desperate defense, of wonderful cross-examination and masterful argument, of wise and witty sayings, of humor and satire, of imperturbable self-possession and poise, of swift insight, of courage and audacity, told by judges and lawyers and jurors and court officers, were repeated wherever lawyers gathered, and became a part of the common professional knowledge of the history of the Bar.

"As he grew older in the profession, his attention as a lawyer became less exclusively concentrated upon the interests of particular cases, and was broadened in scope to include the administration of justice as a whole. The public duties of the Bar, the ethics of the profession, the lessons of its history, the inspiration of its great examples, attracted more of his thought as his experience increased. In his addresses as President of the State and National Associations of the Bar, in his speeches to the Bar when from time to time it met upon casual occasions, in the memorials read before this Association, in his speeches to the Constitutional Convention, in many of his formal public addresses, first among which stands the noble address upon the unveiling of the statue of Rufus Choate in the Court House in Boston, he expressed so clearly the underlying spirit and purpose of the American Bar, he represented with such cogency and command the Bar at its best of real devotion to justice and liberty, that the finest thought and feeling of the profession came to follow him, and to look to him as a leader, not merely because he tried causes more skilfully, or argued them more powerfully than others; but also, because he put the power and prestige of his great reputation in the courtroom behind the thrust of advocacy for the honor and public service of the Bar as a whole. He has told us what his conception of advocacy was and his whole life helped mightily to establish that high standard. He said:

" 'I maintain that in no other occupation to which men can devote their lives is there a nobler intellectual pursuit or a higher moral standard than that which inspires and pervades the ranks of the legal profession. To establish justice, to maintain the rights of man, to defend the helpless and oppressed, to succor innocence, and to punish guilt, to aid in the solution of those great questions legal and constitutional which are constantly being evolved from the ever varying affairs and business of men are duties that may well challenge the best powers of man's intellect and the noblest qualities of the human heart.'

"Thus, the recognition of power and promise which he commanded from his seniors in the 60's was gradually succeeded by universal admiration, deference, and pride in his leadership among the juniors of his later years. Wherever the class consciousness of the Bar of New York sought expression in the comradeship of social intercourse, in protest against abuse, in repelling assaults upon the administration of justice or demands for its improvement, in concerted action upon any great public question, his came to be the sympathetic leadership, his the clear voice, the commanding authority, the unimpeachable representation of the noblest impulses of the profession. The great leaders and colleagues of his early and middle life passing from the stage left him alone without an equal or a rival, the most eminent, the most admired, and the most revered advocate and counsellor of the Bar, not only of New York but of our country.

"In this country of popular self-government, however, it did not satisfy him to be successful in the trial of causes, or to win the respect and admiration of the Bar alone. To be a great American lawyer in the broadest sense, one must be a great citizen, and Mr. Choate was that. He realized that our system of law striking its roots far back in the customs and struggles in which the liberties of England were developed, shaped by the fathers of the Republic to suit the conditions of a freer life, adapted from generation to generation to meet the new requirements of National growth, rests always upon the foundation of general public conviction that it is fit and adequate to secure justice and to preserve individual liberty. He knew that public respect for law, public confidence in the judicial system through which the law is administered, public faith in the wisdom and rightfulness of those great rules of conduct which we have written into our Constitutions for the limitation of official power in its relation to the life, the liberty, and the property of the private citizen, are essential to the maintenance of the most vital rights which from day to day we assert in the courts. He welcomed the privilege of the American lawyer not merely to insist upon the application to his client's case of the principles of American law, but to assert and defend the principles themselves before the great governing body of American citizens who make and can unmake the law. He understood that American lawyers cannot rightfully be a separate body cultivating a mystery, that they ought to be an active part of the citizenship of the country sharing in the formation and expression of its opinion, in its social and political life, and by virtue of their special knowledge and training, leaders of opinion among their fellows in the community. He said to the Chicago Bar in February, 1898:

" 'But at all times, and especially in this our day, great public duties await us. So long as the Supreme Court exists to be attacked and defended (that sheet anchor of our liberties and of our Government), so long as the public credit and good faith of this great Nation are in peril, so long as the right of property which lies at the root of all civil government is scouted and the three inalienable rights to life, to liberty, and the pursuit of happiness which the Declaration of Independence proclaimed and the Constitution has guaranteed alike against the action of Congress and of the States, are in jeopardy,—so long will great public service be demanded of the Bar.

" 'Let us magnify our calling. Let us be true to these great occasions, and respond with all our might to these great demands, so that when our work is done, of us at least it may be said that we transmitted our profession to our successors as great, as useful, and as spotless as it came to our hands.'

"These functions of the American lawyer Mr. Choate performed with unwearying interest and devotion, and with signal distinction. He received from his Massachusetts ancestry and brought with him from his old Salem home a large measure of that amazing formative power, which, proceeding from the few scanty settlements on the Atlantic shore, has moulded this vast Continent with its hundred millions of people according to the course of the common law, and to conceptions of right inspired by the spirit of Magna Charta, and of the immortal Declaration of rights unalienable, to secure which governments are instituted.

"The blood in his veins, the influences of early environment, of education and training, the foundations of his political belief, all made impossible for him the conception of a free community in whose public affairs it was not the duty of every private citizen to take an active part. He took such a part as a matter of course, and with an effectiveness natural to his exceptional powers. His intense and instinctive patriotism made him keenly alive to the welfare of the Nation, and of the State and City in which he lived. The strain of labor in the Courts never prevented him from doing his full share both in government and in the public movements and private enterprises, through which a democratic community develops the best side of its nature.

"He was not a dreamer to reject the natural agency of political parties in popular self-government, and he did not hold himself aloof from the activities of the Party which seemed to him the best agent of government. He never changed or wavered in his political allegiance. He made his first public political speech for Frémont in 1856, and his last for Hughes in 1916; but he conceived of a political Party as an organization by which many citizens, agreed upon major questions of principle and policy, may give practical effect to their opinions in actual government. His interest was in the public effect of Party control, not in office or emoluments. His activity was in the leadership of opinion, not in Party management; he took little or no part in that. He sought no office, and he entered into no combinations. He held no Party office. I remember that moving some 40 years ago into a new neighborhood, and attending for the first time the Republican Association of the old 21st Assembly District, I found him there attending to his duties as a citizen; and he was there as one of the rank and file. He was always in the ranks. But, when the time of conflict came between opposing Parties or against misleading leadership in his own Party, when serious decisions were to be made by the instructed judgment and conscience of the people, then he was wont to come as a champion from the ranks with all the weapons in the armory of debate, with clarity of statement and destructive satire, and power of appeal, and charm of persuasion, against things sordid and corrupt, against the follies of ignorance and prejudice, against indifference and decadence and for the cause he deemed just, for the living spirit of American institutions.

"He did not reserve himself for great occasions and great efforts; but gave without reserve to the everyday activities which taken together fill so great a part of the life of the community. In the multitude of gatherings half public half social through which the members of a community are welded together in sympathy of good fellowship and of opinion, he played a leading part for almost half a century. It is hard to understand how any man engaged in the exhausting labors of a crowded professional life could find the strength and resiliency of body and mind to make speeches in vast number at

public dinners and luncheons and meetings for all sorts
of objects, where he delighted and instructed the crowd
year after year during his long active life; yet, he did so
with undiminished brilliancy until the end. It would
have been impossible but for a strong and active interest
in the life of the world, in everything that went on in
the community, and a genuine liking for the people among
whom he lived, sympathy with their feelings, and understanding of their characters. He was never uninterest-
ing. His wit and humor never obscured or belittled his
serious thought, and his serious thoughts were never
dull. He richly merited the great fame he acquired as
an after-dinner speaker. In viewing that phase of his
activity as a whole, it is plain that he made it the means
of great influence and useful service. He promoted causes
and institutions in which he was interested, and inspired
in the tens of thousands who listened to him not merely
admiration and grateful remembrance, but respect for
his authority, and acceptance of his ideas.

"The reputation of many great lawyers is confined
to their own profession; but the wide range of his activities extended a knowledge of his great abilities and
commanding character to the public at large, and brought
appreciation from the general body of good citizens.
To achieve a commanding position in the public life of
this great Country ordinarily requires the holding of
high office. The office itself cannot give the holder such
a position, but it carries to the minds of the great multitude who have to form their judgments chiefly upon
hearsay, a presumption of a right to be heard in public
affairs. The presumption may not be justified and may
fade out of existence, but it is the door of opportunity,
and few men acquire great public consideration with-

out it. Almost entirely without the aid of office, Mr.
Choate acquired universal recognition as a great public
character, a significant figure in the public life of his
time, speaking with authority and entitled to leadership
of opinion. This position was fully established before
he was appointed Ambassador to Great Britain, and he
was appointed to that office because of it. The basis
of that great position was achievement at the Bar, and
the devotion of powers trained at the Bar to the duties
of a private citizen in the service of the community and
the Country.

"Nature was very kind to him. She gave him a sound
body, a constitution capable of enduring without injury
the strain of long continued and severe effort, and a temperament which saved him from the exhausting effect
of worries and fears and passions and vain regrets, and
she gave him a physical presence most impressive and
attractive. He was tall, fully six feet in height, slender
and erect in his early years, broad shouldered, and carrying an impression of poise and balanced strength; the
leonine head was set perfectly in its place, and his face
was luminous even in repose with the beauty of intellect
and nobility of character, sublimated and manifestly
active and dominant. His voice was clear, pleasing to
the ear, and far carrying. I do not recall that he ever
strained it, or seemed to be forcing it unduly. He was
never oratorical even in passages of greatest force and
feeling. His manner was dignified and courtly, but perfectly simple and unaffected, and it was the same everywhere and to everybody. Forty odd years ago, when we
were in the beginnings of a friendship which has been
for me one of the chief satisfactions and joys of life, I
used to think that he was the most beautiful and splen-

did specimen of manhood I had ever seen. I have revised my judgment upon this; for, after the Declaration of War with Germany, when he knew that the manhood and honor of his Country had re-asserted themselves, in the benign and radiant face with its lines of old experience and wisdom, made purer and gentler by trial and high endeavor, still alert with intelligence and feeling, shining with the joy of unselfish patriotism, and in the massive form bowed under the weight of a noble life, there was a beauty surpassing that of conquering youth; and the memory of it is a benediction.

"His mind was strong, well balanced, and wonderfully alert and rapid in action. Its response to the emergencies which so continually arise in court was instantaneous, and apparently intuitive. Extraordinary power of discrimination and a sense of material and crucial questions relieved him of the burden of bothering over immaterial matters, and enabled him to work with great ease. This faculty, combined with his vast experience, led some younger men who were with him as juniors to think that he worked very little; but that was a mistaken idea. He worked very hard and with great intensity, but he was happy in escaping the great mass of unnecessary work which most of us have to do. When he came to New York in 1855 he brought a letter from his father's cousin Rufus Choate to Mr. Evarts. He prized this letter very highly, and I am sure that he would not have exchanged it for any patent of nobility. I will reproduce it here:

" 'MY DEAR MR. EVARTS,

" 'I beg to incur one other obligation to you by introducing the bearer my friend and kinsman to your kindness.

" 'He is just admitted to our bar, was graduated at Cambridge with a very high reputation for scholarship and all worth, and comes to the practice of the law, I think, with extraordinary promise. He has decided to enroll himself among the brave and magnanimous of your bar, with a courage not unwarranted by his talents, character, ambition and power of labor. There is no young man whom I love better, or from whom I hope more or as much; and if you can do anything to smooth the way to his first steps the kindness will be most seasonable and will yield all sorts of good fruits.

Most truly,

Your servant and friend,

RUFUS CHOATE.'

"The particular expression of this letter which he valued most was the reference to his 'power of labor,' and he never regarded as a compliment the suggestion that he reached his results without the exercise of that power.

"This letter points to one of the chief influences in the development of his character and the direction of his life. No one who has watched his career and has read the address in which he paid his tribute to the majestic and lovable personality of Rufus Choate can fail to be convinced that widely as they differed in temperament and in their surroundings, admiration, and reverence for his great kinsman was one of the controlling influences of the younger life. Much as they differed, there was a striking resemblance in the standards of life, the intensity of application, the tenacity of purpose, the ardor of conflict, combined with the broad and kindly view, the strong sense of humor, the love of literature and reliance upon its broadening and humanizing influence to correct the narrowing effect of exclusively professional interests, the impulse for public service and the intense love of Country: all these were found in both the older and the younger Choate. One was the spiritual successor of the other. Rufus Choate came to the Bar in the year 1823, and he continued for four years after his young relative's admission. Thus, for almost a hundred years these two men of the same name and family, products of the same influences, and inheritors of the same traditions and the same ideals, adorned and ennobled the American Bar, and each in his turn rose to great heights of honor and renown. The younger man was fortunate also in associating during the formative period of his career with really great leaders whose influence tended along the same lines of development. How could there be broader scope or loftier spirit than he found in Mr. Evarts, the advocate and statesman, eloquent, philosophical, delightful companion, the wittiest lawyer of his time, and Mr. Southmayd, the typical solicitor, learned, logical, cautious, independent in judgment, stubborn in opinion, caustic in expression. They were not merely partners, they were friends, and nothing could be more delightful than the intercourse between them.

"Our friend was enabled to use his intellectual power to the highest advantage by two qualities of the first importance. One was his clear and instinctive courage. He was wholly free from any impediment of timidity. This quality did not impress one as being the kind of courage which overcomes fear, but, rather, as a courage which excluded fear. With him, no such emotion as fear seemed to exist. The other closely allied quality was a universal and invincible cheerfulness. In all my varied opportunities for observation for many years, he was the same. I never knew him to be sullen, or sour, or bitter, or cross, or fretful. He strongly condemned some things and some men with force and picturesque expression, but never with the least tinge of malevolence. He had his griefs, which sank deep in his heart, but his buoyant spirits and high courage forbade them to control his conduct; and, through them all, he presented the same bright and cheerful face to the world. He brought to the breakfast table always the same genial and cheery lifting of spirit which made him such a welcome guest at the banquet tables of New York. He was as lively and interesting with a dozen friends, or with one friend, as with five hundred, because he was entirely free from false pretence, and he was the same man with the public audience that he was with his close and private friends. He had a most serene and imperturbable temper. He never lost his self-possession or entire control of his powers. Safe upon this ground of vantage, he took special delight in making his adversary angry, and in reaping the benefits.

"He was a loyal and devoted friend, as he was loyal to every cause he espoused, and to every case he undertook; and he left no debt of friendship unpaid. No trouble was too great, no labor too arduous for him to help a friend. His power of satire and ridicule were terrible weapons, and he used them unsparingly, always most fatally when he was most gentle and childlike in manner. When engaged in battle he used all his weapons without respect of persons, and his thrusts often wounded his friends at the Bar more deeply than he probably knew. Yet, I think he never lost a battle through friendship, or lost a friend through what he said or did in battle. It was impossible to cherish resentment against him. He fought as those gay and debonaire youths of Dumas, who drew their swords with alacrity, and, rejoicing in their skill, fought joyously upon all suitable occasions without anger or malice, to death or victory or eternal brotherhood. Before a jury he was a master of the art of appearing surprised, and of appearing indifferent; but nothing was further from his habit than personal display. Any one with his appearance and talents might be pardoned for thinking of so agreeable a subject as his own person; but he never appeared to do so. He was thinking always of his object, and carefully studying the minds and feelings of those to whom he spoke. He studied his juries, his judges, and his audiences with sympathetic insight, and his favorite method of capturing their judgment was by boldly invading the field of their personal experience and interest, making himself at home with them, and when he departed leaving his own ideas with his audience as a part of their household goods. He very seldom told a story. His wit and humor did not percolate through him from the *gesta Romanorum*, or from the pages of American humorists. They were the natural reaction of his own mind from his perception of the persons and events that surrounded him at the time. He was a fountain, not a conduit, of humor. His speeches were interesting because his way of looking at men and life was fresh and original.

"It is quite inadequate to say that he was always cheerful and interesting. He had in him something far beyond that, which I cannot describe to myself better than by calling it the eternal boy in him. He rejoiced in life. He spurned dull care. He bubbled over with fun. He dearly loved a little boyish mischief. That was rather a dangerous faculty, but the danger gave it zest. There is an old story (I think it belonged to Mr. Evarts) of an American assuring an Englishman that Washington could throw a dollar across the Potomac because he had thrown a sovereign across the Atlantic. Mr. Choate would never have deigned to tell that ancient joke here, but when he got to England and before an English audience he could not resist the desire to see his English friends contemplating the aerial flight of their sovereign, and he told it I think several times. It befell me to sit near him at a famous St. Patrick's Day dinner, and he stopped at my chair and made a remark which indicated that he was having huge enjoyment with himself over something he was going to say. When he suggested that the Irish in America should redeem poor unhappy Ireland by going home, he was following the same kind of boyish impulse for mischief which leads school boys to carry their disconcerting pranks to the limit of audacity.

"He had great force and nobility and purity of character. He made the world his debtor by great usefulness in many fields. He deserved and received great praise and admiration for his achievements; but, after all, I think it was the delightful 'boy' in him that made us love him. It was that which, joined to his other qualities, made him so different from ordinary men. It was that blithe spirit which gave color and life and light to the whole character."

At the annual meeting of the New York State Bar Association, January 12, 1918, Judge Hughes presiding, Judge Alton B. Parker, Judge Cullen, Judge Ingraham,

Mr. John G. Milburn, and Judge A. T. Clearwater told their memories of Mr. Choate and appraised his qualities as lawyer, man, and friend. A minute prepared by Mr. Wickersham, Mr. Guthrie, and Mr. Root was adopted.

Out of Judge Clearwater's recollections came a story bearing on a side of Mr. Choate as to which information is somewhat to seek. Telling of casual foregatherings one summer with Mr. Choate and others at August Franzen's studio at Bar Harbor, Judge Clearwater said:

"One foggy morning there came up for discussion the failure of men to erect artistic and lasting monuments of the greatness of their achievements, Mr. Choate citing the ruins of the civilizations of antiquity, Nineveh, Babylon, Antioch, Corinth, and many other cities where such monuments had been erected and disappeared, and thus the conversation gradually drifted to the subject of immortality.

"In October, 1916, Rutgers College celebrated its one hundred and fiftieth anniversary, and decided to honor itself by conferring the Degree of Doctor of Laws upon Mr. Choate and other men of distinction. To me was assigned the duty of accompanying Mr. Choate to New Brunswick. Sitting in the Pullman on the way down, he reminded me of the conversation at Franzen's studio some years before, and said: 'Somebody, I think Frank Stetson, tells me you are attending a church at Kingston with which your family has been connected for two hundred and fifty years.' I said that was true. He said: 'As you are a trustee of Rutgers, I assume you are a Calvinist.' 'Well,' I said to him, 'I was born of a Calvinist family which has attended the Reformed Dutch

Church since the Reformation, a church which I have attended from my infancy, and I suppose I am a Calvinist.' 'Then,' said he, 'you believe in the immortality of the soul.' Now he said this with that compression of the lips and intensity of look which characterized his utterances when he was deeply in earnest. I said to him: 'You remember Stedman being at Franzen's studio when that subject was discussed.' He said he did very well. 'Well,' I said, 'when that portrait which you reviled was sent to my home at Kingston, Stedman and Franzen came up to visit us, and while they were there Stedman received from Thomas Wentworth Higginson a letter written by the Colonel on his eighty-fourth birthday in answer to one which Stedman had written congratulating him upon that event, and in that letter Colonel Higginson said that as the years went by, and the shadows lengthened, more and more he thought of the great question of the immortality of the soul. He had read the Darwins, Huxley, Spencer, Tyndall, Haeckel, and the other evolutionists and materialists, and there was a time in his life when he had discredited any notion of survival after death. Subsequently he had oscillated like a pendulum from unbelief to belief, and back again, but now as the time was approaching when he finally must solve the great problem, his mind was at rest. He believed that the soul of man survived physical death. That,' said I to Mr. Choate, 'is my experience and conclusion.' He put his hand on my knee, and said: 'Clearwater, I have pondered much and long over this great question. I, too, have read the evolutionists and the materialists, the ancients and the moderns. You know I was born and brought up in Salem, a singularly puritanical community, and always the atmosphere,

spiritual and intellectual, of Salem has to some extent
influenced my life, but I, too, am of the view of Colonel
Higginson, and have concluded, as I soon must solve
that grave question, that man does survive physical
death, that his soul is immortal.' Said he: 'Have you
ever thought as you worship in that old church at Kingston that possibly the spirits of your long line of ancestors
also were present? Don't misunderstand me,' said he,
'I don't for a moment believe there is any communication between the spirits of the departed and the living,
but it may be possible that they do frequent the scenes
of their former activities, especially the place where they
worshipped.' He went on to talk most beautifully of
the consolation afforded by a belief in immortality, of
the emptiness of a life where such a belief was absent,
of the vanity of human wishes and ambitions, the shal-
lowness of worldly honors, and the absence of incentive
to high and better living if man were destitute of a conviction that his soul was immortal.

"He received the degree at Rutgers amid the thunder-
ous applause of the alumni and the undergraduates.
We came back together, and parted late that afternoon
at the Union League Club here in New York."

Of course Mr. Choate, who thought about everything,
thought about immortality, and doubtless mused on it
the more in those later years, when the shadows were
lengthening for him, and the war's mortalities made
every one ask himself what became of the dead. The
talk at dinner on May 12, his talk with Judge Clearwater
seven months earlier, and such allusions as are in his
words about Mrs. Lowell, all suggest that having lived
long as life goes, and done what he could and got what

he might, he felt that what he had got and done and been was not enough, and that further adventures lay before him. One writes "The End" to his biography, but that only means the end of a book.

THE END

INDEX